SECRETS OF REVELATION

To order additional copies of
Secrets of Revelation, by Jacques B. Doukhan, call 1-800-765-6955

Visit our Web site at *www.reviewandherald.com*
for information on other
Review and Herald® products.

SECRETS OF REVELATION

The Apocalypse Through Hebrew Eyes

Jacques B. Doukhan

REVIEW AND HERALD® PUBLISHING ASSOCIATION
HAGERSTOWN, MD 21740

The author assumes full responsibility for the accuracy of all facts
and quotations as cited in this book.

Unless otherwise noted, Bible texts in this book are from the *Holy Bible,
New International Version.* Copyright © 1973, 1978, 1984, International Bible
Society. Used by permission of Zondervan Bible Publishers.

This book was
Edited by Gerald Wheeler
Copyedited by Jocelyn Fay and James Cavil
Designed by Leumas Design/Willie Samuel Duke
Electronic makeup by Shirley M. Bolivar
Type: Bembo 12/14

PRINTED IN U.S.A.

06 05 04 03 02   5 4 3 2 1

R&H Cataloging Service
Doukhan, Jacques B.
    Secrets of Revelation: the Apocalypse through Hebrew eyes.

    1. Bible. N.T. Revelation—Commentaries.   I. Title.

                        228

ISBN 0-8280-1645-3

CONTENTS

TO MY DAUGHTER ABIGAIL,
WHO SHARED THE BURDEN OF THE WORD,
AND THE LIGHT OF THE VISION.

A STRANGE BOOK

(Revelation 1:1-3)

The Mishnah tells the story of four famous sages who entered the *Pardes,* the mystical paradise of the apocalyptic vision.[1] No one survived the visit, however. The first died right away, the second lost his faith, and the third became demented. As for the fourth . . . he proclaimed himself the Messiah.

This parable brings us—with a smile—an important warning: the concept of the apocalypse is, indeed, a dangerous one. It has an aura of death, doom, and fear about it. At times the fear has become so paralyzing that some cannot even bear to think about it. Someone once said that "either the apocalypse finds a man mad, or it leaves him mad." From David Koresh in the United States, Shoko Asahara in Japan, and Luc Jouret in Europe—to all these "mystics" who still rush to Jerusalem[2] to find the Messiah or to be one—the concept of apocalypse has inspired many mad men and even greater delirium.

Before we venture into the biblical book of Apocalypse, we need, therefore, to prepare ourselves and make sure that we will read it and understand it the way God meant it to be. For that purpose, the first three verses indicate the nature of the book and serve as guidelines as to how we should approach it—and enjoy it and survive.

First of all, the author is a Jew himself. His Hebrew name *Yohanan* (YHWH is gracious) was relatively common among his people. It appears in biblical times,[3] and Flavius Josephus mentions 17 different men with the name. It is also the name of famous ancient rabbis such as Yohanan ben Zakkai (first century) or Yohanan the Sandal Maker (second century). Our Yohanan is probably the same person who wrote the Gospel of John, Yohanan ben Zebedeh, James's brother and Jesus' (or Yeshua's) beloved disciple. Christian tradition is unanimous on this matter. Polycrates, bishop of Ephesus (130-196 C.E.), clearly attests to Yohanan's presence in Ephesus, which might explain the author's particular concern with the church of Ephesus and Asia.[4] The author of the Apocalypse is real. The place where he was, "Patmos," was a small island of 16 square miles surrounded by the Aegean Sea (the word "sea," *thalassa* in Greek, appears 25 times in the Apocalypse). According to tradition, Domitian, the first emperor (81-96 C.E.) who took his own divinity seriously and requested that his people adore him as God, exiled Yohanan there and sentenced him to hard labor in the quarries. The Jews and Christians, whom he called "these atheists" since they refused him the honor of deity, particularly annoyed him. According to Jerome,[5] the Romans deported Yohanan 14 years after the persecution of Nero (94 C.E.) and liberated him two years later upon the death of Domitian (96 C.E.). Such deportation was common under the Roman regime, and usually involved political figures. The prisoners lost all their civil and property rights. In the introduction to the Apocalypse, Yohanan identifies himself as a witness, a *"martus"* (Rev. 1:2), who was "suffering" and "was on the island of Patmos because of the word of God" (verse 9). Uprooted from his past, his family, friends, abode, and familiar surroundings; crushed from hard work and humiliation; having nothing left but hope, the author of the Apocalypse was then a "martyr" who achieved *Kiddush ha-Shem* (sanctification of the name) in the perfect manner of Jewish tradition. And his nostalgia for his homeland and the daily confrontations with his oppressors served only to enhance Yohanan's Jewish identity.

A Hebrew Book

The Apocalypse is, therefore, more Hebrew than any other book of the New Testament. It contains more than 2,000 allusions to the

Hebrew Scriptures, including 400 explicit references and 90 literal citations of the Pentateuch and the Prophets. With regard to textual citations, the Apocalypse is more faithful to the original Hebrew than to its Greek translation, the Septuagint. Ernest Renan observed that "the language of the Apocalypse is traced from the Hebrew, thought in Hebrew, and can hardly be understood by those who do not know Hebrew."[6] This characteristic invites us to consider the book's Hebrew background and perspective. To understand the Apocalypse, we must read it in the light of the Hebrew Scriptures. This is the main perspective of the present commentary. As we seek to find the author's intentions, we will analyze the references to the Hebrew Scriptures in their own Hebrew and Jewish contexts. Our interpretation of the Apocalypse will then include not only a direct exegesis of the Hebrew Scriptures when necessary, but will also take into consideration the specific Jewish world and traditions that the book reflects.

A Revealed Secret

From the very beginning the book is rooted in the "secrets of Daniel." Even the first word, "revelation," puts us in the presence of a secret about to be revealed. "Revelation," or "apocalypse,"[7] comes from the Greek apokalupto, "to reveal a secret." This verb "reveal" happens also to be one of the key words of the book of Daniel (glh), in which it occurs seven times. Like the first word of the Apocalypse, it too introduces prophetic visions[8] and is associated with the word "secret" (razah). This echo of the book of Daniel in the first word of the Apocalypse suggests a special connection between the two prophetic works. The "revelations of Yohanan" refer us back to the "secrets of Daniel."

Moreover, the Apocalypse begins with a beatitude that echoes the last beatitude of the book of Daniel: "Blessed is the one who reads the words of this prophecy, and blessed are those who hear it and take to heart what is written in it, because the time is near" (Rev. 1:3). Daniel declared: "Blessed is the one who waits for and reaches the end of the 1,335 days. As for you, go your way till the end. You will rest, and then at the end of the days you will rise to

11

receive your allotted inheritance" (Dan. 12:12, 13).[9]

From the very first, the author of the Apocalypse places himself in the same perspective as the prophecy of Daniel, as hinted at by the title "Revelation" and the first beatitude that introduces the book and orients its reader. The Apocalypse alludes more to the book of Daniel than any other portion of the Hebrew Scriptures.[10] Even the technical expression "I Yohanan," which the prophet uses to introduce his vision,[11] echoes the "I Daniel" of the Old Testament book.[12] Both books have similar phraseology. And both have the same visions, the same themes, the same ethical implications, and the same prophetic perspective covering the same time span.[13]

The similarities between the book of Daniel and the Apocalypse offer our first clues to how we should read the latter book. The references to the book of Daniel guide us as we attempt to interpret the Apocalypse. I recommend all to read the book of Daniel and my commentary *Secrets of Daniel*[14] as background for the way the Apocalypse employs its themes and allusions.

Also, the beatitude that introduces the Apocalypse suggests from the outset the methodology that should characterize any approach to this book. The passage divides into three verbs: "read," "hear," and "take to heart" (or "keep").

The book first summons us to read. "Blessed is the one who reads." The blessedness emerges from a revelation, "a revealed secret," an Apocalypse. The beatitude suggests that happiness implies the need for a revelation. Otherwise we could miss the point. In fact, the nature of the reading of this book is essentially religious. Interestingly, the verb "to read" is the only one in the singular form: *"he* who reads." The other verbs are in the plural form: *"those* who hear," *"those* who keep." The reader has an audience—he is not alone. The words he reads must be heard by the multitude—"those who hear," according to the liturgical practice of the synagogue. We are in the sacred context of corporate worship. The Apocalypse is to be read as a liturgy; as an emotional and mystical experience; as poetry, with its rhythms, symbols, and spiritual lessons.

But the Apocalypse is much more than a liturgical exercise. Scripture calls its words "prophecy." Dealing with more than emotions, the book does not just address mystics and poets. Indeed, its words resonate far beyond the walls of the temple, far beyond the premises of the worship service. More than a liturgy, the Apocalypse is a book its audience must study and understand. But this approach requires intellectual effort. We have to "hear" the prophecy, which means in the context of Hebrew thinking, that we have to understand it (1 Kings. 3:9; Neh. 8:3; Jer. 6:10; Rev. 2:7; 3:22). Only then will it "reveal secrets" and illuminate the tormented course of history up to its ultimate fulfillment, as suggested in the last words of the beatitude: "because the time is near" (historicoprophetic approach). The Hebrew conception of "hearing" also implies a willingness to live up to what one has understood. The *Shema Israel* (Deut. 6:4-9) is more than a pleasant melody to enjoy. In Hebrew, the verb "to hear" (to listen, to understand) is synonymous with the verbs "to keep" and "to obey." This is precisely the message of the last words of our passage: "Blessed are those who hear it and take to heart what is written in it." Beyond the liturgical reading that sings to our ears and the prophecy that challenges our minds, the book aims to lead us to surrender our lives to God, to make them in tune with "what is *written* in it" (existential approach). The beatitude points then to the first words of the book, identifying the written message as a revelation from above, "the revelation . . . which God gave" (Rev. 1:1). We should understand the "revelation of Yohanan" (the earliest title of the book)[15] as a revelation *to* Yohanan. The Apocalypse is thus divine truth in the flesh of the written word, calling for the painful effort of passionately and religiously searching for the meaning of the text (exegetical approach).

A Menorah Structure

This multiplicity of approaches we should use to study the Apocalypse we find already hinted at by the very structure—what I call the *menorah,* or sevenfold pattern—that supports the whole book (see the Menorah table, p.14). The structure of the Apocalypse has the following characteristics:

1. It unwinds in seven cycles of visions, parallel and simultaneous, not unlike the book of Daniel,[16] in chiastic form (from the

Greek letter *chi,* having the form of an X), meaning that the second half of the cycle is the inverse parallel of the first (ABC/C'B'A').

2. At the beginning of each of the seven cycles the vision returns to the temple with a liturgical note that alludes to the calendar of Israel's high holy days (as prescribed by Leviticus 23). The book thus places each prophetic cycle within the perspective of a Jewish festival, one often alluded to within the cycle itself.[17] The author invites us to read the Apocalypse in the light of the Jewish festivals,[18] rituals that shed symbolic meaning on history.

The Menorah Form of the Apocalypse[19]

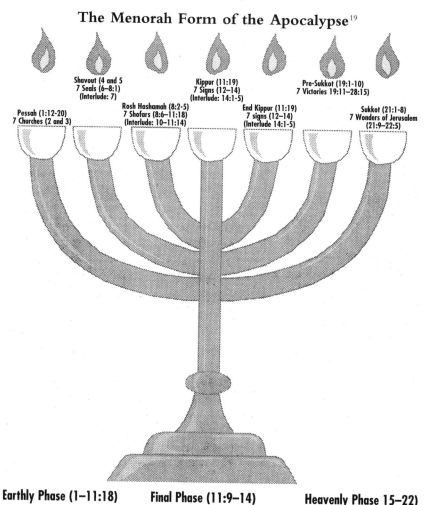

Shavout (4 and 5
7 Seals (6—8:1)
(Interlude: 7)

Kippur (11:19)
7 Signs (12—14)
(Interlude: 14:1-5)

Pre-Sukkot (19:1-10)
7 Victories 19:11—28:15)

Rosh Hashamah (8:2-5)
7 Shofars (8:6—11:18)
(Interlude: 10—11:14)

Pessah (1:12-20)
7 Churches (2 and 3)

End Kippur (11:19)
7 signs (12—14)
(Interlude: 14:1-5)

Sukkot (21:1-8)
7 Wonders of Jerusalem
(21:9—22:5)

Earthly Phase (1—11:18)   **Final Phase (11:9—14)**   **Heavenly Phase 15—22)**

3. Moreover, as in the book of Daniel, the Apocalypse divides into two main sections (historical/terrestrial and eschatological/celestial), at the middle of which appears God's judgment during the end of times and the return of the Son of man (Rev. 14; cf. Dan. 7).[20] The first part of the Apocalypse is primarily a prophetic vision of history from the time of Yohanan's life to the coming of God, while the second part deals with the epoch from the coming of God to the descent of the heavenly city. Instead of interpreting the Apocalypse as a mere reflection of the contemporary events of its author (preterist interpretation),[21] we would rather interpret it according to his own perspective, as a vision of things to come (historicoprophetic interpretation), with all the risks of faith and responsibility that such a reading entails (existential approach). This "historicoprophetic interpretation" is not only the one most faithful to the author's intentions, but is also the most ancient interpretation.[22]

The book gradually expands, develops, and intensifies its apocalyptic themes. Yohanan here follows the example of Daniel, who repeated and expanded his visions (see especially Daniel 2, 7, and 8). The "revelations of Yohanan" are also one single revelation. The title *Apocalypsis* implies both a singular and a plural. Our interpretation of the visions should, therefore, take into consideration this literary feature of repetition and intensification (recapitulatory interpretation). Such an interpretation obviously challenges a chronological understanding of the Apocalypse that sees the events predicted by the seals as following those predicted by the letters; those predicted by the shofars after the seals, and so on (futurist and dispensationalist interpretation).

All these preliminary observations about the nature, purpose, and form of the Apocalypse indicate that this mysterious book was not designed to be frightening and strange, but instead a clear revelation to answer our questions and soothe our fears about the future.

---

[1] *Hag.* 14b; cf. *TJ Hag.* 2:1, 77b.

[2] See Yair Bar-El, Rimona Durst, Gregory Katz, Josef Zislin, Ziva Strauss, and Haim Y. Knobler, "Jerusalem Syndrome," *The British Journal of Psychiatry* 176 (January 2000): 86–90.

[3] Jer. 40:16; Eze. 8:12; Neh. 12:23; 1 Chron. 3:15; etc.

[4] Polycrates, *From His Epistle to Victor and the Roman Church Concerning the Day of Keeping the Passover* (*Ante-Nicene Fathers,* vol. 8, p. 773), quoted in Eusebius, *Church History* 5. 24. 3 (*Nicene and Post-Nicene Fathers,* Second Series, vol. 1, p. 242).

[5] Jerome, *Lives of Illustrious Men 9* (*Nicene and Post-Nicene Fathers,* Second Series, vol. 3, pp. 364, 365).

[6] Ernest Renan, *Antichrist: Including the Period From the Arrival of Paul in Rome to the End of the Jewish Revolution,* trans. and ed. Joseph Henry Allen (Boston: 1897), p. 17.

[7] The word "apocalypse" has given its name to an important literary trend, both in the Jewish and in the Christian traditions, and applies to both biblical and nonbiblical sources. In the Hebrew Scriptures, examples include Daniel, Ezekiel, Haggai, Zechariah, and some parts of Isaiah, etc.; in the New Testament we find the genre in Matthew 24; Mark 13; 1 Thessalonians 4:13-18; 2 Thessalonians 2:1-12; 1 Corinthians 15:20-26, 51-53. Outside of the Bible (apocryphal and pseudepigraphical writings), we classify the Jewish writings 1 Enoch, 2 Enoch, 4 Ezra (2 Esdras 3-14), 2 Baruch, the Ascension of Moses, the Apocalypse of Abraham, the Apocalypse of Adam, the Apocalypse of Elijah, the book of Jubilees, the Testaments of the Twelve Patriarchs, and some texts of the Dead Sea manuscripts as apocalyptic. Among Christian writings, we consider the Apocalypse of Peter, the Apocalypse of Paul, the Apocalypse of Isaiah, etc., as apocalyptic. We must, however, remark that the classification of the above works as "apocalyptic" remains arbitrary and artificial. Moreover, the Apocalypse retains certain characteristics that differentiate it from the other "apocalyptic" writings (its prophetic intention, its ethical implications, its optimism, its author [whose name is not a pseudonym from a more illustrious predecessor], etc.).

[8] Dan. 2:19, 22, 28, 29, 30, 47; 10:1.

[9] The Apocalypse contains seven beatitudes (Rev. 1:3; 14:13; 16:15; 19:9; 20:6; 22:7, 14). All seven allude to the God who comes.

[10] See Henry Barclay Swete, *The Apocalypse of St. John: The Greek Text With Introduction, Notes and Indices,* 3rd ed. (London: reprint 1917), p. cliii.

[11] Cf. Rev. 1:4, 9; 22:8.

[12] The book of Daniel employs the expression seven times to introduce the apocalyptic visions (Dan. 7:15, 28; 8:15, 27; 9:2; 10:2, 7).

[13] For parallels and connections between Daniel and the Apocalypse, see Richard Lehmann, "Relationships Between Daniel and Revelation," in *Symposium on Revelation— Book 1,* ed. Frank B. Holbrook, Daniel and Revelation Committee Series (Silver Spring, Md.: Biblical Research Institute, General Conference of Seventh-day Adventists, 1992), vol. 6, pp. 131-144. Cf. Jean-Pierre Ruiz, *Ezekiel in the Apocalypse: The Transformation of Prophetic Language in Revelation 16, 17-19, 10,* European University Studies, Series XXIII, Theology (Frankfurt am Main: 1989), vol. 376; and G. K. Beale, *The Use of Daniel in Jewish Apocalyptic Literature and in the Revelation of St. John* (Lanham, Md.: 1984).

[14] Jacques B. Doukhan, *Secrets of Daniel: Wisdom and Dreams of a Jewish Prince in Exile* (Hagerstown, Md.: Review and Herald Pub. Assn., 2000).

[15] The *Canon Muratori,* a second-century document, and the writings of the Church Fathers attest to it (see David E. Aune, *Revelation,* Word Biblical Commentary [Dallas: Word Books, 1997], vol. 52, p. 4).

[16] See Jacques B. Doukhan, *Daniel: The Vision of the End,* rev. ed. (Berrien Springs, Mich.: Andrews University Press, 1989), pp. 3-6.

[17] The Jewish festivals indicated in the titles shall be in the original Hebrew: Shabbat (the Sabbath), Pessah (Passover), Shavuot (Pentecost), Rosh Hashanah (New Year, or Feast of Trumpets), Kippur (Day of Atonement), Sukkot (Feast of Tabernacles).

[18] For a similar pattern of the Jewish feasts in the Gospel of John, see George R. Beasley-

Murray, *John,* 2nd ed., Word Biblical Commentary (Nashville: 1999), vol. 36, p. lix.

[19] Cf. K. A. Strand, *Interpreting the Book of Revelation: Hermeneutical Guidelines, With Brief Introduction to Literary Analysis,* rev. and enl. ed. (Worthington, Ohio: Ann Arbor Publishers, 1976), p. 51.

[20] See Doukhan, *Secrets of Daniel,* p. 100.

[21] The Spanish Jesuit Luis de Alcazar (1554-1614) first introduced this interpretation. In contrast to the Reformers who apply this prophecy to the Papacy, the Jesuit theologian applies it instead to Judaism and to pagan Rome contemporary to Yohanan. German rationalism in the nineteenth century further developed this view, and it paved the way for the historical-critical method.

[22] Irenaeus of Lyon (130-202 C.E.) held this interpretation. Born only a few years after the appearance of the Apocalypse, this Church Father was the disciple of Polycarp, a martyr who met Yohanan personally (see Eusebius *Church History* 5. 20. 6 [*Nicene and Post-Nicene Fathers,* Second Series, vol. 1, pp. 238, 239]). The church, under the influence of Hippoltus and Origen, discarded the perspective during the Middle Ages for a more allegorical, spiritual, and moral interpretation, but it reappeared in the sixteenth century with the Reformers.

"HE IS COMING"

(Revelation 1:4-10)

The God of Israel

From the book's very first words of greeting, the author grounds his prophecy in the God of Israel: "From him who is, and who was, and who is to come" (Rev. 1:4). The phrase reminds us of the way God announced Himself to Moses (Ex. 3:14): "I AM WHO I AM." The God of Israel presents Himself as the God that cannot be captured by, or limited to, a theological definition. He is simply the God "who is" right here in our present. But the God we worship today is the same as that worshiped in ancient Israel. The second verb, "who was," reminds us that He was the God of Abraham, Isaac, and Jacob. Yet He "is" in the present just as He "was" in the past and will more than just "be" in the future. Instead of using the existential verb "to be" for the future, Yohanan changes the verb, switching from the verb "to be" (conjugated in the past and present tenses) to the verb "to come." Indeed, God exists. But in spite of all the knowledge we have acquired about Him, and of all that we have experienced as He intervenes in history, He remains ever remote, because He has not yet come. Only the future holds the promise of His coming. The future holds out to us much more than the past and the present. More than the God of memory, more than the God of existence, of spirituality, and of communion, He is the God "who is to come."

The book further confirms its message by a reference to the

Spirit "before his throne" (Rev. 1:4). The predictions of the Apocalypse are not the product of some astrological or psychic reading. They are certain because they proceed from the throne of God, from the sovereign Judge of the universe, who knows all things.

When the prophet Isaiah enumerates the seven Spirits that are to crown the Messiah, he does so to illustrate the Messiah's clear and just judgment that will precede the establishment of the kingdom of God: "He will not judge by what he sees with his eyes, or decide by what he hears with his ears. . . . The wolf will live with the lamb. . . . They will neither harm nor destroy on all my holy mountain, for the earth will be full of the knowledge of the Lord" (Isa. 11:3-9).

As the Spirit from above reveals the secrets of the salvation and judgment of the world, the book defines itself once more as an Apocalypse—an unveiling. The prophet's words then take on a warmer, more intimate tone as he declares that such secrets come "from Jesus Christ" (Rev. 1:5). Johanan describes three attributes of Christ ("faithful witness," "firstborn from the dead," and "ruler of the kings of the earth" [verse 5]) that are related to three actions ("him who loves us," "has freed us," and "has made us to be a kingdom" [verse 6]).

The three attributes of Yeshua allude to the three main stages of salvation: (1) His incarnation, as a witness for God among humanity; (2) His death, which saves us, and His resurrection; and finally (3) His royalty, which guarantees our citizenship in His kingdom.

The apostle Paul, as he reflected upon the Resurrection, described the same three stages: "But Christ has indeed been raised from the dead, the firstfruits of those who have fallen asleep. . . . Then the end will come, when he hands over the kingdom to God the Father. . . . For he must reign until he has put all his enemies under his feet" (1 Cor. 15:20-25). And we have the same thematic progression in Peter's address to the crowd at Pentecost (Acts 2:22-25; cf. Acts 7:56).

The whole plan of salvation, as understood by the early Jewish Christians, serves as a prelude to the prophecy. The God who comes is none other than the Messiah Himself. But the prophecy holds more than just the good news of deliverance. We do not wait merely for an event, but also for a person whom we love and whom we know,

19

and who loves and knows *us.* This personal relationship makes the wait all the more intense.

The first prophecy the Apocalypse presents is that of the Messiah's coming. The book depicts the Messiah as He was in the book of Daniel: "He is coming with the clouds" (Rev. 1:7; cf. Dan. 7:13). The expression seems far-fetched and has at times elicited smiles and even sneers. Some have thought it well to interpret it in a spiritual sense, as God inhabiting one's heart and soul. Others have understood it as being little more than mythology. Yet clearly the prophet has in mind something quite real as he goes on to state: "Every eye will see him, even those who pierced him" (Rev. 1:7). The text here refers to a prophecy pronounced by Zechariah: "They will look on me, the one they have pierced, and they will mourn for him as one mourns for an only child, and grieve bitterly for him as one grieves for a firstborn son. On that day the weeping in Jerusalem will be great, like the weeping of Hadad Rimmon in the plain of Megiddo" (Zech. 12:10, 11).

The allusion to Zechariah evokes the idea and imagery of weeping and mourning. Facing "a kingdom and priests" (Rev. 1:6), those who passionately wait for the coming of the Messiah from above, Yohanan sets up another camp—"the kings of the earth," who rely only on immediate and tangible earthly powers. It includes not only the Romans who drove in the nails and saw Him die with their own eyes, but also those who indirectly contributed to His death: the priests jealous of His popularity; the "Christian" disciples who cowardly kept silent; and ultimately the whole crowd of men and women who, through the ages, have in one way or another participated in His murder. Yohanan predicts that they will be disappointed. Instead of becoming kings and inheriting eternal life, they will mourn for Him, not because He will actually die, but because at His coming they will then realize the extent of their misjudgment. Scripture compares their sorrow with that deep emotion we have when a loved one dies. It is indeed an ironic note. The one they had wished dead—the one they actually murdered—they now mourn even though they will see with their own eyes that He is no longer dead.

A liturgical response confirms that the Messiah will return: "So shall it be! Amen" (verse 7). The words seem to proceed directly from the mouth of the pierced, and it is He who now speaks: " 'I am the Alpha and the Omega,' says the Lord God, 'who is, and who was, and who is to come, the Almighty' " (verse 8). He is the "Lord God," the YHWH Elohim of Creation (Gen. 2), the God of both the beginning and end of time; "the Alpha and the Omega" (the first and the last letter of the Greek alphabet); the one "who is, and who was" and especially the one "who is to come"; and "the Almighty," the *El Shaddai.*

This last name is one of the most ancient names for God in the Hebrew tradition. Israel would come to remember Him, the God of the patriarchs, as the God of promises and blessings (Gen. 28:3; 35:11).

Shabbat

Yohanan receives his vision on the "Lord's Day" (Rev. 1:10). Most Christian readers think immediately of Sunday, forgetting that the writer is Jewish, nourished by the Hebrew Scriptures and steeped in the tradition of his ancestors. Moreover, history does not begin to refer to the "Lord's Day" as Sunday until the second century C.E. Thus it is more plausible to think of the "Lord's Day" as the Sabbath day, also called a day "to the Lord" in the Hebrew Scriptures (Ex. 20:10; Deut. 5:14). Moreover, the frequent use of the number 7 in the Apocalypse justifies our allusion to the Sabbath day as the opening festival of the book. Furthermore, the Sabbath introduces the yearly cycle of festivals outlined in Leviticus 23: "There are six days when you may work, but the seventh day is a Sabbath of rest, a day of sacred assembly. You are not to do any work; wherever you live, it is a Sabbath to the Lord" (Lev. 23:3).

According to biblical tradition, the Sabbath was the first festival of God that humanity observed (Gen. 2:1-3). It was also the only day God sanctified before He gave the commandments at Sinai (Ex. 16:23, 29), and the only day that does not depend on the seasons, the movements of an astronomical body, or any historical event. Thus it is perfectly natural to begin with the Sabbath.

It is likewise highly probable that Yohanan is alluding to the other "Day of the Lord," the *Yom YHWH* of the ancient Hebrew prophets (Isa. 13:9-13; Eze. 30:1-5; Joel 2:1-11; Amos 5:18-20; Zeph. 1:14-18; etc.), the day of judgment and the day of His coming at the end of times. The eschatological context of our passage confirms such an interpretation.

In other words, Yohanan received his vision about the day of the Lord (day of the final judgment and of the *Parousia*) during the Sabbath day (the other day of the Lord). That the prophet has associated the two days is not unusual. The Sabbath has always had eschatological overtones in the Bible (Isa. 58:14; 61:1-3), as well as in Jewish tradition, which understands the Sabbath as the sign of the day of deliverance and "the foretaste of the World-to-come."[1]

Suddenly Yohanan hears a loud voice behind him (Rev. 1:10). Hebrew thought situates the past "before" one's eyes, because it is spread out in front of our perception, while the future is yet to happen and consequently comes from *behind* us.[2] Thus by implication the loud voice represents the future.

For Yohanan, the voice sounds near, familiar. It is the voice of the Messiah he knew personally and whom he loved, the voice of the resurrected Yeshua of the present. But it is also a voice that arrives from far away, from the future—the voice of the God who is coming.

---

[1] Midrash Rabbah, *Genesis* 17. 5.

[2] The Hebrew word *qedem,* meaning "before," designates what has already taken place, the past; the Hebrew word *ahar,* meaning "behind," indicates what comes after, the future. In contrast, modern Westerners tend to see the past as behind and the future as ahead. On this notion, see Thorleif Boman, *Hebrew Thought Compared With Greek* (New York: reprint 1970), pp. 149, 150.

STORMS

Yohanan now sketches a portrait that depicts Yeshua (Jesus) as having a dual identity. The Yeshua of the prophet's vision resembles an ordinary "son of man," like the Yeshua of the Gospels,* a being of flesh and blood dwelling among the men and women of that time. But He also has the characteristics of the glorious "Son of man" of Daniel, who, with His woolen hair (Dan. 7:9) and fiery eyes (Dan. 10:6), participates in the final judgment and returns upon the clouds to inaugurate the kingdom of God (Dan. 7:13).

We thus encounter both the God who is near, present on a personal level in the flesh of Yeshua the Messiah, and the God who is far off, the God of future glory. When He addresses Yohanan, the prophet falls at His feet "as though dead." But this God also reassures: "Do not be afraid" (Rev. 1:17).

It is this tension between the future God who comes and the present God who is that kindles hope within us. Without the certainty of a hereafter beyond the anguish of the present, we would have no reason to wait. And without the daily surge of hope produced by a renewed encounter with God, we would have no desire to wait. Hope requires the categories of both the present and of the future.

The first series of visions reflects this tension. We hear about the faithful martyr and the unfaithful oppressor. God both praises and judges the history of the church. Rain has two faces—it is both a blessing and a curse, a shower of life and a storm of death—and the church has two faces as well.

---

* Matt. 8:20; 10:23; 17:9; Luke 7:34; John 6:53, etc.

CHAPTER 1

OPEN LETTER TO THE CHURCHES

(Revelation 1:11–3:22)

Pessah

It is no coincidence that the introductory vision of the seven churches transports us into the midst of candelabras. It would have reminded the reader of how the Temple candelabra had become just another item of booty taken after the Roman army destroyed the Temple in 70 C.E., a fact attested by its presence on the relief on Titus's arch celebrating his victory over Jerusalem. The imagery of the vision means that the end of the Temple does not have to imply the end of humanity's relationship with God. The candelabra that had apparently disappeared into the Roman treasury was still present in the seven churches, and in their midst walks the God of heaven. He has not left His people to fend for themselves or to endure the tortuous course of history without Him. God is still with His people as the *shekinah* was with Israel: "I will walk among you" (Lev. 26:12). Yeshua's last words before His ascension held the same promise: "And surely I am with you always, to the very end of the age" (Matt. 28:20). It was the *shekinah,* the fiery cloud, that guided the Exodus (cf. the burning bush in Exodus 3). Likewise, it is the presence of the Son of man, with eyes like "blazing fire" (Rev. 1:14), a face "like the sun shining in all its brilliance" (verse 16), and feet "like bronze glowing in a furnace" (verse 15), who perpetuates the light of the candelabras and guides the course of the people. This vision of the golden-clad Son of man melts into the brilliant glow of the candelabras in a flash of light pointing to the gleam of the future golden Jerusalem.

After the Sabbath, the Apocalypse now proclaims the message of Passover through an allusion to the death and resurrection of Yeshua (verse 18)[1] and to the *shekinah* in the midst of the people. Passover is the festival that directly follows the Sabbath in Leviticus 23 (verses 4-14) and is the first festival of the Jewish yearly calendar (Ex. 12:2). Indeed, Passover commemorates the Exodus and the creation of Israel. But it entails more than a day of remembrance—it speaks of Messianic hope. The sacrifice of the lamb symbolizes the *pessah*, the angel "passing over" the households set apart by blood, and renews the hope of deliverance to come (verses 7, 13). The prohibition to break the bones alludes to the Resurrection.[2] The eating of unleavened bread, *matzah,* reminds us of the nomadic origins of a people whose sole hope lay in the Promised Land (verse 11). Even the Jewish liturgy, the *haggadah,* repeats from generation to generation Israel's profound sigh, "Next year in Jerusalem" *(leshanah habaah birushalayim).* Likewise, in Christian tradition, the Communion service—the Eucharist, commemorative of the Lord's last *Pessah*—repeats the same liturgical formulas with the promise "I tell you the truth, I will not drink again of the fruit of the vine until that day when I drink it anew in the kingdom of God" (Mark 14:25), a promise that the apostle Paul would later understand in an eschatological sense: "For whenever you eat this bread and drink this cup, you proclaim the Lord's death until he comes" (1 Cor. 11:26). It is also noteworthy that the ancient Christian eucharistic liturgy concluded with the Aramaic greeting *Marana tha,* "Come, O Lord," testifying to the hope of the early Christians.[3]

The Seven Churches

The tension between the future and the present lies at the very core of the prophetic vision and is the key to our understanding it. The prophet sees "what is now and what will take place later" (Rev. 1:19). We must read the message to the churches contemporary to Yohanan also in a prophetic perspective—as a message to the churches to come. The passage already hints at this type of interpretation. It compares the seven churches to seven stars, held in the Son of man's right hand (verses 16, 20). The ancients believed that the stars directed human destiny, thus the popularity of astrology, especially in Mesopotamia, as a means predicting the future. The authors of the Bible were well aware of such beliefs, as attested in the book of Job: "Can you bind the beautiful Pleiades? Can you loose the cords of Orion? Can you bring forth the constellations in their seasons or lead out the Bear with its cubs? Do you know the laws of the heavens? Can you set up God's dominion over the earth?" (Job 38:31–33). Later Judaism believed that every person had a celestial body, a *mazzal,* i.e., a particular star that presided over his or her destiny.[4]

God's holding the stars in His hands amounts to His controlling their destiny. In speaking of his God as the God of the heavens, Daniel made the same point to the Babylonian astrologers: his God was the deity who controlled the stars, thus human destiny.[5] Going beyond the churches of his time, Yohanan alludes to those of the future. Indeed, their very number, seven, confirms such an interpretation.

From the most remote times the number 7 has had symbolic value. The Sumerians, Babylonians, Canaanites, and Israelites[6] regarded the number 7 as the symbol of totality and perfection. During the intertestamental period, under the influence of Pythagoras (fifth century B.C.E.), number symbolism, especially of the number 7, was very popular.[7] The Apocalypse makes extensive use of number symbolism, including the number 7. The number 7 occurs 88 times in the New Testament. Fifty-six of them appear in the Apocalypse: seven candelabras, seven stars, seven seals, seven spirits, seven angels, seven plagues, seven horns, seven mountains, etc. In its very structure, Yohanan molded it around the number 7.

We should not take the seven churches on a strictly literal level. Indeed, their number hardly reflects the actual count of Asian churches, which were far more numerous. The Apocalypse does not include the two churches of Colossae and Hierapolis, both mentioned in the New Testament.[8] Indeed, the seven churches of the Apocalypse represent the church as a whole, an interpretation attested by a third-century C.E. manuscript.[9] The concluding statement of each letter, "He who has an ear, let him hear what the Spirit says to the churches,"[10] seems to address a larger audience. The letters speak to all the churches, and anyone may benefit from their content, a point explicitly brought out in the fourth letter to Thyatira. It contains the phrase "all the churches" (Rev. 2:23).

The seven churches were chosen not only as part of the prophet's familiar surroundings (he'd been there and knew them), but also for their symbolic meaning. Extracting prophecy from a geographical location was common practice in Israel. Micah wove his whole vision of the future around the names of Palestinian cities.[11] Likewise, Daniel used the geographical and strategic situations of the north and south to express his prophetic vision.[12] Even the sequential order of the churches follows a certain geography—the route of a traveler.[13]

As we progress from one letter to another, we notice Yeshua's presence growing more intimate with each letter:

1. *Ephesus:* "him who . . . walks among the seven golden lampstands" (Rev. 2:1).

2. *Smyrna:* "him who . . . died and came to life again" (verse 8).

3. *Pergamum:* "Repent therefore! Otherwise, I will soon come to you and will fight against them" (verse 16).

4. *Thyatira:* "Only hold on to what you have until I come" (verse 25).

5. *Sardis:* "If you do not wake up, I will come like a thief" (Rev. 3:3).

6. *Philadelphia:* "I am coming soon" (verse 11).

7. *Laodicea:* "I stand at the door" (verse 20).

But it is only by penetrating to the very heart of the letters that we may grasp the prophetic intention. And indeed, the Christian scene is not rosy. Instead, Christianity finds itself in the midst of crises and storms as the curtain lifts on a revelation of complex and troubling details.

As we read the letters we will note their prophetic overtones as well as their pastoral message. As pointed out earlier, the letters to the seven churches concern both the churches contemporary to Yohanan (preterist interpretation) as well as anyone equipped with ears to "hear what the Spirit says to the churches" (idealist or symbolic interpretation). And now as we enter the third millennium, we find ourselves on the far horizon of the prophetic series. In addition to the preterist and idealist interpretations, a prophetic interpretation—one that we may check against actual events—is ever more relevant.

Ephesus

From the island of Patmos, the first stop is Ephesus, one of the most important ports of the time. Sailors could see its lights far out at sea. It is no coincidence that Ephesus represents the first church, the first candelabra. Yohanan begins his cycle of letters with an allusion to the Garden of Eden, just as Daniel had done in his introduction to the first kingdom, Babylon:[14] "To him who overcomes, I will give the right to eat from the tree of life, which is in the paradise of God" (Rev. 2:7).

Ephesus is indeed the first love, its name in Greek meaning "desirable." The passion is still alive, and the memory is fresh (Rev. 2:5). It is the church of the apostles (verse 2) and also the church of the first pagan conversions. Former pagans must acknowledge with humility where they have come from (verse 5). Paul similarly warned the pagans in Rome (Rom. 11:18). For the Christians of Ephesus— the place of the goddess Artemis, the famous "Diana of the Ephesians" (Acts 19:28, KJV)—this call is significant. Ephesians were well known for their superstition, and they had a prominent amulet business. The crime rate of Ephesus had reached the point that the philosopher Heraclitus allegedly wept over it and afterward carried the title of the "weeping philosopher." Ephesus is thus the church of beginnings.

Yet, while still embedded in its spiritual source, it is on its way to perdition. Already the nervous pacing of its "him who holds the seven stars" hints to the danger of the situation (Rev. 2:1). Peter uses the same verb (peripatei) to describe the worried behavior of Satan at bay.[15] Ephesus' problem lies in the fact that its fire has died and has not been rekindled: "You have forsaken your first love" (verse 4). "Repent and do the things you did at first" (verse 5). These "first deeds" allude to the teshuvah, the prophetic call for repentance. The angel couples the exhortation with a warning: "If you do not repent,

29

I will come to you and remove your lampstand" (verse 5). The first church's purity does not guarantee it from losing its light. The fact that God established the church Himself does not absolve it from its future deeds. The church is apt to stumble. It may even fall and knock over its candelabra and extinguish its light, a point that we need to ponder. The risks of error and failure ever remain. We cannot equate the church with God. It is not enough to be a church member to be saved: "Even within the church, there is no salvation."

Yet the letter does not linger on threats. In spite of its errors, the church maintains a certain spiritual integrity. It hates "the practices of the Nicolaitans" (verse 6), an attitude all the more virtuous since God also shares it: "which I also hate."

The evil that threatens the first Christians recalls the fate of the Nicolaitans. An early church tradition considered them followers of the Nicolas mentioned in Acts 6:5. Whoever they were, the Nicolaitans were, according to the Church Fathers, well known for their depravity.[16] A distortion of Paul's new stand on grace and law had led them to reject all the principles of the Torah. By the grace of Yeshua the Messiah, they set themselves free from the Torah and fell into debauchery.

They based their ideas on the dualistic view prevalent among the gnostic Christians of their time.[17] They despised the human body and, in fact, anything belonging to the physical creation, as basely material and evil while regarding the spirit as pure, good, and divine. One could therefore dispose of one's body at will, torture it, or gratify it, while remaining pure in spirit. Dualism ties the body to the domain of the law and rejects it, while the soul, connected to the domain of grace, is upheld.

According to the prophetic testimony of the first letter, the first seeds of apostasy must have emerged out of the devaluation of both Torah and physical creation. But the conclusion of the letter declares: "To him who overcomes, I will give the right to eat from the tree of life" (Rev. 2:7). On the one hand, it affirms the physical act of eating and thus creation[18]—a response to the dualists who cared only about the spiritual and despised physical life and creation. On the other hand, "the tree of life" (ets hayyim) upholds the Torah, of which it has become a classic symbol since both biblical times[19] and later Jewish tradition.[20] It even came to designate the wooden rollers holding the parchment Torah scroll.

Smyrna

Our second stop takes us to Smyrna, 40 miles from Ephesus. Known as a commercial city of striking beauty, it was one of the rare cities of antiquity to have undergone extensive planning, and later, reconstruction. The Greeks built it in 1000 B.C.E., then the Lydians destroyed it in 600 B.C.E. Later Lysimachus, one Alexander the Great's generals, reconstructed it (200 B.C.E.). The city was literally "resurrected" from the ruins. It is thus no coincidence that the themes of death and resurrection permeate the letter to the church of Smyrna. The author of the letter introduces himself as "him who . . . died and came to life again" (verse 8). The recipients of the letter are bound for death, yet are promised life (verses 10, 11). The very name, Smyrna, has been popularly associated with the word "myrrh," the balm of death.

Beyond the allusions to the city's fate, the letter to Smyrna evokes the persecution endured by the Christian martyrs. In addition to the threat of death, the Christians of Smyrna struggled with poverty. The Christianity of Smyrna hardly reflects the crimson robes and jeweled crowns of later Christendom. It is still the time when to be a Christian did not imply success and fame. Christians, for the most part, came from the poor of the city and endured the hostility of the pagan masses.

The fate of the church of Smyrna is one of persecution. People suspected Christians of the most outrageous crimes. The pagans associated the rite of Communion with cannibalism, during which they believed that Christians drank blood and ate human flesh. Non-Christians also viewed the agapes, celebrations of Christian fellowship, as orgies of debauchery. Because God was invisible, Christians faced charges of atheism. The state suspected them because of their refusal to pledge allegiance to the emperor as Lord. Some even accused them of having foretold the end of the world by fire, a charge later exploited by the emperor Nero. Many despised Christians because they identified them as Jews, a religion considered backward and remote.

The Jewish situation was just as miserable. Jews who proclaimed a Messiah were suspect from without and from within. Internal division as to the Messiah's validity tore the Jewish community apart, as we see in the case of Saul of Tarsus, later known as Paul.[21] The letter to Smyrna reproaches them for their calumny and questions the authenticity of their Jewishness: "those who say they are Jews" (verse 9). The allusion to Jewishness hints to the fact that the early Christians still considered themselves Jews. Today we would accuse our fellow believers of not living up to their "Christianity," and call their gathering place a "church of Satan." The Christians of Smyrna were closer to the Jewish community than to their pagan counterparts. Christian anti-Semitism had not yet ignited. Thrown in jail and tortured by the pagans, suspected by their Jewish brothers and sisters, the early Christians were left to their own wretchedness.

The persecution reached alarming proportions under the reign of Diocletian, the historical era of martyrdom. In an edict (303 C.E.) the emperor ordered the Christian communities dissolved, their churches demolished, and their books burned.[22] Numerous Christians died for their beliefs. Many found themselves reduced to slavery. A number of the church's revered saints date from that epoch: Saint Sebastian, who died pierced by a hundred arrows while tied to a tree; Saint Cecil, patron of sacred music; and Saint Agnes, burned at the stake. The last wave of persecutions lasted until 311. In 313 the emperor Constantine released an edict that established Christianity as an official religion.

Interestingly, the time of persecution lasted a total of 10 years, as predicted by the letter (one day equals one year, according to prophetic calculations).[23] But the language is also symbolic. In the Jewish and biblical traditions, the number 10 came to symbolize the idea of test or trial. For example, we remember Daniel's 10-day trial (Dan. 1:14, 15). The Jewish calendar retained the symbolism. Ten days of trial separate Rosh Hashanah, the Feast of Trumpets, from Kippur, the Day of Atonement, during which Jews prepare for the great day of judgment. The Mishnah employs the same language when speaking of the 10 generations from Adam to Noah, and from Noah to Abraham; the 10 ordeals endured by Abraham; and the 10 plagues in Egypt, concluding that, indeed, the number 10 is the symbol of trial and testing.[24] But it is merely a test, which by definition implies reward. Failure and death shall not have the last word, and hope exists. God has reserved the crown of victory (*stephanos*) for the martyrs of faith (Rev. 2:10).

Irony permeates the passage: vanquished by the gladiator's sword, the Christians nevertheless receive the crown of victory. They have died, yet they have the "crown of life," an image often reproduced on the sepulchers of Greco-Roman antiquity to symbolize victory over death.[25] It was, however, no allusion to the immortality of the soul, a notion cherished by the Greek mind and one that would later infiltrate the Judeo-Christian tradition. The next verse further specifies that the martyrs "will not be hurt at all by the second death" (verse 11), an expression found only in the Apocalypse.[26] Rabbinical literature and the Targum, however, support the concept.[27] In all these passages, the "second death" consists of the final death of the wicked, without hope of resurrection. A later passage of the Apocalypse (Rev. 20:6) speaks of two resurrections. The first belongs to the just, at the coming of the Messiah. The second involves the wicked. Only the first resurrection results in eternal life. The second, on the other hand, leads to eternal death. Everybody shall endure the first death, but only the wicked shall know the second death.[28]

To exempt the martyrs of Smyrna from the second death is to assure them of a true resurrection that leads to eternal life. For the Bible, deliverance from death does not affect merely the soul, but the whole flesh and blood individual, denying any dualistic assumptions.

Pergamum

Our voyage continues northward 30 miles from Smyrna. The city of Pergamum welcomes us in all its grandeur and majesty—a city on a hill—thus its name, "citadel" or "glorious city." Situated somewhat outside of the main commercial routes of Asia, the city of Pergamum remained nonetheless the greatest city of Asia Minor.

The Greek geographer Strabo (about 63 B.C.E. to about 21 C.E.) called it the "illustrious city," and the Roman historian Pliny the Elder (23–79 C.E.) considered it the "most famous city of Asia." A political center, Pergamum was renowned as a cultural and religious hub as well. It was in Pergamum that parchment was first manufactured. Shelving 200,000 rolls of parchment, the library of Pergamum rivaled that of Alexandria. The city was also famous for its religious life. Its hospitals and temples of healing in honor of the god Asclepias attracted thousands of pilgrims from around the world, as testified by the archeological finds of a wide range of currencies.

The city of Pergamum reflects the situation of the third period of church history. In contrast with its predecessors, the church of Pergamum exhibits great success and glory. The Christians of Pergamum are respectable citizens. The era of martyrdom has ended. References to those miserable times occur in the past tense: "even in the days of Antipas, my faithful witness, who was put to death in your city" (Rev. 2:13). The time is one of prosperity and of comfort.

But Pergamum does have problems. The letter denounces a practice reminiscent of the dealings of Balaam, the prophet responsible for leading the people of Israel into syncretism.[29] Balaam, whose name means "to devour the people," recognized that compromise was the best way to "devour" or neutralize the chosen people. Introducing them to foreign cultural elements did more harm to the people of Israel than persecution or death. Compromise with evil can be more dangerous than pure evil. It is easier to identify the enemy while they are still outside the ramparts than when they have infiltrated the secret chambers of the city. Such was the situation with the church of Pergamum. Paganism and error mingled with truth. Since Ephesus, the church had strayed greatly. The Nicolaitans, once hated by the church, now preach within its walls: "You also have those who hold to the teaching of the Nicolaitans" (verse 15). Both Balaam, "who devours the people," and the Nicolaitans, a name that was the Greek equivalent of Balaam and signifying "the conqueror of the people," now ravage the church.

History confirms this tendency to compromise. To strengthen its political status, the church adopted an attitude of flexibility and openness, molding itself around the political power elite. Imperial decrees promulgated at that time reflect the church's art of compromise. For example, Sunday, the Roman day of the sun, came to replace Saturday as the God-given Sabbath day.[30]

The prophet Daniel had already pointed out this tendency to compromise in the visions of the statue and of the four beasts. The vision of the statue (Daniel 2) represented the church by both clay, symbolizing the religious dimension, and iron, symbolizing political power.[31] In the vision of the four beasts a horn—political power—bearing human features—spiritual dimension—stood for the church.[32]

The same call for repentance we heard in Smyrna the angel now repeats here. The double-edged sword in the mouth of the Son of man (Rev. 2:16) represents the word of a God who judges, separating truth from error (cf. Isa. 49:2). The reward of the just, the "hidden manna," and the "white stone" (Rev. 2:17), likewise allude to a judgment context. The manna evokes the Exodus and the perspective of the Promised Land. This bread fallen from heaven becomes the sign of hope.[33] According to an old Jewish legend, during the destruction of the Temple (sixth century B.C.E.) the prophet Jeremiah hid the pot of manna kept in the holy ark.[34] Only in the time of the Messiah would anyone find the pot of manna and again eat it as food.[35] According to this legend, only the end of time would reveal the identity of the selected few to be saved. In the meantime, it is impossible to determine who are saved and who are not.

The same lesson is engraved on the white stone bearing a "new name" (verse 17). The white stone alludes to Roman judicial proceedings that used black and white stones to indicate the verdict. White signified acquittal, and black condemnation. To receive a white stone means then to be acquitted. As for the "new name," it represents the act of re-creation from above, the sign of a new beginning and of a new destiny. In this way, Abram became Abraham, bearing the promise of a generous offspring,[36] and Jacob became Israel, with the responsibility to wrestle with God.[37] Geographical locations acquire new names: Jerusalem receives the new appellation of "The Lord our righteousness" in virtue of God's eternal presence among His people.[38] In the same manner, the chosen of Pergamum receive a new name "known only to him who receives it" (verse 17). The Bible and Jewish tradition speak of God's name as unutterable and incomprehensible.[39] This is in fact the interpretation given in a later letter: "I will write on him [who overcomes] the name of my God and the name of the city of my God" (Rev. 3:12). This "new name" is the very name of God and, by extension, the name of the new Jerusalem that God would bring from heaven (verse 12). This association of the name of Jerusalem with the name of God Himself already appears in the book of Jeremiah, in which the prophet gives a new name to the city, "The Lord our righteousness" (Jer. 33:16). On the basis of this verse the Talmud and the Midrash will later elaborate and associate Jerusalem and the Messiah, "for they both carry the name of the Holy Blessed Be He."[40] Likewise the Midrash notices that "just as [God] calls the Messiah with His own name, He will also call Jerusalem with His own name."[41] We find the same concept at the very heart of the Apocalypse. The chosen few, the 144,000 citizens of the New Jerusalem, receive a name identified with that of God (Rev. 14:1; cf. 22:4).

In the introduction to the letter the faithful were those who remembered the name of God. Then, in its conclusion, the chosen of Pergamum receive the name of God as their own (Rev. 2:17). Israel's responsibility is to bear His name, because His people are the sign of the invisible God. The mention of Antipas, meaning "him who represents the father," had already alluded to this. The mission of the son is to carry the name of his father and to represent him in his absence. This is why this name is known only to those who receive it. Likewise, if the elect of Pergamum are the only ones who know the name of God recorded on the white stone, it is because of their personal relationship with Him. At the time represented by Pergamum the visible church begins to lose its identity and its mission as the bearer of God's name.

Thyatira

Our attention has now shifted to the east, 40 miles from Pergamum. Thyatira is quite an insignificant city in contrast to Ephesus and Pergamum. Pliny calls it a "mediocre city." Yet, this

36

letter holds the most brazen accusations (Rev. 2:20-27), and very few compliments (verse 19).

Already evil had infiltrated Pergamum. The situation worsens with Thyatira. Evil now permeates every area of the church. The angel depicted the heresy in Pergamum through the symbol of Balaam, whose influence had remained external to the church. In the church of Thyatira, however, evil reigns, embodied by Queen Jezebel (verse 20). Jezebel was the wife of Ahab, king of Israel. Originally from Phenicia and daughter of Ethbaal, king of the Sidonians (1 Kings 16:31), priest of Baal and Astarte,[42] she single-handedly led the king and the people of Israel into Baal worship. Personally supporting 450 prophets of Baal, she is also known for her bitter hatred of the prophet Elijah and of anyone else who remained faithful to YHWH. Her influence continued through the rule of her sons and then her daughter, Athaliah.[43]

The reign of Jezebel is characteristic of the church of Thyatira. Heresy has become official and coincides with the church's power elite. The church has now established itself as a political power and clad itself with robes of royalty. And indeed, the city of Thyatira was renowned for its purple dyes, the color of royalty[44] and of priesthood.[45] We remember Lydia of Thyatira, who worked in the dye business.[46]

But the city of Thyatira also had a reputation for its worship of the god Tyrimnos (god of the sun), which later developed into the cult of the Roman emperor. Ironically, the author of the letter presents Himself in an aura of resplendent brightness, eyes like "blazing fire," feet like burnished bronze, thus outshining the sun-god and denouncing its presumptuous pride. The symbolic Jezebel usurps God's authority as the church makes decisions that are God's alone.

The letter mentions "all the churches" (Rev. 21:23). Often God's witnesses forget whom they represent and replace the object of their testimony with their own selves. It is a risk faced by all religions and all prophets. People may substitute their own voices for God's. Traditions and institutions may prevail over the truth that originated them. When human beings and institutions take the place of God and truth, the result is always the same: intolerance and persecution. Such became the characteristics of the church of Thyatira, the church of the medieval era, officially instituted in 538 C.E. after the last Arian threat,[47] and dismantled in 1563, with the Council of Trent. It was the church of the Inquisition and of the Crusades. Never has human history witnessed such prolonged and consistent persecutions. One understands the anger of the Son of God as He brings a judgment of intense suffering (verse 22). The church shall pay dearly for its intolerance.

We must, however, note that God does not direct His wrath against the men and women of Thyatira but at the church as a human institution. Even within the church of Thyatira countless men and women remained faithful and did not know "Satan's so-called deep secrets" (verse 24). This expression echoes a similar one about God: "the deep things of God" (1 Cor. 2:10), characterizing those who put their trust in the Spirit of God rather than in "men's wisdom" (verse 5). As in the times of the original Jezebel, they have not "bowed down" to the new Jezebel's will (1 Kings 19:18), but have remained faithful to their God. The letter acknowledges these exceptions and praises them profusely. It also mentions four virtues: love, faith, service, and perseverance (Rev. 2:19). The church of Thyatira is also the church of Francis of Assisi (1182-1226) and of the French King Louis (called the Saint), who founded some of the first schools, hospitals, and universities. It is a time of change and of reformation. We remember Peter Waldo (1140-1217) in Italy, John Wycliffe (1320-1384) in England, and John Huss (1369-1415) in Bohemia. Then came Martin Luther (1483-1546) in Germany. The angel encourages all these men, all these movements: "Only hold on to what you have until I come" (verse 25).

The Apocalypse holds out the eschatological hope as the ultimate comfort and reward. It first represents the gift of "authority over the nations" (verse 26), a promise derived from Psalm 2:8, 9, which announces the Messianic era. According to the ancient rabbis, that would be the coming of "the Messiah son of David."[48] Since the letter to this church depicts a human attempt to usurp God's authority, we need to be reminded who alone has ultimate power.

The hope of the Second Coming is also the gift of "the morning star" (Rev. 2:28), an allusion to Numbers 24:17 ("a star will come out of Jacob"), a passage traditionally interpreted in Judaism as referring to the Messiah: "Numbers 24:17, I see him: this applies to the King Messiah, 'a star shall come out of Jacob,' the star from the dark . . . this is the star of the Messiah."[49] This last promise encouraged all those who struggled during the Dark Ages and longed for a new dawn.

Sardis

Forty miles to the south of Thyatira, the town of Sardis stretches out on two levels, thus the plural form of its name (*Sardeis* in Greek). Originally the city was built on a plateau, but in the course of its development it flowed into the lower valleys and slopes. The topography of Sardis testifies to its decadence. Sardis is the perfect example of the contrast between a glorious past and a wretched present. At the time of Yohanan's exile, Sardis's glorious past was history. Five centuries earlier it stood among the most prestigious cities of the world. The wealthy Croesus had been its last king (reigned 560–546 B.C.E.). Then it fell into the hands of Cyrus. When his army approached the summit of the plateau, they found the city doors open and unguarded. Distracted by his wealth, Croesus had not prepared for war. The city of Sardis soon withered away to a dusty monument of the past, reminding its dwindling people of the painful price of their lack of vigilance.

The tragedy of the city's history now inspires the letter's exhortations: "Remember, therefore, what you have received and heard; obey it, and repent" (Rev. 3:3). The whole letter appeals to the church to return to a past of true and authentic faith.

The author of the letter now introduces Himself—as He had done in the letter to the church of Ephesus—as "him who holds the . . . seven stars" (verse 1; cf. Rev. 2:1). Sardis, like Ephesus, is the only church that "has" something. In spite of all the accusations against them, the two churches still "have" something to their credit. The same Greek word *alla* ("but," Rev. 2:6; "yet," Rev. 3:4) introduces the praise, the "have" within the body of reprimands. Both churches receive the promise of life—"the tree of life" for Ephesus (Rev. 2:7) and the "book of life" for Sardis (Rev. 3:5). And both partake of the celestial banquet—for Ephesus (Rev. 2:7) the right to eat of the tree of life, and for Sardis (Rev. 3:4, 5) mention of the white garments, an image that evoked the concept of feasts and celebration (Eccl. 9:8).

The church of Sardis represents a return of Christianity to its sources. The church of the Reformation, its people rediscover the original message of the Bible. Minds open as the quest for truth reignites. The Reformation movement established direct access to the biblical documents, removing the barriers of priest and tradition. Scholars encouraged the reading of the Bible in its original languages, Greek and Hebrew, and began to produce the first Hebrew grammars.

But quickly the dynamism of change solidified into dogma. The church introduced new traditions and creeds. A concern for correct doctrine prevailed over a personal relationship with God. Intolerance crept back into church life. The Protestants had their own Inquisitions. Calvin had scholars such as Michael Servetus (1511-1553) executed at the stake, while Luther raged against Catholics and Jews and vowed to exterminate those who chose not to follow his lead. The victims of the religious wars of Europe were not only Protestants as church leaders committed more crimes in God's name. Both the Protestant and the Catholic churches established themselves as powerful institutions. Forgetting the sources of truth, Protestants fell into the same kinds of mistakes they had criticized in the medieval church.

History is bound to repeat itself for those who do not remember. The church that does not remain vigilant loses its reason for existence. The city guards have fallen into slumber. "Wake up!" the divine letter urges. "Strengthen what remains and is about to die" (Rev. 3:2); "if you do not wake up, I will come like a thief" (verse 3).

Imperatives thunder throughout the letter to Sardis: "wake up!" "strengthen," "remember," "obey," "repent." Such language seeks to arouse people who, as had the ancient dwellers of Sardis, retreated into wealth and comfort.

"Yet," sighs the author of the letter, "a few people in Sardis" remain faithful to their beginnings. They have not "soiled their clothes" (verse 4). A minority endures. The notion of a "remnant" permeates the biblical tradition. From Seth, the third son of Adam, to the builders of the Temple under Ezra and Nehemiah; from the patriarchs Abraham, Isaac, and Jacob to the disciples of Elijah, the history of God's covenant with His people is constantly reorganized around these precious few, this surviving "remnant."

God made the same promise of a surviving remnant to the prophet Isaiah, who proclaimed it in the name of one of his sons, Shear-Jashub (a remnant will return), as a sign to his slumbering people (Isa. 7:3). Yohanan also plays on the name *Sardis* to convey his prophetic message through the alliteration *"sterison!"* ("Wake up!"). Within the name of Sardis we can hear the resonant *sterison,* the powerful outcry to awaken those threatened by the slumber of death.

Philadelphia

Just 40 miles to the east of Sardis, Philadelphia lies scarred by its tumultuous past of earthquakes. The great volcanic plain that surrounds bears the name Katakaumena (burned earth). Colonists from Pergamum who wanted to propagate the Greek language and culture founded the city during the reign of Attalus II (159-138 B.C.E.). The city of Philadelphia ("brotherly love") owes its name to the great love of the king for his brother Eumenes II. Yet it bore other names as well. In gratitude to Tiberius (Roman emperor from 14 to 37 C.E.), who aided its reconstruction after devastating earthquakes, it adopted the name of Neo-Caesarea (new city of Caesar), then changed it again to Flavia in gratitude to the later emperor (Flavius) Vespasian (ruling from 69-79 C.E.). The letter to the church of Philadelphia reflects its tormented past. Again, prophecy takes over historical detail to illustrate its message. Like the city of Philadelphia, colonists have founded the prophetic church of Philadelphia. The church of Philadelphia is the church of missions, expanding beyond the European frontier to Africa and the Americas (end of the eighteenth century to the beginning of the nineteenth). A renewal of its spirit and the enthusiasm and the zeal of the beginning characterize the spirit of its Christianity: "I know that you have little strength, yet you have kept my word and have not denied my name" (Rev. 3:8).

41

The elect of Philadelphia walk in the steps of the remnant of Sardis. They too have kept the word. But the church of Philadelphia is in a better condition. Although it has a righteous remnant, the letter to Sardis calls for "strengthening" what remains of the word. But the letter to Philadelphia has only praise for the endurance of those who have "kept" (verses 8, 10) the word. The situation in Philadelphia has progressed beyond that of Sardis. What believers in Sardis only dreamed of now becomes reality in Philadelphia. In Sardis the coming of the Messiah might be like that of a thief; one does not wait, let alone long for, the arrival of a thief. The letter to Philadelphia, though, mentions the Messiah's return without a negative tone, and the wording suggests that believers await it with impatience: "I am coming soon" (verse 11).

The church of Philadelphia is a time of revival between God and His people. Even the church's enemies will acknowledge its status as God's beloved: "I will make them come and fall down at your feet and acknowledge that I have loved you" (verse 9; cf. Ps. 23:5). We see the reciprocity between the covenant and the love of God suggested by the echo between the two verbs: "you have kept" (Rev. 3:10) and "I will also keep you" (verse 10). The prophets had already proclaimed this relationship: "I will be your God and you will be my people" (Jer. 7:23). In the Song of Songs it takes on the language of love: "My lover is mine and I am his" (S. of Sol. 2:16; cf. S. of Sol. 6:3; 7:10, 11). This relationship of exclusive love resonates in the church's very name—Philadelphia, "brotherly love."

Here again the Apocalypse affirms the eschatological hope: "I am coming soon" (Rev. 3:11). The promise made to "him who overcomes" reaches beyond the one given to the church of Sardis. It is now one of everlasting duration in the new kingdom inaugurated by the arrival of the Messiah. "I will make [the overcomer] a pillar in the temple of my God. Never again will he leave it" (verse 12). The "pillar" conveys already by association the idea of continuation. In the Jewish world it was customary to erect a pillar as a monument to help remember a person beyond his or her death and thus immortalize the individual in the memory of the living. Such pillars, for instance, formed part of the ancient synagogue of Chorazin and Kefar Nahum

(Capernaum). Being identified as a pillar means then that a person will remain forever an essential part of the temple of God. But the promise goes even further—they will also be identified with God Himself, since the name of God will be written on them. Like the ancient Greco-Roman city, the overcomers of Philadelphia receive the name of their benefactor—of their God. This reward, however, will deeply affect the identity and the fate of the righteous as it transforms their very being. The righteous has forever become a person identified in relationship to God and His temple. The Talmud resonates with the same associations. "Three are called by the name of the Holy One Blessed Be He, and they are the following: the righteous, the Messiah and Jerusalem."[50]

The church of Philadelphia is characterized by its hope in the kingdom of God. This is the time in history probably the most pre-occupied with eschatological hope. Such hope seized people in the United States, Germany, Scandinavia, France, Switzerland, and the Netherlands. A historian of the time, John B. McMaster, reports that nearly 1 million people out of the 17 million in the United States participated in this movement.[51] Their expectations were all the more serious because they seemed reinforced by biblical prophecy. Religious leaders even determined a precise date for the prophetic calculations: 1844.

Interestingly, the same fever also gripped Jews and Muslims. In Judaism, the rebirth of European Jewry through Hassidism included a prediction of the Messiah's coming for the year 5603 (1843/1844).[52] The Baha'i Muslims reached a similar conclusion. The *bab* ("the door," opening to the hidden *iman*) would appear in the year 1260 of the *hegira,* that is, in 1843/1844.[53] And in the sec-ular world, the birth of Marxism, with its hopes and optimism in human progress, also proclaimed the expectation of a new world.

We understand better the significance of the letter's promise: "See, I have placed before you an open door that no one can shut" (Rev. 3:8). The image of an "open door" reoccurs in the next chapter (Rev. 4:1). The period of the church of Philadelphia, as portrayed by the open door to heaven and to earth, is thus one of hope and expectations—a time of preparing for salvation coming from above.

Laodicea

After Philadelphia, the prophet's gaze journeys 45 miles south to Laodicea. It is the last stop, the time of the end—our time, an idea already brought out by the fact that it is the seventh letter, a symbol of the end. The idea of finality permeates the message. Already the author presents Himself as the "Amen" (Rev. 3:14). Here we have the last word, the fulfillment of all the promises, of all the prayers. The prophet Isaiah had long ago described the Lord as the "God of the Amen" (Isa. 65:16, literal translation).[54] In both texts a reference to Creation follows both amens.

The God of the Amen in Isaiah swears to "create new heavens and a new earth" (verse 17). In the letter to Laodicea, the God of the Amen defines Himself as the "beginning of God's creation" (Rev. 3:14, an alternate translation to the NIV). The Greek word *arche* for "beginning" renders the Hebrew word *bereshit* (beginning) in Genesis 1:1.[55] The God of the end is also the God of beginnings. He is present from the beginning to the end.

During these last days God's coming has never been so close. The letter depicts Him as knocking on the door (Rev. 3:20), as sung in the Song of Solomon, whose beloved is also pictured at the door (S. of Sol. 2:8, 9; 5:5). Yeshua is at the door, which means in the language of the New Testament that the end is near (Matt. 24:33; Mark 13:29). The next allusion to the intimate meal has the same connotation: "I will come in and eat with him, and he with me" (Rev. 3:20).

The meal has long symbolized the longing for the final reunion. The idea of longing flavors every sacred meal of the Levitical calendar.[56] It appears in Psalm 23, in which the banquet table honors the one who has remained close to God even to the point of death. The meals taken by Yeshua and His disciples in the New Testament have the same connotation.[57] The last supper they shared, the *seder,* they did so in the hope of their final reunion in heaven, and it has come to embody hope for all Christians.[58]

The final banquet of reunion is one of the central themes of the Apocalypse.[59] The hope of the Bible is real, it is concrete. It affects all of our senses. Touch, smell, sight, and taste each contribute to the enjoyment of this hope. The presence of the guest enriches the experience all the more. The traditional expression: "I will come in and eat with him, and he with me" (Rev. 3:20) further indicates the intimacy and mutuality of the relationship. In the Middle East people customarily sit on the floor together and eat with their hands from the same dish, touching and sharing each other's food, a risky business indeed. The meal was truly an act of communion. We must expect the reunion with God to be a concrete event, one to experience physically and historically. Interestingly, the one who hopes in our passage is not humanity, but God. It is God who knocks, who pleads, not us: "Here I am! I stand at the door and knock. If anyone hears my voice . . ." (verse 20).

God is the one who must be invited in. The meal is first to be partaken in our midst. In contrast to the situation in Philadelphia, only we may open the door: "If anyone hears my voice and opens the door, I will come in." After a long plea for change and repentance (verses 15-19), it is God's last request, which is all the more pathetic because Laodicea does not even feel the need for change. The church thinks itself righteous, as indicated by its name "righteous people," and as the letter explicitly mentions: "You say, 'I am rich; I have acquired wealth and do not need a thing'" (verse 17).

This is precisely the attitude of the ancient city of Laodicea, renowned for its riches and elaborate banking system. When the Roman statesman Cicero (106-43 B.C.E.) traveled through Asia Minor, he would always stop there to retrieve his letters of credit. The people of Laodicea had produced their own currency since the second century B.C.E. bearing the image of their local gods. Wholly self-sufficient, Laodicea needed no outside intervention. The historian Tacitus (55-120 C.E.) had marveled that, after its devastation by an earthquake in 61 C.E., the city of Laodicea had reconstructed itself without any aid from the Roman government.[60]

Laodicea also owed its wealth to its fertile farmland and pastures, where grazed the sheep whose pure black wool had made the city's fame.[61] It was the center of a flourishing textile industry. The city was also renowned for its exports of medicinal eyesalve.

But the prophetic letter considers all the city's wealth as worthless. Laodicea's gold is tarnished, its purity dubious. The letter advises it to buy gold "refined in the fire" (verse 18). Likewise God scoffs at the church's wardrobe, counseling it to clothe itself. Blinded by its own sense of self-worth, it cannot even see that it is naked. The snobs of Laodicea are ridiculous—they walk around puffed up, full of the illusion that they are well dressed, when they are in fact just naked and miserable. The letter then urges them to purchase eyesalve to help them see their own wretchedness.

God has found the riches of Laodicea—its gold, textiles, eyesalve, all of its possessions—lacking. The reason is simple: Its riches come from the wrong source. The church must "buy from me" (verse 18)—from Yeshua. The wealth of these last-hour believers is rubbish, because it does not come from God. Their situation is all the more tragic because they are unaware of it and believe they are rich. Their mentality is but the symptom of a civilization that prides itself in its secularism and humanism while excluding God. Its riches—even spiritual and religious—it accumulates by the prowesses of reason. Religious issues have been stripped of all references to the supernatural. Miracles belong to ancient myths and beliefs. The kingdom of God has become a human construction. The institutional church—if not the nation—has replaced the city of God. Politics takes the place of religion, and reason that of revelation. The human has usurped the divine on all levels. This attitude has infiltrated even those who are supposed to wait. The certainty of the truth and the high level of morality and spirituality they have achieved only sinks them into self-satisfaction and pride. Material wealth—the successful outcome of missionary, administrative, and ecclesiastical projects—conceals the actual wretchedness of the situation. And even when they do sense their need, the passion is lacking. Indifference accompanies ignorance. After diagnosing their problem, the letter to Laodicea declares: "Because you are lukewarm—neither hot nor cold—I am about to spit you out of my mouth" (verse 16). The ancient city had mineral springs nearby. Nothing is more nauseating than lukewarm sulphur water, and it symbolized the church's spiritual condition.

We don't need to mention any names, since we all fit the profile. The letter to Laodicea is also a "judgment of the people," the other meaning of the name "Laodicea." What can be done? For the author of the letter, the solution lies beyond human means. There is no point in organizing yet another colloquium, another committee, or even resorting to the game of power or of money. The answer lies elsewhere and involves a reversal of roles. The poor play rich, and the rich play poor. The people of Laodicea pass as rich. God answers by taking the rags of a beggar. The solution lies beyond the door, which may be opened only from the inside, as in the Song of Solomon (S. of Sol. 5:5). Those who run this risk—"him who overcomes"—do not just receive the name of God, as in Sardis, but now receive God's privilege and power to rule with Him: "I will give the right to sit with me on my throne" (Rev. 3:21).

Those who open the door of the heart will penetrate through the doors of heaven, and become part of a new order, another sovereignty, a new delight in things that no one deserves.

Interestingly, the very next chapter begins with a door: "And there before me was a door standing open" (Rev. 4:1) and revealing God's throne. The Apocalypse speaks of two doors. One is here below that God knocks passionately upon, as the beloved does in the Song of Solomon: "Listen! My lover is knocking: 'Open to me my sister, my darling'" (S. of Sol. 5:2). In this context, the knocking is extremely violent. The Hebrew verb used here, *dafaq*, denotes heavy pounding. Scripture uses the same word of the shepherd who hurries his sheep along.[62] This text suggests that Yeshua is pounding on the door. His passion indicates the urgency and seriousness of the situation. Opening the door of our hearts is our responsibility. Religion grapples with the reality of everyday existence and is concerned with our struggles and choices. It is our response to God's plea to become part of our lives.

The other door opens into the heavens. Only God can unlock it. It gives us access to His forgiveness and His kingdom. Religion is not merely existential, with ethical and emotional implications. Nor is it only the concern of the individual and the present. The kingdom of God is not just in our midst (cf. Luke 17:20, 21). The Apocalypse speaks of another door, a door in heaven that only God

47

may swing open. The kingdom of God has cosmic aspects. The Apocalypse uses the same image of the door to suggest a relationship between individual and universal realms. The kingdom of God begins here below when we open the door: "I will come in and eat with him" (Rev. 3:20). The banquet has already started in our existence. God comes down among us and eats at our table. But in His presence we come to long for more. Our communion with Him creates a desire for a deeper intimacy. The meal becomes a mere appetizer to the main course. The closer we approach God, the more we crave His presence; the more we come to realize what is missing in this meal, the more we yearn for the banquet up there. And the more we open our door here, the more we sigh for God to swing aside the other door in heaven.

---

[1] Only in Revelation 5:6 does the book specifically mention the lamb, "looking as if it had been slain." The death of the lamb precedes the scene of the throne in chapter 5.

[2] In the biblical and Jewish tradition, bones allude to resurrection (see Eze. 37:1-14; 2 Kings 13:21; cf. Job 10:11; Ps. 34:20; Isa. 66:14; Gen. 50:25). In the pseudepigraphon of Jubilees (second century B.C.E.), the prohibition to break the bones of the Passover lamb seems linked to the miracle of resurrection: the bones of Israel are to remain whole, apparently for the resurrection (Jubilees 49:13).

[3] *Didache* 10. 6; cf. 1 Cor. 16:22.

[4] Babylonian Talmud, *Shabbath* 53b.

[5] See Dan. 2:28; cf. 2:37, 44, 45; Doukhan, *Secrets of Daniel,* p. 27.

[6] See Gen. 1; Ex. 34:18; Lev. 23:36; Num. 28:11, 19, 27, etc.

[7] See 4 Ezra (2 Esdras) 13:1; Ecclesiasticus (or Sirach) 7:3; 20:12; 22:12, etc.

[8] Col. 1:2; 4:13.

[9] *Canon Muratorianus: The Earliest Catalogue of the Books of the New Testament,* ed. Samuel Prideaux Tregelles (Oxford: 1867), pp. 19, 45.

[10] Rev. 2:7, 11, 17, 29; 3:6, 13, 22.

[11] Micah 1:10-16.

[12] See Dan. 11; cf. Doukhan, *Secrets of Daniel,* pp. 171-174.

[13] See W. M. Ramsay, *The Letters to the Seven Churches,* updated ed., ed. Mark W. Wilson (Peabody, Mass.: 1994), pp. 131-133.

[14] Dan. 2:37, 38; cf. Gen. 1:28; Doukhan, *Secrets of Daniel,* p. 30.

[15] 1 Peter 5:8; cf. Job 1:7 in the Septuagint.

[16] See Hippolytus (died about 226 C.E.) *The Refutation of All Heresies* 7. 24 (*Ante-Nicene Fathers,* vol. 5, p. 115); and Epiphanius (died in 403 C.E.) *Adversus Haereses* 1. 2. 25 (*Patrologicae Graecae,* vol. 41, cols. 319-330). See also D. M. Beck, "Nicolaitans," *Interpreter's Dictionary of the Bible* (1962), vol. 3, pp. 547, 548.

[17] On the early views of Christian gnosticism, see R. M. Grant, "Gnosticism," *Interpreter's Dictionary of the Bible* (1962), vol. 2, p. 404.

[18] See Gen. 1:29. Cf. Dan. 1:16; Doukhan, *Secrets of Daniel,* pp. 19, 20.

[19] See Prov. 3:1-18.

[20] See Babylonian Talmud, *Ketubot* 111b; cf. *Zohar* 2. 151a-151b.

[21] See Acts 7-9.

[22] Donald Kagan, Steven Ozment, and Frank M. Turner, *The Western Heritage,* 3rd ed. (New York: 1987), pp. 191, 192.

[23] See Doukhan, *Secrets of Daniel,* pp. 108, 109, 143-145.

[24] *Aboth* 5. 1-9.

[25] Franz Cumont, *Études syriennes* (Paris: 1917), pp. 63ff.

[26] Rev. 20:6, 14; 21:8.

[27] Targum of Jeremiah 51:39, 57; cf. Targum of Deuteronomy 33:6 and of Isaiah 22:14; 65:6, etc.

[28] Daniel probably alludes to the two types of death and resurrection in Daniel 12:2.

[29] Num. 25:1-5.

[30] See Samuele Bacchiocchi, *From Sabbath to Sunday: A Historical Investigation of the Rise of Sunday Observance in Early Christianity* (Berrien Springs, Mich.: 1977), and Kenneth A. Strand, "The Sabbath and Sunday From the Second Through the Fifth Centuries," in *The Sabbath in Scripture and History,* ed. Kenneth A. Strand (Hagerstown, Md.: Review and Herald Pub. Assn., 1982), pp. 323-332.

[31] Doukhan, *Secrets of Daniel,* pp. 34, 35.

[32] *Ibid.,* pp. 106-111.

[33] Ex. 16:15; Ps. 78:25.

[34] Ex. 16:33, 34; Heb. 9:4.

[35] Mekhilta 16. 25; cf. 2 Baruch 29:8; Babylonian Talmud, *Hagigah* 12b.

[36] Gen. 17:5.

[37] Gen. 32:28.

[38] Jer. 33:16.

[39] See Ex. 3:13-15; cf. Gen. 32:29, 30; Judges 13:17, 18, which led to the prohibition against pronouncing the divine name (see Babylonian Talmud, *Kiddushin* 71a; Mishnah, *Sanhedrin* 10. 1).

[40] Babylonian Talmud, *Baba Bathra* 75b.

[41] *Midrash on the Psalms,* Psalm 21, section 2.

[42] See Josephus *Antiquities of the Jews* 7. 13. 2.

[43] 2 Kings 8:18, 26, 27; 10; 11.

[44] 1 Maccabees 8:14; Homer *The Illiad* 4. 141-145.

[45] Ex. 25:4; 28:5, 6; 39:29; Josephus *Wars of the Jews* 5. 5. 4.

[46] Acts 16:14, 15, 40.

[47] See Doukhan, *Secrets of Daniel,* p. 109.

[48] Babylonian Talmud, *Sukkah* 52a.

[49] *Pesiqta Zutarta,* Num. 24:17.

[50] Babylonian Talmud, *Baba Bathra* 75b.

[51] *A History of the People of the U.S. From the Revolution to the Civil War* (New York: 1920), vol. 7, p. 136.

[52] See especially Menahem Mendel, *Zemah Zedek* (1870-1874).

[53] See Mírzá Husain Hamadani, *The Táríkh-i-jadíd, or New History of Mírzá 'Alí Muhammad, the Báb,* trans. and ed. Edward G. Browne (Cambridge: reprint 1975), p. xxxv.

[54] The NIV translates "God of truth." The word *amen* has same root as the word *emet,* truth.

[55] See also John 1:1.

[56] Gen. 14:18-20; 31:54; Deut. 12:5-7, 17, 18; 14:23, 26; 15:20; Ex. 18:12; 24:11; 1 Sam. 9:11-14; Prov. 9:1-5.

[57] See Matt. 5:6; 9:11; 22:1-14; Mark 6:35-44; Luke 13:29.

[58] Mark 14:25; 1 Cor. 11:26.

[59] Rev. 2:7; 3:20; 19:7, 9; 22:2.
[60] *The Annals* 12. 27.
[61] Strabo *The Geography of Strabo* 12. 8. 16.
[62] See Gen. 33:13.

CHAPTER 2

THE CHRISTIAN JIHAD

(Revelation 4–8:1)

Shavuot

And, indeed, the door of Revelation 3 responds to another door: the "door standing open in heaven" of
Revelation 4. The voice of the Son of man again grips
Yohanan. This time, however, Yeshua tells the prophet
to "come up here" (Rev. 4:1). And when he does he sees that "before me was a throne in heaven with someone sitting on it" (verse 2).

The Apocalypse is the New Testament book that has the most
references to a throne. Among the 62 occurrences of the Greek word
for "throne" in the New Testament, 47 appear in the Apocalypse,
followed by only four in the Gospel of Matthew. The throne motif
is important to Yohanan. The allusion to the throne concerns both
the prophet's contemporaries—preoccupied with earthly thrones, especially that of Caesar—and people today who have discarded the
notion of throne as nothing more than a monarchic vestige. The
Apocalypse multiplies the allusions to the throne of God to remind
us that there is indeed a "throne in heaven," one exalted above all
other thrones. "Throne" is the key word of chapter 4. Of the 47 uses
of the word in the Apocalypse, it has 14 of them.

Yohanan merely mentions the throne and does not attempt to
describe it. As for the Person seated on the throne, Yohanan also
finds himself incapable of portraying Him. Here, however, he becomes poetic and compares the individual to three precious stones:

51

jasper, carnelian, and emerald. This specific combination is significant, since the chest-piece of the high priest of Israel contains the
same three stones (Ex. 28:17-19). It is the only place that Scripture
mentions the three gems together. Yohanan does not see much of
the mysterious Being seated on the throne except for the three jewels. The intention is again to evoke the temple.

The rainbow above the throne adds to its grandeur. It also reminds us of the rainbow of hope after the Flood. A symbol of grace,
the rainbow serves to temper the aura of justice represented by the
throne. In the midst of "lightning, rumblings and peals of thunder"
(Rev. 4:5)—precursors of the upcoming historical chaos and the
wrath of God [1]—the rainbow is the sign of God's love that, with His
justice, saves and gives hope. The rainbow is also the "appearance of
the likeness of the glory of the Lord" (Eze. 1:28); that is, of His infinite greatness and power. The great arc embraces the heavens and
the earth—the totality of the universe.

Around the throne sit 24 elders. Their age identifies them with
the white-maned judge (see Rev. 1:14), and their position—they,
like Him, sit on thrones—reveal their quality as judges. The 24 elders then represent the ones who "overcame" in the letter to
Laodicea—those invited to sit with the Son of man on the throne
(Rev. 3:21) to help Him judge. But not until chapter 20 will the
Apocalypse describe them as judging. For now, they present praise
and adoration (Rev. 4:9-11). Their duty a little later involves trans-
mitting "the prayers of the saints" (Rev. 5:8), and one of them even
helps Yohanan identify the last remnant (Rev. 7:13, 14). Such re-
sponsibilities reflect those of priests rather than of judges. Yet the
two roles are not necessarily incompatible. Seated upon thrones,
they are, like the high priest, invested with the double duty of priest
and judge, a linkage that dates from the time of Moses, when the
priest was also judge.[3]

Of course, the number 24 is symbolic. It is related to the number 12, the number of the covenant (four, number of the earth,
times three, number of God). The 12 tribes of Israel, as well as the
12 disciples of Yeshua, have the same connotation, one clearly attested in the Apocalypse (Rev. 21:12, 14). The number 12 repre-

sents the people of the covenant, the remnant, the whole of Israel, the Israel of the Apocalypse. The number 24 also evokes the Jerusalem Temple service with its 24 divisions of priests (1 Chron. 24:1-19). A "chief" (1 Chron. 24:5, called an "official" in the NIV), led each group. Interestingly, the Mishnah calls them "elders."[4] Like the priests, the singers belonged to 24 groups (1 Chron. 25:1-31) and, like the "elders," they adored God by playing the harp (Rev. 5:8; cf. 1 Chron. 25:1, 6, 7). The activities of the elders are nothing else than a heavenly service of adoration, of which the earthly Temple service was the mere reflection.[5]

The sea of glass, clear as crystal, appears to extend ad infinitum before the throne (Rev. 4:6) and thus evokes the cosmic dimension of the situation. Also, the image of the throne of God suspended above water proclaims the power of God over the elements. The Apocalypse here represents God as the Creator. The book of Genesis describes the creation of the world in terms of a victory over the element of water, a symbol of emptiness and of darkness.[6]

The latter theme occurs also in the Psalms[7] and in the book of Isaiah.[8] Psalm 104 places God's throne above water to signify His sovereignty over creation: "And lays the beams of his upper chambers on the waters" (Ps. 104:3). It is probably this image that inspired the sea of bronze that Solomon had cast for the Temple (2 Chron. 4:2). The divine Judge, King of the universe, was thus identified as the Creator.[9]

Interestingly, a reference to the Spirit of God (Rev. 4:5), the active agent of Creation (Gen. 1:2), introduces the sea of glass, the symbol of Creation. Moreover, the description of the four beings, which represent the earth, follows the imagery of the sea of glass. In the Bible, as in the rest of the ancient Near East, the number 4 symbolizes the terrestrial dimension. We recall the four cardinal points[10] and the four corners of the earth.[11] The prophet Daniel speaks of the four winds of heaven (Dan. 7:2), which again represent the earth in its totality. He also recounts the history of the human race (Dan. 2 and 7) through the symbolism of four kingdoms.

What is most striking about the four beings is their appearance. The first resembles a lion, the second an ox, the third a man, and the fourth an eagle. An ancient Jewish story, a midrash, borrows the same language. According to Rabbi Abahu, there are four powerful creatures: the eagle, the most powerful among the birds; the ox, the most powerful among domesticated animals; the lion, the most powerful among wild animals; and man, the most powerful among all animals.[12] Tradition regards these four beasts as representing the whole of creation, as the 24 elders exemplify more specifically the human race. The Apocalypse sets the creation of the universe at the heart of the vision of the throne.

The liturgy chanted by the 24 elders in response to the incantations of the four beings also alludes to Creation. First, the four beings hover over the throne, singing in triple meter: "Holy, holy, holy, . . . who was, and is, and is to come" (Rev. 4:8). This parallelism suggests that the holiness of God manifests itself in the three components of time and of history: the past, the present, and the future. In other words, God is ever holy. The prophet Isaiah received a similar vision (Isa. 6:1-3). It too emphasized the sanctity of God three times: "Holy, holy, holy is the Lord Almighty; the whole earth is full of his glory" (verse 3).

Then the 24 elders fall down in adoration, throwing their crowns before the throne. And the cycle resumes. The four beings keep singing God's holiness. Their liturgy never ends.

The scene engulfs space and time. The objects, the voices, the images, the persons—all typify the same adoration to the glory and honor of the Creator-God: "You are worthy, our Lord and God, to receive glory and honor and power, for you created all things, and by your will they were created and have their being" (Rev. 4:11).

What makes God worthy of adoration as judge and king is that He is Creator of the universe—that He is our Creator. Were He not our Creator, our adoration would be idolatry. One can adore the Creator or idolize the creation. Only God, because He has created us, may judge our destiny and our salvation.

"You are worthy" (Rev. 4:11) anticipates the question in chapter 5: "Who is worthy?" (Rev. 5:2). This question comes as a shout, and concerns a sealed book held in the right hand of the divine Judge seated upon the throne: "Who is worthy to break the seals and open the scroll?" (verse 2). The question is left hanging as the universe is silent. "But no one in heaven or on earth or under the earth could open the scroll or even look inside it" (verse 3). The fact that no one responds leaves Yohanan devastated, but one of the elders reassures him: "Do not weep! See, the Lion of the tribe of Judah, the Root of David, has triumphed. He is able to open the scroll and its seven seals" (verse 5).

And then he sees Him, the Worthy One, standing in the midst of the heavenly beings, "in the center of the throne" (verse 6). But its appearance hardly resembles that of a mighty lion—the Lion of the tribe of Judah that has triumphed. Instead, in the center of the throne sits a feeble lamb—a sacrificed lamb at that. This paradox—the uniting of force with weakness—is also evoked by the dual character of the lamb. It has seven horns. In the Bible horns symbolize strength.[13] The lamb also has seven eyes, "which are the seven spirits" (verse 6) and symbolize the divine capacity to see and understand everything everywhere. The allusion to Zechariah 4:10 is clear: "These seven are the eyes of the Lord, which range throughout the earth."

Obviously, the sacrificed lamb represents Yeshua Himself as the Messiah, son of David and Lion of Judah (verse 5), triumphant over death and evil precisely through His humility and sacrifice. The lamb approaches the sealed book: "He came and took the scroll from the right hand of him who sat on the throne" (verse 7).

Next Yohanan sees Yeshua standing at the right of "him who [is sitting] on the throne," an image that closely resembles Peter's description during Shavuot (Pentecost), the Feast of Weeks, concerning the Messiah's enthronement after His death: "God has raised this Jesus to life, and we are all witnesses of the fact. Exalted to the right hand of God, He has received from the Father the promised Holy Spirit and has poured out what you now see and hear" (Acts 2:32, 33).[14]

This scene from the Apocalypse follows the traditional ritual of enthronement found throughout ancient Near Eastern culture. It was customary for the new king to read the covenant that bound him to his suzerain out loud.[15] Likewise, in Israel, the newly crowned king inaugurated the enthronement ceremony by reading the "book of the covenant,"[16] thus expressing his dependence on his suzerain God.

The covenant ceremony at Sinai (Ex. 19 and 20) followed the same scenario. There also, God's people received a document written by Him on both sides (Ex. 32:15; cf. Rev. 5:1). Similarly, flashes of lightning, thunder, and trumpets (Ex. 19:16; 20:18; cf. Rev. 4:1, 5) accompany the event. In addition, the Lord summoned the prophet to "come up" and receive God's revelation (Ex. 19:24; cf. Rev. 4:1) and also called the people to be a nation of priests (Ex. 19:6; cf. Rev. 5:10). Finally, the occasion is that of the inauguration of the sanctuary (of the earthly one in Exodus 19 and 20, and of the heavenly one in Revelation 4 and 5).[17]

The prophet of the Apocalypse interprets the enthronement of Yeshua as an inauguration of the sanctuary. The Epistle to the Hebrews sheds some light on the significance of such an association: "The point of what we are saying is this: We do have such a high priest, who sat down at the right hand of the throne of the Majesty in heaven, and who serves in the sanctuary, the true tabernacle set up by the Lord, not by man" (Heb. 8:1).

Such language saturated with Levitical terminology was designed to impress the Christian Jews of New Testament times, to make them understand the role and the actual value of the sacrifice of a Messiah who was still active: Yeshua is still alive and intercedes for us to this day.

Interestingly, the enthronement of Yeshua takes place in the liturgical context of Pentecost, a point already hinted at by the numerous parallels between our passage and Exodus 19 and 20, the main liturgical reading during Pentecost. The book of Acts further confirms this association by pairing the event of the Christian Pentecost with Yeshua's enthronement (Acts 2:1, 34). In the Apocalypse, Pentecost, which prepares for the breaking of the seven seals, recalls the Passover of the preceding chapter, which introduced the reading of the seven letters. The Apocalypse thus follows the Jewish liturgical calendar. Pentecost follows Passover, and marks the end of the 50-day countdown from the second day of Passover (Lev. 23:15, 16). From this fact comes its English and Greek names, which derive from the Greek word for 50, and the Hebrew name *Shavuot*, signifying "weeks" and referring to the seven weeks (7 x 7) covered by this time span.

Virtually all the lessons of the Jewish Shavuot are present in the Christian Pentecost. Shavuot is the Feast of Harvest or the day of the firstfruits (Ex. 23:14-19; Lev. 23:9-22). Likewise, the Christian Pentecost celebrates the first conversions, the firstfruits of the Christian proclamation. Pentecost realizes God's dream for Israel: "You have made them to be a kingdom and priests to serve our God" (Rev. 5:10; cf. 1:6; and Ex. 19:6).

The Christian Pentecost celebrates the first mass dispensation of the Spirit.[18] Our passage here in the Apocalypse alludes to it by mentioning the "seven spirits of God" (Rev. 4:5; 5:6). But Pentecost is especially connected to the resurrection of Yeshua and to His glorious enthronement in heaven. The Apocalypse identifies the lamb with the "Lion of the tribe of Judah, the Root of David" (Rev. 5:5), thus fulfilling the ancient promise of an eternal Davidic dynasty.[19] The ritual enacted by the Son of man standing at the right of God inaugurates Him as eternal Davidic king to the praise of the heavenly hosts.

The voices of the heavenly host, joyous in liturgical praise of the worthiness of the lamb, now answer the question of "Who is worthy?" The liturgy revolves around this theme in a four-part crescendo.

1. The first voices are those of the four beings and of the 24 elders who sing "You are worthy" "because you were slain, and with your blood you purchased men for God from every tribe and language and people and nation" (verse 9).

A harp accompanies the song. Music mingles with incense, which is linked to the prayers of those who hope (verse 8). Truly a "new song" (verse 9), never before sung, it is a new poem with new emotions and a new melody. The psalms often use this expression to express a radical change of heart from darkness to light, from death to life. Usually the expression appears in the context of creation.[20]

2. The next voices that we hear are a chorus of angels: "Worthy is the Lamb . . . to receive power and wealth and wisdom and strength and honor and glory and praise" (verse 12). The seven attributes echo the seven horns, symbols of power.

3. The whole universe now breaks into song with "every creature in heaven and on earth and under the earth and on the sea, and all that is in them" (verse 13) joining their voices with the immense

chorus of angels, echoing their last words, but in reverse order. The angels had sung: "strength and honor and glory and praise" (verse 12). The creatures of the earth now answer: "praise and honor and glory and power" (verse 13), in harmony with the preceding chorus.

4. Finally, the four beings conclude with a powerful "Amen!" (verse 14). The elders fall down and worship, and the service concludes with silence. Words are not enough. Only silence may express the inexpressible.

The Seven Seals

The destiny of the universe is at stake. From the very first words, the trumpetlike voice had said so: "I will show you what must take place after this" (Rev. 4:1). Thus the vision of the seven seals is in this sense different from that of the seven churches. In the letters to the churches the prophet also saw "what is now" and not only "what will take place later" (Rev. 1:19).[21] But the vision of the seven seals is a turning point in the Apocalypse. From now on, the visions concern primarily the future.

The passage has already hinted at this. God holds the scroll in His right hand, the hand that controls the course of history.[22] The Apocalypse does not give the scroll's content,[23] but indicates only its form. It is an "opisthograph," a manuscript inscribed on both sides, as were most legal documents of the time.[24] Also, all the seals must be broken before the scroll may be opened. It is only at the seventh seal that we shall understand the scroll's purpose, and only then will hope take on its full significance.

"Come," the leitmotif that occurs in the seven seals, suggests a progression in time just as in the letters to the churches:

First seal: "Come" (Rev. 6:1)
Second seal: "Come" (verse 3)
Third seal: "Come" (verse 5)
Fourth seal: "Come" (verse 7)
Fifth seal: "How long?" (verse 10)
Sixth seal: "has come" (verse 17)
Seventh seal: silence (Rev. 8:1)

The "come" repeated by each of the four beings does not involve Yohanan, and is only partly directed at the horses that then appear. In fact, the "come" addresses the Lamb and involves the second advent of the Messiah, the *parousia*. The Greek verb *erchesthai* is the technical term used in the Apocalypse to designate the return of the Messiah.[25] The imperative form of this verb, *erchou*, translated in the breaking of the first four seals as "come," also occurs in the conclusion of the book as a pleading prayer (Rev. 22:17, 20). In the fifth seal the cry "How long?" (Rev. 6:10) quivers with urgency. It is the plea of those who approach the end.[26] With the sixth seal Yohanan experiences the coming as a current event: "has come." Finally, the seventh seal has no allusion to the "coming," only silence: the time has indeed come.

The seven seals thus punctuate the course of history, paving the way for the return of the Lamb. As with the seven churches, we must interpret the seven seals in a prophetic sense.

The vision of the seven seals runs parallel to that of the seven letters. They recount the same story but with a different emphasis. While the seven letters denounced the heresies of the churches, the seven seals condemn their oppression, violence, and persecution.

The White Horse

The Lamb opens the first seal, and a white horse appears—a symbol of conquest and victory. When Roman generals celebrated their triumphs, they paraded at the head of their armies on a white horse. The prophet understood the vision in a similar sense: "He rode out as a conqueror bent on conquest" (Rev. 6:2). Interestingly, the first being, resembling a lion (Rev. 4:7), introduces the imagery of the white horse, reminding us of another triumph, that of the Lion of Judah, of Yeshua Christ's victory enabling Him to open the seals (Rev. 5:5). Moreover, He receives a "crown" of victory (*stephanos*). In Revelation 19 the same image reappears to represent Yeshua Christ's victory: a white horse mounted by a rider also wearing a crown (verses 11-16). But the crown in that context is a royal one (*diadema*). The image of Revelation 6 concerns Yeshua the Messiah, but it does not necessarily apply to the coming of His kingdom. Yeshua is merely victorious, not yet king. He has won a battle, but the war is not over. In our text the rider is departing, not arriving: "he rode out." The history of Christianity is only beginning. We find ourselves in the time of early Christianity (first to third centuries).

The church is still relatively pure of its compromises, politics, and violence. It is a time when the emphasis is still on the fresh victory of Yeshua, and its implications for the life of the Christian. Interestingly, He has not achieved His victory through bloodshed. The crown of victory *(stephanos)* is "given"—it is a grace from above. The rider has a bow but no arrows. His victory is a peaceful one.

The Red Horse

The breaking of the second seal—introduced by the oxlike being—releases a red horse. Its rider has as his mission "to take peace from the earth and to make men slay each other" (Rev. 6:4). He receives "a large sword."

The history of Christianity has now undergone a change from peace to war. The context is not that of persecutions but of reciprocal butcheries. The red color of the horse resembles spilled blood (see 2 Kings 3:22), while the ox (calf) evokes the imagery of the butcher (Luke 15:27), and the sword announces the upcoming massacres. The same word, *machaira,* is used in the book of 1 Enoch, in which Israel receives a "great sword" to combat the infidels and to kill them.[27]

The church is fighting for its supremacy (between the fourth and fifth centuries) against the Arians. For the first time, the emperors support the church politically and militarily. The Roman emperor Constantine (306-337 C.E.), and later the Frankish emperor Clovis (481-511 C.E.), fight for it. It is the time described by Jules Isaac during which "the persecuted church rose up (or sank) to the status of office and victory."[28]

The Black Horse

The third seal opens on a scene of darkness: the black horse. Its rider holds in his hand a scale for the rationing of food, a symbol of famine, as expressed by Ezekiel: "Son of man, I will cut off the supply of food in Jerusalem. The people will eat rationed food in anxiety and drink rationed water in despair" (Eze. 4:16).

The black horse follows the red horse, as famine does war. The voice that surges from the midst of the four beings seems to be the voice of the Lamb, since He is also situated "in the center of the throne, encircled by the four living creatures" (Rev. 5:6). The voice of the judge seated on the throne is thus the voice of the Lamb, tempering justice with grace. And indeed, the voice orders that the oil and the wine be preserved (Rev. 6:6). Usually the olive tree and the vine, because of their deeper roots, can resist periods of drought better than wheat and barley. Moreover, grain, oil, and wine usually represent the three main products of the land of Israel.[29] The appearance of the third being, with its human face, already alludes to such an interpretation. It represents the spiritual dimension versus the natural and nonreligious aspects depicted by the other three beasts (see Dan. 4:16, 34; cf. 7:8, 13).[30] The famine therefore symbolizes spiritual drought. Moreover, grain, wine, and oil all have their distinct connotations in the Bible.

Grain symbolizes the Word of God.[31]   also Christian
Wheat vs tares
Oil symbolizes the Holy Spirit.[32]
Wine symbolizes the blood of Yeshua.[33]

The famine and drought affect only God's Word, sparing the Holy Spirit and the blood of Yeshua. Of the two components of the covenant, the human one—the Word of God—and the divine one—the Holy Spirit and the blood of Yeshua—the famine touches only the human one. On the human level, the church has lost its calling. It does not meet the spiritual and theological needs of its members. The people are not spiritually fed. The church neglects the study of the Word of God, and understanding is limited.

On the divine level, however, the influence of the Holy Spirit and the grace of the blood of Yeshua remain active among God's people, providing a balm of relief. Interestingly, the ancients traditionally used oil and wine as treatment for wounds.[34] The symbols are rich in connotations, and the two meanings of wine and oil are not mutually exclusive. Biblical symbolism often functions in this way. The wine and the oil represent the redemptive action of the Messiah, and constitute, as such, a balm upon the church's self-inflicted wounds.

61

The prophecy of the third seal recounts the time in history during which the church became so preoccupied with establishing itself as an institution that it forgot the spiritual needs of its members. The "grain" being measured and bought suggests this preoccupation with material wealth. Again, the grain has two connotations—that of the church's materialistic obsession and of the spiritual famine of Christians.

During this period the church established itself as a political power, with its own territory. Italy had just been liberated from the Arians (538 C.E.), and the church appropriated the region. Y. Congar would later note that the church was building "the basis for a vertical hierarchy, and finally a theocracy of power." [35] History has considered Gregory the Great (pope 590-604) as the first pope "to accumulate both political and religious functions." [36]

The more the church prospered materially and politically, the more impoverished it became spiritually. The institution itself and its traditions gradually came to replace the study of God's Word. It is a lesson important even today for churches seeking to establish themselves. Each time the church has sought to embellish its structure, to add to its grandeur and style, it has plunged itself into spiritual poverty. When the form rules in place of the content, the sense for the absolute, what really counts gets lost. But there is even a greater risk. Intoxicated by its political status, the church began to consider itself the criterion of truth. Dogma replaced the Word, creating an open invitation for oppression and intolerance.

The Pale Horse

The opening of the fourth seal brings a horse of a pale color *(chloros)*, suggestive of death and terror. The being resembling an eagle, a bird of prey and a biblical symbol of persecution and death, [37] precedes this horse. The church now embodies death to its most murderous degree. Not only does the Apocalypse call the rider "death," but another rider described as *Hades* (the dwelling place of the dead) immediately follows him. The Septuagint uses this Greek word to translate the Hebrew word *sheol,* that is, the place or state of the dead. The Apocalypse often combines the two words "death" and "dwelling place of the dead." [38] This last plague contains and surpasses all others. Sword and famine bring death. As for the "wild beasts," they only intensify the reference to death. The Bible often represents the dwelling place of the dead, *sheol,* as inhabited by wild beasts.[39]

It is the period of history when the church became the oppressor, persecuting all those suspected of heresy. We enter the time of the Crusades, the Inquisition, and the religious wars. On the horizon looms the shadow of the Nazi oppression, nurtured by the church's "teaching of contempt."[40] The pale horse also evokes the Holocaust, with its sophisticated death camps. Such an interpretation may seem somewhat disturbing. Yet Hitler's anti-Semitic rage is but the continuation of 18 centuries of denigration and persecution of the Jews by the church. Hitler was dead serious when he declared to two Catholic bishops that his intentions were to take over and finish the church's lethal work against the Jews.[41] And even if the *Shoah* (the Nazi massacre) was but indirectly related to the church, it remains nevertheless a consequence of its religious policy. Even if the church did not implement the Holocaust, we know today of its silent complicity.[42] The fourth horse therefore represents the culmination of the church's jihad.

Its conquest of the world had started with the triumph of peace. The scene had opened on a white horse, whose rider, Yeshua the Messiah, bore an empty bow. From the second horse, however, the momentum turned into violence. Whereas the Messiah had fought for the church, the church now considered it its duty to wage war for the Messiah. The religious wars and Crusades testify to a shift in the church's mentality. Action from below replaces revelation from above. The church assumed the prerogative to speak and act on God's behalf. Intolerance always stems from this type of usurping attitude, when God's witness comes to identity himself or herself with God; when success obliterates the revelation from above; when an imperialistic mentality replaces an evangelical concern; when statistics and the number of baptisms prevail over the genuineness of conversion; and when the church seeks the answer to its problems in strategies and marketing plans rather than in spiritual guidance. When humanity replaces God, anything goes. The reason is simple. The need for security always opts for the visible and concrete versus a humble trust in the incomprehensible and invisible God. The success of worldly achievements then lead only to pride and intolerance.

Violence and oppression are the natural consequences when we usurp God's role. From the Crusades to the concentration camps, each time people have hoisted themselves to God's level to fight in the name of the cross, or for the *"Gott mit uns,"* millions of victims have suffered, and their shouts to the heavens for justice still ring in our ears.

The Victims

The fifth seal marks a turning point. The opening of the first four seals revealed four horses, beckoned by each of the four living creatures to "Come!" In the opening of the next three seals we will find no more horses. The prophetic vision will be directly concerned with prophetic events themselves.

The outcry of history's victims shatters the fifth seal. The perspective now shifts from that of the oppressor to that of the victims. The moans of the men and women trampled replaces the hoofbeats of the conquering and oppressive horses.

From the point of view of the victims, only two questions matter: Why? and How long?

The first is the eternal question of the righteous victim. But the victims in our passage have even more reason to cry out—they are suffering "because of the word of God" (Rev. 6:9). It was the cry of the exiled Hebrews in Babylon thrown into the burning furnace because of their refusal to adore an idol; the cry of the early Christians thrown into the roaring stadiums because of their faith in the God of love; the cry of the Christian outcasts, thrown in prison or in the flames for having opened the Bible or proclaimed the truth revealed to them from above. But it is also the cry of the Jews, from the Middle Ages to our own times, denigrated, oppressed, pursued, massacred, and gassed, solely because of their being Jews and of their testifying to the ancient God.

Crucified because of God, the victims in the Apocalypse have died for God. Our text is deliberately ambiguous, describing their death as a holocaust, a sacrifice on an altar (Lev. 4:7). Their souls cry to God for vengeance just as the blood of Abel did (Gen. 4:10). The Apocalypse borrows language from Leviticus, which identifies the soul with the blood (Lev. 17:11), to better express the sacrificial character of their suffering. The blood of the martyrs is poured onto God's altar as a sacrifice, and as such, cannot go unheeded by Him. Justice shall be done.

The prophet swears not only to the salvation of the victims—they receive white robes—but also vengeance against the persecutors. Salvation implies justice. To save, God must judge. Too often Christians overemphasize the cross, grace, and the love of God to the detriment of His justice. Boiling religion down to emotions or spirituality, they forget the historical repercussions of salvation. But the crushed victim has a different perspective. Tender words of love, beautiful smiles, and charitable ideas do not suffice. Only the saving hand, which tears the victim from his suffering, really matters. The oppressed have no use for gentle, comforting words. Their obsession lies with deliverance, leading to their cry: "How long?"

Neither the consolation of religious experience, nor faith in the God of the past or of the present can silence the plea for justice. It demands that God intervene in the reality of history: "How long . . . until you judge?" (Rev. 6:10). The judgment has not yet come to pass, and God's people await it as a temporal event. This same cry resonates through the Psalms,[43] with the same impatience for God's judgment. But the outcry in the book of Daniel (Dan. 8:13)[44] is the strongest echo to the plea in our passage. In Daniel also, the cry is that of the persecuted saints (Dan. 8:12) and leads into the judgment of God.

To the question of "How long?" in the book of Daniel, the angel answers, "It will take 2,300 evenings and mornings; then the sanctuary will be reconsecrated" (Dan. 8:14). The reconsecration of the sanctuary alludes to the Day of Atonement, or Kippur,[45] that celebrates the cosmic judgment of God. This is the moment when, according to the parallel passage in Daniel 7, "the court was seated, and the books were opened" (Dan. 7:10).

The fifth seal opens on a judgment scene that takes place in heaven. According to this vision, however, it does not yet signify the end of suffering. Salvation is postponed "until the number of their fellow servants and brothers who were to be killed as they had been was completed" (Rev. 6:11). For salvation to be effective, everyone must be present, a concept based on the biblical principle of totality. God does not save one without the other. The salvation of the individual necessarily entails the salvation of the universe. Salvation is cosmic or it is not at all. In the present state of affairs, salvation is impossible. The kingdom of justice necessitates a reconsecration, a recreation—the fundamental lesson of Kippur.[46]

God is not simply the Lord of grace, of existence and of mystical experience, but also the God of justice and of holiness—the "Sovereign Lord, holy and true" (verse 10). We have already encountered this type of language in the letter to Philadelphia (Rev. 3:7). The two visions are moreover linked by the theme of "brothers," *adelphoi* (Rev. 6:11), implied in the very name of Philadelphia. These allusions help situate our passage in history. Indeed, the two passages cover the same time span: we are in the nineteenth century.

The prophecy's historical implications are intriguing. We are accustomed to reducing Christianity to a spiritual and nontemporal truth. But the God we encounter here is the only answer to the cry of the victims. God is love, but His love is not indifferent to suffering. It is a love coupled with justice that intervenes in favor of the oppressed.

Cosmic Chaos

To the moans of the trampled victims, answer the shrieks of terror of the oppressors as they tremble before God's wrath. The opening of the sixth seal reveals the other aspect of the justice of God. In the fifth seal we saw God's judgment from the victims' perspective as they cried out for vengeance (Rev. 6:10). The judgment was an event of salvation and of grace that dressed the victims with "white robes." Now the judgment turns against the oppressor in raging fury. These two aspects are complementary, two facets of salvation. To truly save, God must create anew, and the creation of the new necessitates the destruction of the old.

Humanity's sin has had repercussions throughout the universe. The event of Creation has already hinted at the interdependence between humanity and its environment. The human race and nature are inseparably linked. The effect of Adam's disobedience spread to nature in the form of thorns and weeds. The iniquity of the first generations of humanity led to the Flood. The perversity of the inhabitants of Sodom and Gomorrah consumed them in sulphurous fire. The land of Canaan vomited its inhabitants because of their iniquities.

The prophets of Israel also emphasized the principle of co-dependence. Moses, Hosea, Isaiah, and Jeremiah all reminded Israel of its responsibility for the cosmos. Sin affects plants, animals, time, mountains, and especially men and women. In the New Testament the death of Yeshua the Messiah shakes the earth and turns the light of day into the darkness of despair.

Every crime is against both humanity and the universe. God thus directs His wrath against the whole earth, against all people. The eye of the prophet traces this wrath to the very heart of our civilization. The time of the end splits in two phases:

The first affects the earth: "There was a great earthquake. The sun turned black like sackcloth made of goat hair, the whole moon turned blood red, and the stars in the sky fell to earth" (Rev. 6:12, 13). One remembers the natural phenomena that occurred between the end of the eighteenth century and the first part of the nineteenth century. The Lisbon earthquake (Nov. 1, 1755) killed 70,000 people, half the city's population. Unusual darkness affected areas of the United States and elsewhere between the years 1780 to 1880. And people observed meteorite showers of exceptional intensity between the years 1800 and 1900 in Europe, the Americas, Africa, and Asia.

Interestingly, the events coincide with the end of the time of trouble, as predicted by the prophet Daniel, a period already noted in the prophetic calendar as a time of remission for the oppressed by the church. We are at the end of the three and a half times (Dan. 7:25).[47] The French Revolution has neutralized the church's threat. The cosmic signs thus take on new meaning in the light of the prophetic vision, confirming that history is marching to its end. From the time of the end, we move to the end of time.

We must superimpose the vision of the sixth seal upon that of the fifth seal. Both seals occur in the same time span and account for the same events, but from a different perspective. In the fifth seal the prophetic vision revealed the suffering of God's people as they sighed "How long?" and joined voices with the oppressed of Daniel 8. This leads us into the middle of the nineteenth century. The vision had then flashed a scene beyond human history, one of grace and of judgment in which the oppressed received white robes.

Likewise, the vision of the sixth seal anticipates, beyond the end of the time of trouble (eighteenth and nineteenth centuries), the final extermination of the oppressor. This second phase occurs in heaven: "The sky receded like a scroll, rolling up" (Rev. 6:14). The event now encompasses the whole earth. The language already alludes to the event's universal character through the typical Hebrew way of citing the parts to express the totality of a thing: "Every mountain and island" (verse 14); "kings of the earth . . . generals . . . every slave and every free man" (verse 15). God's wrath invades the earth in its totality. The fate of the universe lies in His hands. His wrath encompasses everything and everyone. The sixth seal closes with the vision of God "who sits on the throne" (verse 16) and with the anguished question that concludes the oracle: "Who can stand?" (verse 17).

Yet this very question kindles the spark of hope—the paradox of biblical hope, which occurs when there is no more hope. The Apocalypse borrows the question from the prophets Nahum and Malachi, who use it to assure the faithful: "Who can withstand his indignation? . . . the rocks are shattered before him. The Lord is good, a refuge in times of trouble. He cares for those who trust in him" (Nahum 1:6, 7; cf. Mal. 3:2, 3).

Likewise, in the Apocalypse, the question opens on an interlude that concerns the survivors of the great cosmic chaos.

Interlude: The Survivors of Jacob

The destruction suddenly halts, and the prophetic eye zooms in on those who "withstood" (cf. Rev. 6:17). These survivors bear a sign, or mark, that will protect them from divine wrath. It reminds us of events in Egypt when the children of Israel were spared by the sign of the blood sprinkled on their door frames (Ex. 12:23). But this time the four winds of the earth, which carry the wrath of God, threaten the "four corners of the earth," that is, the whole earth.[48]

The chiastic structure (ABA') of the announcement to the angels identifies the survivors. The first action (A) spares the earth, sea, and trees (Rev. 7:1). The second action (B) threatens the earth and the sea (verse 2). And the third action (A') spares again the earth, sea, and trees (verse 3).

A (7:1)	B (7:2)	A' (7:3)
spares:	threatens:	spares:
the earth, sea, trees	earth and sea	earth, sea, trees

The center of the chiasm reveals the element of nature spared by the winds. The command explicitly limits destruction to the earth and the sea, representing the whole earth.[49] The trees are the sole survivors of the disaster. The text already hints, on the syntactic level, of their exceptional character. In the first action that introduces the other two, the Greek word for "tree" receives a different declination from the other two words "earth" and "sea," although each is preceded by the same Greek preposition. "Tree" is in the accusative, whereas the words "earth" and "sea" are in the genitive. This difference suggests that the winds relate differently to the earth and the sea than they do to the trees.

These stylistical and syntactic indications help distinguish the trees from the other elements, setting them apart. The trees represent persistence. Their roots, growing deep into the earth, protect them from the winds. In the Bible trees symbolize the righteous (Ps. 1:3; Jer. 17:8), whereas straw, easily carried off by the wind, stands for the wicked (Ps. 1:4; Job 21:18).

We must understand the angel's safeguarding of the trees as the divine protection of the righteous. But curiously, the trees/righteous do not owe their salvation to the strength of their roots. Their survival is a gift from above. An angel from the east—the direction symbolic of the sun that brings life and light; the Garden of Eden (Gen. 2:8); the human deliverer King Cyrus (Isa. 41:2); and the saving God Himself (Eze. 43:2)—marks their foreheads with a seal.

In contrast with the other seals in the Apocalypse that carried death, this one is the seal of life (Rev. 7:2). The other seals announced judgment and destruction. This one signifies salvation and creation. The other seals guaranteed the confidentiality of a document, but this one indicates ownership.

The ancients often marked their merchandise with a seal to designate whom it belonged to. Generally the seal used to mark the clay or wax consisted of a piece of metal or a precious stone (Ex. 28:11; Esther 8:8) that bore the engraved name or symbol of the owner. In our passage, the seal marks the forehead. It reminds us of Cain, who also received a mark on the forehead for his own protection (Gen. 4:15). But a passage in Ezekiel comes closest to ours: "[The Lord] said to him, 'Go throughout the city of Jerusalem and put a mark on the foreheads of those who grieve and lament over all the detestable things that are done in it.' As I listened, he said to the others, '. . . Slaughter old men, young men and maidens, women and children, but do not touch anyone who has the mark'" (Eze. 9:4-6).

Those who receive the mark on their foreheads are the faithful ones who react to the "detestable things" (verse 4) done by their contemporaries. The preceding verses use the same words, "detestable things," to speak of idolatry of the sun (Eze. 8:16, 17). The mark on the forehead then represents the adoration of the true God, the living God, the Creator. The meaning seems to be the same here in Revelation 7. The earth, sea, and trees sequence (cf. Gen. 1:9-13) intensifies the allusion to Creation. The seal marks those who believe in the Creator. To confess God's ownership of our lives is to recognize Him as our Creator. The psalms praise God as the owner of all things because He is the Creator: "The earth is the Lord's, and everything in it, the world, and all who live in it; for he founded it upon the seas and established it upon the waters" (Ps. 24:1, 2).[50]

To recognize God as the owner of everything amounts to acknowledging Him as Creator. His seal alludes to a whole way of thinking. To be sealed is to show that we owe everything to God, a theme that permeates the entire Bible. The tithe represents our giving back to God what is already His, a point already understood by Melchizedek, who justified Abram's giving his tithe with the proclamation of God as "Creator of heaven and earth" (Gen. 14:19). The book of Leviticus makes the same association. Before they entered the Promised Land God told the people of Israel that they must remember that the land belonged to Him: "The land is mine and you are but aliens and my tenants" (Lev. 25:23). Because of this fact "a tithe . . . belongs to the Lord" and is "holy to the Lord" (Lev. 27:30).

It is no coincidence that the Sabbath occupies the central place in the Decalogue, normally reserved for the seal in ancient covenant documents.[51] The Sabbath celebrates the Creator and His work—it is God's seal on Creation. We distinguish again the seal of God in the dietary choices of Daniel and his companions as they sought to show their dependence on the Creator rather than on the king (Daniel 1).[52]

The seal on the forehead represents God's mark on the whole person, the sign that we belong to Him. The image of God, if reflected in the human creature, constitutes, in a way, His seal. To belong to God is to live with Him. Through this image the Apocalypse designates those who confess the God of Creation in every facet of their lives. The Sabbath, the tithe, dietary choices, and respect for the law of God—all could indicate the presence of God's seal, but they do not magically produce it. The seal of God is both invisible and alive, just as the Creator God it represents.

Likewise for those who carry the seal. They constitute a spiritual entity. Their number, 144,000, composed of 12 x 12, is symbolic. The number 12 represents the number of the covenant between God and His people (4, number of the earth, x 3, number of God). It is also the number of the 12 tribes of Israel, explicitly mentioned (Rev. 7:4-8). Each tribe consists of 12,000 people. As for the number 1,000, which multiplies 12, it symbolizes not only the multitude[53] but also the tribe. In Hebrew, the word *elef* (thousand) stands for the tribe, the crowd, the clan, or even the regiment.[54] The number 12,000 thus depicts the tribe in its totality. In Yohanan's time, however, the records of who belonged to most tribes had disappeared with the destruction of the Temple. All that anyone could be sure about were those who claimed to be part of Judah, Benjamin, and Levi. Thus we should not take the Israel mentioned here in a literal sense. The rhythmic regularity of the list—like that of a parading army—reinforces the impression of completeness and perfection. The word *ochlos*, rendered in verse 9 by "multitude," also means "army."[55] And indeed, verses

9 and 10 describe a victorious army. White robes and palms were part of the ritual of celebrating military victory.[56] The style, language, and the numeric symbolism of the text all testify to the presence of all Israel. The 144,000 depict Israel marching as a whole. It is the "all Israel" dreamed by the apostle Paul (Rom. 11:26), the "complete" number of the saved, as alluded to in the fifth seal (Rev. 6:11). Also it is the great multitude, multicultural and multinational, that Yohanan sees adorned by the white robes (Rev. 7:9; cf. 6:11), survivors of the oppression (Rev. 7:14; cf. 6:9, 11).

The incomplete group of the fifth seal and the 144,000 are the same people. They are all present. Refugees of history, whose only point of reference was the heavens above, condemned to roam the earth always foreigners, citizens of the beyond, they are now re-united in the discovery of their lost identity, of their roots, of their people—their Israel. Sharing memories of hardship and suffering, they now belong together body and soul. Emotion wells up from broken hearts and escapes as a great cry of glory, a cry of victory (Rev. 7:10).

To their cry of victory, the angels, the elders, and the four living creatures answer "Amen!" in a sevenfold adoration: "Amen! Praise and glory and wisdom and thanks and honor and power and strength be to our God for ever and ever. Amen!" (verse 12).

The vision now takes place in heaven, in the far future, when the heavens shall join with the earth in adoration; when God shall truly live among His people. The latter shall serve Him "day and night in his temple" (verse 15) as did the ancient priests and Levites (1 Chron. 9:33). The vision unfolds with the image of the tent that God spreads over them (Rev. 7:15), evocative of the desert sanctuary. In Greek, *skenoun* (to spread the tent) sounds like the Hebrew word *shekinah* (from the verb *shakan,* to dwell), which designated the cloud of fire, a symbol of God's "dwelling" among His people (Ex. 40:34-38).

God's presence is a fact. He is physically with His people. The text concludes by an allusion to Psalm 23: "For the Lamb . . . will be their shepherd; he will lead them to springs of living water. And God will wipe every tear from their eyes" (Rev. 7:17).[57] God is not content just to provide for the needs of His creatures, but also yearns for an intimate relationship with them. Not only will He wipe out hunger, thirst, heat, and suffering from our existence, but God will comfort us by His very presence.

Silence in Heaven

The prophet now gazes at the final seal. Breaking it would at last reveal the contents of the scroll. But it is not opened like the others. Each time, Yohanan had been personally involved in the vision. The expression "I heard" had introduced the first four seals and "I saw" or "I looked" the fifth and sixth seals. But Yohanan does not need to see or hear the seventh seal. For the first time the events triggered by the seal occur exclusively in heaven. The first six concerned worldly events and followed the course of human history. The seventh seal, however, describes a very short moment recorded in only one verse (Rev. 8:1). And, finally, what it depicts is fundamentally different. After the shrieks of war, the roars of wild beasts, the moaning of men and women, the chaos of natural disasters (Rev. 6:12-16), suddenly we are met with silence—total silence.

Neither seen nor heard, the incident is beyond description. Silence expresses what even words, music, and art cannot. Only silence can communicate the unutterable. And only silence may express the infinite God.[58] The silence lasts for a good half hour. In prophetic language, in which one day stands for one year,[59] this amounts to a whole week (if one 24-hour day equals one prophetic year, one hour equals 365 divided by 24—that is, 15 days—and one-half hour stands for a week). Human history finishes as it had begun—by a time of creation. The week of silence of the end echoes the week of silence of the beginning (Gen. 1), a concept further confirmed by Jewish tradition.[60] The opening of the seventh seal reveals the scroll's content: the coming of God and the promise of a new creation, of a new world—the only solution to our questions, to our longings, and to our suffering.

---

[1] See Job 37:4; cf. Rev. 11:18, 19; 14:2, etc.
[2] Cf. Rev. 20:4.
[3] Deut. 17:9; cf. Jer. 18:18.

[4] See *Taanith* 2. 6; *Sukkah* 5. 6-8; *Yoma* 1. 5.

[5] See Ex. 25:40; cf. Heb. 8:5; 9:23.

[6] See also Eze. 26:19-21; Jonah 2:6; Hab. 3:10; cf. Philippe Reymond, *L'Eau sacrée, sa vie, et sa signification dans l'Ancien Testament,* Vetus Testamentum, Supplements (Leiden: 1958), vol. 6, p. 231. The image also appears in other contemporary cultures and in different myths. A Babylonian account describes the origin of the world in terms of the victory of Marduk, god of Babylon, over Tiamat, god of water.

[7] Ps. 136:6.

[8] Isa. 27:1; 40:12.

[9] Ps. 74:12, 13; 89:13-15.

[10] Jer. 49:36; Dan. 7:2.

[11] Rev. 7:1; 20:8.

[12] Hermann L. Strack and Paul Billerbeck, *Kommentar zum Neuen Testament aus Talmud und Midrasch* (Munich: 1922-1961), vol. 3, p. 799.

[13] See Ps. 132:17; Jer. 48:25; Dan. 7:8, 11, 21; Zech. 1:18, 19, etc.

[14] See also Acts 7:55, 56; Phil. 2:9-11; Heb. 8:1, 2; 10:19-22, etc.

[15] See Leslie C. Allen, *Psalms 101-150,* Word Biblical Commentary (Waco, Tex.: 1983), vol. 21, p. 80; Gerhard von Rad, "The Royal Ritual in Judah," in *The Problem of the Hexateuch and Other Essays* (London: 1966), pp. 103ff.

[16] Ex. 24:7; 2 Kings 23:2, 21; Deut. 17:18; 2 Kings 11:11-13; 23:3, etc.

[17] We would like to note that our passage in the Apocalypse, like the text in Exodus dealing with the inauguration of the tabernacle (Ex. 40), refers to elements present in all parts of the sanctuary (the lamps, bowls of incense, the horns, the cherubim). The only other occasion listing all these elements appears in the context of the Day of Atonement, during the purification of the sanctuary (Lev. 16). But the presence of the lamb excludes any reference to the Day of Atonement here since the lamb is traditionally sacrificed at the inauguration ceremony of the sanctuary (Ex. 40:29; cf. Lev. 1:10) and not at the Day of Atonement. There is likewise no allusion to the ark of the covenant, a key figure in the Day of Atonement (Lev. 16:11-15). Moreover, the word *naos,* the technical term designating the holy of holies where the ark of the covenant is kept, is absent in Revelation 4 and 5. It is, however, mentioned later in chapter 11. Interestingly, we find an extensive use of this word in the second part of the Apocalypse: Revelation 11:2, 19 (twice); 14:15, 17; 15:5, 6, 8 (twice); 16:1, 17; 21:22 (twice). The only two passages that use this word in the first part of the Apocalypse concern a time in the future.

[18] Acts 1:8; 2:38, 39; Eph. 5:18.

[19] Gen. 49:10; 2 Sam. 7; 1 Chron. 17; Dan. 9:24-27; Luke 1:32, 33.

[20] Ps. 33:3-9; 96:1, 4-6; 98:1-9; 149:1, 2, etc.

[21] Revelation 1:19 explains the expression "after this" (Rev. 4:1), "this" being the time of the seven churches in a literal sense; "after this" concerns then the time after the era of the first Christians contemporary to Yohanan. Note also that the NIV has translated the same Greek phrase as "later" in Revelation 1:19 and as "after this" in Revelation 4:1.

[22] Job 40:9; Ps. 45:4; Luke 6:6; Acts 3:7; Isa. 48:13; Ex. 15:6-12; Ps. 17:7, etc.

[23] Several elements indicate that the scroll concerns the Messiah's future reign, which remains under a higher authority, that of Him who controls history, just as the "book of the covenant" bound the kings of Israel to their suzerain at the moment of their enthronement (see above). Another parallel with a passage in Ezekiel that mentions such a scroll—held by a right hand from the throne of God (Eze. 1) and likewise written on "both sides" (Eze. 2:9, 10; cf. Rev. 5:1)—confirms this interpretation. The passage in Ezekiel further mentions that this scroll contained "words of lament and mourning and woe" (Eze. 2:10), interpreted as judgments and warnings about Israel's future (see Eze. 3). Likewise, Yohanan

sees the scroll in his vision as containing warnings and judgments concerning God's people during the reign of Yeshua the Messiah. Perhaps the prophet witnesses beforehand judgments that shall be fully revealed only later in the Apocalypse. The two documents, the Apocalypse itself and the "scroll" of chapter 5, are designated by the same term: *biblion* (referring to the Apocalypse in Revelation1:11; 22:7, 9, 18, 19) and to the scroll in Revelation 5:1, 2, 3, 4, 5, 7, 8). Yeshua the Messiah gives both to make known "what must soon take place" (Rev. 1:1; cf. 22:6). The fact that the Apocalypse is not sealed receives an eschatological interpretation, for it is related to the fact that the "time is near" (Rev. 22:10). In this sense, we can compare the Apocalypse to the book of Daniel, which is also sealed until the "time of the end. Many will go here and there to increase knowledge" (Dan. 12:4; cf. verses 9, 10).

[24] See the scrolls discovered at Qumran among the letters of Bar Kokhba. Yigael Yadin, *The Finds From the Bar Kokhba Period in the Cave of Letters,* Judean Desert Studies (Jerusalem: 1963), p. 118; cf. Frank Moore Cross, "The Discovery of the Samaria Papyri," *The Biblical Archaeologist* 26 (1963): 111-115.

[25] Rev. 1:4, 7, 8; 2:5, 16; 3:11; 4:8; 16:15; 22:7, 12, 17, 20.

[26] See Doukhan, *Secrets of Daniel,* pp. 186-190.

[27] 1 Enoch 90:19, in a section written about 161 B.C.E.

[28] *Genèse de l'Antisémitisme* (Paris: 1956), p. 133.

[29] Deut. 11:14; 14:23; 28:51; 2 Chron. 32:28; Neh. 5:11, etc.

[30] See Doukhan, *Secrets of Daniel,* pp. 65, 66, 72.

[31] See Deut. 8:3; cf. Matt. 4:4; John 6:46-51; Neh. 9:15; Ps. 146:7.

[32] Ps. 45:8; Zech. 4:1-6.

[33] Luke 22:20; 1 Cor. 11:25.

[34] Luke 10:34.

[35] *L'Eglise de saint Augustin à l'époque moderne* (Paris: 1970), p. 32.

[36] Isaac, *Genèse de l'Antisémitisme,* p. 196.

[37] See Deut. 28:49; Job 9:26; Lam. 4:19; Hab. 1:8; Matt. 24:28.

[38] Rev. 1:18; 20:13, 14.

[39] See Ps. 22:14-29; 91:13.

[40] The expression is borrowed from Isaac in *Genèse de l'Antisémitisme,* pp. 131ff.

[41] *Hitler's Table Talk,* cited in Rosmary Ruether, *Faith and Fratricide* (New York: 1974), p. 224.

[42] See Saul Friedländer, *Pius XII and the Third Reich: A Documentation,* trans. Charles Fullman (New York: 1966).

[43] Ps. 13:2; 35:17; 79:5; 89:46; 94:1-3, etc.

[44] Cf. Dan. 12:6

[45] See Lev. 16:30; cf. Doukhan, *Secrets of Daniel,* pp. 126-129.

[46] See Doukhan, *Secrets of Daniel,* pp. 129-133.

[47] See Doukhan, *Secrets of Daniel,* pp. 108-110.

[48] See Dan. 7:2.

[49] See Rev. 10:2, 5; cf. Gen. 1:1-9; Ex. 20:11; Neh. 9:6; Ps. 95:5; Matt. 23:15, etc.

[50] See also Ps. 89:12, 13; 100:3.

[51] See Meredith G. Kline, *Treaty of the Great King: The Covenant Structure of Deuteronomy, Studies and Commentary* (Grand Rapids: 1963), pp. 18, 19; Meredith G. Kline, *The Structure of Biblical Authority* (Grand Rapids: 1972), p. 120.

[52] See Doukhan, *Secrets of Daniel,* pp. 18-20.

[53] Judges 15:15; 1 Chron. 12:14; 16:15; Ps. 91:7, etc.

[54] Ex. 18:21; Deut. 33:17; Judges 6:15; Num. 1:16; Joshua 22:21, etc.

[55] See Gerhard Kittel, ed., *Theological Dictionary of the New Testament,* trans. and ed.

Geoffrey W. Bromiley (Grand Rapids: 1964-1976), vol. 5, p. 583.

[56] See 2 Maccabees 11:8; 1 Maccabees 13:51; cf. John 12:13.

[57] See Jacques B. Doukhan, *Aux portes de l'esperance* (Dammarie-les-Lys, France: 1986), pp. 243ff.

[58] See Hab. 2:20; Zeph. 1:7; Zech. 2:13.

[59] See Doukhan, *Secrets of Daniel,* pp. 108, 109, 143-145.

[60] 4 Ezra (2 Esdras) 6:39; 7:30ff.; 2 Baruch 3:7, etc.

CHAPTER 3

THE SHOFARS OF DEATH

(Revelation 8:2–11:19)

Rosh Hashanah

The next vision brings us back to God's throne, where seven angels prepare to sound trumpets (Rev. 8:2). A new cycle of seven events is about to take place. But, as in the seven letters and the seven seals, we have a prelude to the prophetic vision that takes us back to the sanctuary, to the heart of a Jewish festival, one evocative of the mission of Yeshua the Messiah. A vision of Yeshua resurrected, in the context of Passover, preceded the letters to the seven churches, and a vision of the enthronement of Yeshua in the context of Pentecost came before the vision of the seven seals.

Now, just before the sounds of the shofars (the ancient Jewish trumpets), we envision the altar (Rev. 8:3), where an angel burns incense. Suddenly the angel hurls the contents of the censer onto the earth!

The vision has its origin in ancient Temple ritual in which the priest burned fragrant incense continually before God "every morning" and "at twilight" (Ex. 30:7, 8). The ritual took place year-round on a cube-shaped altar. The priest poured hot coals on the altar from a golden censer. Once a year, at Kippur, the incense was directly poured into the coal-filled censer, and carried "behind the curtain" to the Holy of Holies (Lev. 16:12, 13). Our vision transports us to the context of the daily ritual, in which the priest threw the hot coals on the floor between the portico of the Temple and the incense altar. The apocalyptic angel here mirrors the priest's actions. A rabbinical treatise, the *Tamid,* contains material from the first century B.C.E. incorporated into the Mishnah a century later, just a few years after the writing of the Apocalypse.[1] It describes the whole ceremony, and the resemblance to our passage is remarkable. "One of the priests took the spade and threw it between the portico and the altar, and no one could hear the voice of his neighbor because of the noise of the spade."[2] "Then the angel took the censer, filled it with fire from the altar, and hurled it on the earth; and there came peals of thunder, rumblings, flashes of lightning and an earthquake" (Rev. 8:5).

According to another passage in the *Tamid,* the sound of the spade was so loud that it could be heard as far as Jericho, 15 miles from Jerusalem.[3] The shape of the spade (*magrefa*) explains the noise of its fall. According to the Jerusalem Talmud, the *magrefa* was pierced by hundreds of holes (or pipes), each of which could emit several different pitches.[4] With each thrust, the spade could produce a number of different pitches, almost like a pipe organ. In any case, the crashing sound of the spade, associated with hot coals, evokes the idea of God's judgment and wrath.

The prophet Ezekiel further develops this connection when he recounts the same vision of a priestly angel, clothed in linen, hurling hot coals upon Jerusalem (Eze. 10:2). The gesture anticipated the doom that would befall Jerusalem. Indeed, fire would later destroy Jerusalem (Eze. 24:9; 2 Kings 25:9).

The hurling of the coals by the apocalyptic angel carries the same threat. Much like the impact of the spade between the portico and the altar, "there came peals of thunder, rumblings, flashes of lightning and an earthquake" (Rev. 8:5).

The angel's ritual, mirroring the Temple ceremony, is charged with symbolic meaning. The incense burned before the throne of God represents the agonized prayers of the oppressed crying out for justice: "O Lord, I call to you; come quickly to me. Hear my voice when I call to you. May my prayer be set before you like incense; may the lifting up of my hands be like the evening sacrifice" (Ps. 141:1, 2).

Our passage echoes the lamentations in the fifth seal, which also rise up from the same incense altar (Rev. 6:9, 10). The symbolic act of the angel now takes on full significance—it is God's answer to the prayers of the oppressed.

The opening of the fifth seal poured out the blood of the victims crying for revenge against the "inhabitants of the earth" (verse 10). Now the shofars announce the coming of vengeance upon the "inhabitants of the earth" (Rev. 8:13). The intention to avenge clearly resonates in the message of the seventh shofar "Your wrath has come. The time has come for judging the dead, . . . and for destroying those who destroy the earth" (Rev. 11:18).

The shofars answer to the seals as vengeance answers oppression. The seals revealed to us oppression, and now the shofars proclaim judgment.

The image of trumpets is particularly suggestive. Actually, the text speaks of shofars, not of trumpets. The Greek word *salpigx*, rendered in our Bibles as "trumpet," is the translation the Septuagint employs for the Hebrew word *shofar*. The ancients blew the ram's horn on solemn occasions such as war and judgment. The priests sounded the shofar at the conquest of Jericho (Joshua 6:4, 6, 8, 13) to announce victory, and at the feast of expiations (Lev. 25:9) to proclaim the Lord's day of judgment.[5]

Until now the Apocalypse had mentioned the shofar only sporadically—once before the letters to the churches (Rev. 1:10) and once before the seals (Rev. 4:1). Now the shofar blasts have intensified, resonating throughout history. Like the prayers emanating to the heavens, we now hear the shofars constantly. The association between the shofars and the prayers occurs in the context of the feast of the "trumpets" (that is, of the "shofars"). This feast follows Pentecost and is celebrated on the first day of the seventh month (Tishri, September-October) of the Hebrew calendar (Lev. 23:23-25). It is the Jewish New Year (Rosh Hashanah).

For 10 days the use of the shofar reminds the Jews that they are to prepare for the Day of Atonement (the tenth of Tishri). Every morning they recite the *selihot* (requests for forgiveness) as well as the 13 attributes of God's grace (Ex. 34:6, 7). The readings of the Torah

79

include selections from passages concerning the birth and sacrifice of Isaac, evocative of the God who remembers and who answers even impossible requests (Gen. 21 and 22).

In the context of the Apocalypse, the allusion to the shofars enhances the prophetic vision with the same note of hope, judgment, and call to repentance.

The angel in linen who burns the incense before God represents Yeshua, who since His enthronement intercedes before the God of heaven. At the same time the censer of hot coals hurled between the portico and the altar announces a call to repentance, echoing the dramatic blasts of the shofar.

The book of Joel also pairs the sound of the shofar that summons Israel to repentance and the intercession of the priest "between the temple porch and the altar": " 'Even now,' declares the Lord, 'return to me with all your heart. . . .' Rend your heart and not your garments. Return to the Lord your God, for he is gracious and compassionate. . . . Blow the trumpet [shofar] in Zion. . . . Let the priests, who minister before the Lord, weep between the temple porch and the altar. Let them say, 'Spare your people, O Lord' " (Joel 2:12–17).

Through its allusions to the Feast of Trumpets and to the exhortations of the prophet Joel, the vision of the Apocalypse warns us of the upcoming judgment, but it also reassures us of God's answer. It is a call to repentance, a plea to return to God.

In the prophetic perspective, the Feast of Shofars precedes the great judgment day. The enthronement of the Messiah in the context of Pentecost introduced the cycle of the seven seals. The Feast of Shofars, an event supposed to prepare for the judgment, now inaugurates the cycle of the seven shofars. The Feast of Shofars ties the festivals of spring to the festivals of fall (Num. 29:1). The seven shofar blasts that punctuate history serve to warn the people of the earth of God's judgment day. For although the great day of judgment will occur at the end of time, it has implications for our daily lives even now.

The Seven Shofars

The shofars echo the seven seals, and cover the same time span: the church's apostasy and oppression of the others. The first and seventh seals, which frame this time period, have no connection with the oppression. During the first seal the church is still faithful to its beginnings and lets itself be led by Yeshua the Messiah. The last seal marks the end of human history and announces God's descent. The shofars echo the historical period between the second and sixth seals:

First Seal
    White horse

Second Seal
    Fiery red horse, slaying
      (blood implied)

First and Second Shofars
    "Fire," "blood"

Third Seal
    Scarcity of grain
    Black horse

Third Shofar
    Scarcity of water

Fourth Shofar
    darkness

Fourth Seal
    Death ("Death," "Hades")

Fifth Shofar
    Destroyer ("Abaddon,"
      "Apollyon")

Fifth Seal
    Voices at the altar
    Incomplete number of the
      saved
    To be finished later

Sixth Shofar
    Voice at the altar
    Incomplete number of the
      murdered
    To be finished later

Sixth Seal
    "The . . . day of . . . wrath
    has come."

Seventh Shofar
    "Your wrath has come."

Seventh Seal
    Silence in heaven

Moreover, like the seals, the shofars follow a chronological progression characterized by the following: (1) transitions that point to the completion of the events of one shofar and announce the events of the next (Rev. 8:13; 9:12); (2) the structural parallel between the two cycles—like the seals, the shofars subdivide into one group of four visions and another of three visions; and (3) the final note of the last shofar, which announces the coming of the kingdom of God.

These literary considerations give us strong reason to believe that the events of the shofars correspond to the events of the seals.

Fire and Blood

The first and second shofars complement each other. The disasters they bring strike the earth and the sea. The first shofar produces a bloody concoction of fire and hail that burns up the earth (Rev. 8:7). The second shofar releases a solid mass of fire, a "huge mountain, all ablaze," that turns the sea to blood (verse 8). Both disasters achieve the same result: annihilating a third of the earth and sea. Fire and blood represent the violence of warfare and also remind us of the plagues in Egypt.

There, also, fire and hail struck the oppressor (Ex. 9:23-25). As for the "third," it means that the disastrous effect of the plague is only partial and that most of the earth will survive it (Eze. 5:2; Zech. 13:8). The two shofars correspond to the second seal and apply to the time when its wars against the barbarians tore the church apart (fourth and fifth centuries C.E.).

No Water and No Light

Both the third and fourth shofars involve celestial bodies: the stars, the sun, and the moon. Whatever was a source of light now darkens unto death. Curiously, the process begins with a star, contrary to the traditional sequence of sun, moon, and star (Gen. 1:16). The anomaly emphasizes the primacy of the star over the other celestial bodies. It is the star that starts the chain of events.

Another unusual aspect is that "star" is in the singular. The Bible normally employs the word in the plural form and associates them with the sun and the moon. The author here wants us to focus on a particular "star." Interestingly, at times a star is a direct reference to the Messiah in both the Old and New Testaments. In the prophecy of Balaam the star symbolizes the Messiah king, called to save His people Israel from their enemies (Num. 24:17). And in the New Testament the star represents Yeshua as the Messiah (Matt. 2:2; cf. Rev. 2:28; 22:16). The only passage where "star" in the singular does not designate the Messiah appears in the book of Isaiah, which applies it to the fallen angel, Lucifer, personified by the king of Babylon (Isa. 14:12). It represents an evil power that seeks to usurp God's place, as did the builders of the ancient tower of Babel (Gen. 11:1-9), but ends up falling into the abyss: "How you have fallen from heaven, O morning star, son of the dawn! You have been cast down to the earth, you who once laid low the nations! You said in your heart, 'I will ascend to heaven; I will raise my throne above the stars of God. . . . I will ascend above the tops of the clouds; I will make myself like the Most High.' But you are brought down to the grave, to the depths of the pit" (Isa. 14:12-15).[6]

Our text alludes to this passage. We find the same motif of the fallen star, the usurping power. Only the star of our passage lands on the earth and oversees the historical turmoil of the church. The prophet Daniel had already anticipated this in his vision of the little horn that sought to elevate itself to the "host" of heaven and to the "Prince of the host" (Dan. 8:10, 11).

In the Apocalypse, as in the book of Isaiah, the fall of the star symbolizes death. Isaiah even identifies it with death. The star in the Apocalypse pollutes the rivers and springs, causing the death of "many people" (Rev. 8:10, 11) by either thirst or by poisoning. Scripture can employ rivers and springs to represent spiritual nourishment.[7] On the other hand, the identification of the star with wormwood reminds us of the Israelites' disappointment at Marah where the waters were "bitter" (Ex. 15:23; cf. Rev. 8:11). The Bible generally associates "bitterness" with apostasy.[8] The people die of thirst because the waters are polluted. Truth is corrupted and, consequently, cannot nourish the believer.

The fourth shofar says much the same thing but in different terms. Something eclipses the sun, moon, stars—that is, the witnesses of God's revelation (Gen. 37:9; cf. Rev. 12:1). With the third shofar, truth is corrupted, and with the fourth, it is blotted out. The third and fourth shofar depict the Dark Ages, the period of the church's greatest usurpation of divine attributes (sixth to tenth centuries). Rome replaces the "city of God." Tradition and power sweep aside spirituality. Truth becomes a vestige, and the people die of spiritual hunger and thirst, as they did in the third seal (Rev. 6:6). Because of its thirst for power, the church loses its sense of mission and of truth. Having sought to hoist itself up to God's level, it now finds itself, not unlike the ancient city of Babel, condemned to confusion.

As did the seals, the shofars now reach a turning point. After the fourth shofar, Revelation 8:13 marks the transition by introducing the next three shofars with the following admonition: "Woe! Woe! Woe to the inhabitants of the earth, because of the trumpet blasts about to be sounded by the other three angels!"

Locusts

The fifth shofar is situated historically in the same perspective as the preceding shofars. Yohanan again mentions the fallen star (Rev. 9:1), evoking a usurping mentality reminiscent of the ancient power of Babel. Previously the shofars had spoken of events beyond human control, brought about by the hand of God. Now the shofars announce forces that emerge from the depths of the earth, from the "Abyss." "The star was given the key to the shaft of the Abyss. When he opened the Abyss, smoke rose from it like the smoke from a gigantic furnace" (Rev. 9:1, 2). The Septuagint uses the Greek term *abussos* to translate the Hebrew *tehom* (abyss), a word employed to describe the earth before Creation (Gen. 1:2). Significantly, Genesis 1 associates the *tehom* with the concepts of water, darkness, and void. The second account of the Creation parallels it with the words "no" and "yet" (Gen. 2:5).[9] The *tehom/abussos* is the negation of God. Later, the prophets would make it into the abode of His enemy, the great leviathan (Isa. 51:9; Ps. 74:13). The pseudepigraphon of 1 Enoch describes *tehom* as the dwelling place of fallen angels.[10]

The apocalyptic oracle goes even as far as to personify the abyss with the Hebrew name *Abaddon*, or damnation.[11] This word comes from the root *abad* (to die, to disappear), generally used in the Hebrew Scriptures, especially the Wisdom literature (Proverbs, Psalms, Ecclesiastes, etc.), to indicate the fate of the wicked.[12] The Greek word *Apollyon* (Rev. 9:11) comes from the verb *apollynai* (ruin, destroy, lose). Another word from the same verb, *apoleia,* means damnation or perdition, and, like *abussos,* translates in the Septuagint the word *tehom.* The Hebrew word *abaddon* and the Greek word *apollyon* thus share the same connotation of void and of negation of God.

The darkness that invades the scene (Rev. 9:2) differs from that of the fourth shofar. There it resulted from something happening to the luminaries (Rev. 8:12). Now the darkness comes from elsewhere. It is now part of the *tehom,* the darkness of pre-Creation. The locusts crop up from the abyss, forming a thick cloud that blocks the light and the heavens above. The fifth shofar reveals the agencies that dominated the Dark Ages. The star falls into the abyss, opens it, and frees the powers of the void. In other words, the usurpation of God releases the forces of perversion, pretension, intolerance, and oppression that seek to deny God His place and rule in the world.

The fifth shofar also describes God's vengeance. The seeds of the church's punishment lay latent in its own actions. By usurping God on earth through intolerance and oppression, it caused humanity to reject the very God it sought to represent.

History confirms the prophecy. The French Revolution and the anti-clerical movements of the seventeenth and eighteenth centuries constitute humanity's answer to the Crusades, the Inquisition, and the religious wars that marked Western history from the ninth to the sixteenth centuries.

The prophecy uses the locust imagery to convey the nature of this attack. The five months of plague correspond to the insect's life cycle—from its birth to its death. We find the same imagery in the book of Joel. It also compares God's judgment to an invasion of locusts resembling horses (Joel 2:4; cf. Rev. 9:7). The analogy is striking if one considers appearance, speed, and even the military strategy of locusts (cf. Hosea 14:3; Amos 6:12). The locusts destroy the harvests and cover the sky with their cloudlike masses (Joel 1:10), during a whole generation (verses 4, 6).

The effects of the plague predicted by the fifth shofar are limited in both space and time. The locusts attack only those "who did not have the seal of God on their foreheads" (Rev. 9:4). The imagery of the seal derives from their ancient Near Eastern usage to indicate ownership. Merchandise or letters were sealed to identify or attest to whom they belonged. When applied to human beings, the imagery signifies a unique personal relationship. In the Song of Songs, for instance, the Shulammite employs the imagery of the seal to express her special relationship with her beloved: "Place me like a seal over your heart, like a seal on your arm; for love is as strong as death, its jealousy unyielding as the grave. It burns like blazing fire, like a mighty flame" (S. of Sol. 8:6). The lack of a seal would therefore reveal all those who are not really God's. It exposes the church as a hollow institution that has lost its sense of God's sovereignty and ownership. The French Revolution affects the church only as an institution. As for the people, they emerge all the more free and bold in their search for truth.

The locusts, moreover, sting like scorpions though their bite is not deadly (Rev. 9:5). In spite of everything, the church will survive the plague. According to the prophecy, the church's torment will not exceed five months (5 x 30 days), that is, 150 years (according to prophetic rules of one day equaling one year).[13] Such a disaster is without precedent in the history of the church. The French Revolution even dares to imprison the pope (1798). The church would recover only in the period after World War II, thanks to the ratification of the Lateran treaty (1929). Its resurgence would be further strengthened by the spread of new postwar political factions calling themselves "Christian democrats" across the European political scene. Largely dominated by members of the Catholic Church, these factions often formed the head of coalition governments. Today the church has become a superpower. Its influence permeates international relations at every level, from its fight against Communism to its concern for world hunger and its religious vision of ecumenism. Many interpretations of this prophecy exist, but whatever the differences, the message remains the same. We must understand the invasion of the locusts as God's judgment against the oppressor. The Bible consistently employs locusts as a symbol of judgment.[14] It is also hinted at by the five months, a key number in the Flood account, the first universal judgment in human history (Gen. 7:24).

Mounted Troops

The sixth shofar echoes the wailing of the sixth seal. The weeping voices under the altar (Rev. 6:10) receive an answer from the voice that liberates the four angels from the great river Euphrates (Rev. 9:13, 14). Again we must regard the upcoming event as a punishment against an oppressor, identified in our passage with Babylon. Already the mention of the Euphrates alludes to the fall of Babylon.[15] Likewise, the "idols of gold, silver, bronze, stone and wood" (Rev. 9:20) suggests the idolatry of Babylon as depicted by the prophet Daniel on the eve of the destruction of the empire (Dan. 5:23). The "demons" and the "magic arts" (Rev. 9:20, 21) also characterize Babylon, according to the prophet Isaiah, and precipitate its fall (Isa. 47:12).

The fifth shofar had dispatched locusts with scorpion's tails, like an army of horses "rushing into battle" (Rev. 9:9), and the sixth shofar summons them again. Now the Apocalypse compares that invasion to horses whose power lay in their tails (verse 19; cf. verse 10).

The sixth shofar continues where the fifth shofar left off, but the battle now intensifies. Babylon's enemy takes on a more threatening stance. The horses of the fifth shofar had lion's teeth, while now their whole heads are like lions' (verse 17). The power of destruction of the warriors of the fifth shofar concentrated in the tail, but under the six shofar the mouth also is deadly (verse 19). Their breastplates of iron (verse 9) have become "fiery red" (verse 17). The locusts' sting, previously not fatal (verse 5), has turned deadly (verse 18). The cloud of the fifth shofar (verse 2) is now reinforced with fire and sulfur (verse 18). The invasion force has even increased in number. Overwhelmed by its size, the prophet uses the superlative, "two hundred million" (verse 16). The Greek word translated million (in other renditions, 10,000) *myrias*, generally denotes a very great number.[16] The term appears in Septuagint translation of the blessing sung by the sons of Bethuel to their sister Rebekah as they wished her an offspring of "thousands upon thousands" (Gen. 24:60). We also remember the women's praise of David's military performance: "Saul has slain his thousands, and David his tens of thousands" (1 Sam. 18:7). This word is in our passage not merely 10,000 x 10,000, but 2 x 10,000 x 10,000.

Armed forces have never reached such proportions. The forces of the abyss, secular and anticlerical, are overwhelming. Our century has witnessed an explosion of political and philosophical reactions against the church. Ideologies emerging from the French Revolution, Marxism, materialism, evolutionism, and rationalism, permeate our intellectual lives. Secular and atheistic currents penetrate even religious circles. Here we have one of the most striking ironies of human history. In seeking to replace God on earth, the church set itself up for a reaction coming from this very earth—from an abyss that acknowledges no God. The Apocalypse confirms the vision of the prophet Daniel. In chapter 11 of his book he predicted a conflict between the same two powers.[17] One originates from the north and embodies the usurping power of the church, while the other comes from the south and represents the secular and atheistic ideologies that have characterized modern Western thought.

The Apocalypse echoes then Daniel's prophecy, and alludes to both Babylon and Egypt. The fallen star (fifth shofar) by its association to the river of Euphrates (sixth shofar) represents Babylon. The locusts, scorpions, serpents, and darkness all remind us of the plagues that befell Egypt, because of its stubborn denial of the God of Israel (Ex. 5:2). The chariots and horses, characteristic of the Egyptian military arsenal, also point us back to Egypt.[18]

Both Daniel and the prophet of the Apocalypse recount the same event through their allusions to Babylon and Egypt. But the convergence of the two prophetic visions does not stop there. As in Daniel 11, our passage in the Apocalypse predicts the victory of Babylon. It will be the "religious" power that takes the place of God.[19] The warriors of the sixth shofar destroy only a third of humanity (Rev. 9:18). The other two thirds survive, self-confident and idolatrous, far from repentance. We find no more mention of the enemy of Babylon—that is, the "secular" power that denies God's existence. It seems to have been engulfed by the other. As in Daniel 11, the Egyptian forces join the Babylonian (cf. Dan. 11:43).

We hardly dare anticipate the fulfillment of this prophecy. The last events already hint at a weakness in the ranks of secularism. The collapse of Marxism and the failure of rationalism demonstrate the plausibility of the prophecies of Daniel and of the Apocalypse.

It is a process not limited to Christianity in the West. The conflict between the two forces embodied by Egypt and Babylon goes beyond the scope of the Catholic Church and its secular opponents. The influence of the French Revolution extends beyond its religious and political borders. Secularism has penetrated both Islamic and Jewish circles in the spirit of anticlerical humanism. In reaction, we witness today a surge of religious fundamentalism in both religions. More than ever, ayatollahs and rabbis have a say in political matters. In Muslim nations, such as Iran, Algeria, and Egypt, as in Israel, politics surrenders more and more to religious powers.

For some time secularism has discredited religion in Christian circles. But now Christian fundamentalism counterattacks secular, liberal, and rationalistic trends. In the United States, the Religious Right strives for political power in order to help build a "truly" Christian nation. The same tendency has also found fertile terrain in Europe. The new Religious Right has a strong nationalistic spirit that will certainly appeal to many.

In short, we may summarize the church's history as follows:

1. The church unwittingly established itself as Babel when it claimed sole authority over moral and religious issues.

2. In the eighteenth century a new revolutionary spirit reacted against the clergy, encouraging humanist and secular tendencies that would later develop into Marxist, rationalist, positivist, and evolutionist philosophies. It was the attack of Egypt against Babel.

3. During the nineteenth and early twentieth centuries secularism spread to other non-Western religions and cultures through missionary work and colonialism.

4. After World War II the surge of nationalistic movements and the memory of the horrors of war triggered a reaction against rationalism and liberalism and a return to religious and cultural values. It has

been the time of religious best-sellers and evangelical media stars.

We are now in the fourth phase of the cycle, just before the unification of the two camps into one Babel. Already we may witness the first signs of such a development. The revival of religion has anthropocentric overtones, not unlike those that characterized the secular trends of the past century. Religion has been developing toward a more "humanistic" ideal. The "immanent" God, latent in everyone, takes precedence over the transcendent God who reveals Himself from above, usually against human projects.

The popularity of the New Age movement also puts an unexpected twist on the religious revival of our current century. It has affected almost every religion. Both Christians and non-Christians teach its message of tolerance. Father Teilhard de Chardin as well as "ecotheologians" such as Thomas Berry have inspired a new respect for "mother earth." They interpret evolution as a "sacred process" through which God incarnates Himself.

God is thus everywhere—in nature, in the dead, and in the living, a tendency further reinforced by theories on the immortality of the soul, reincarnation, and by activities such as consulting psychics and astrologers. All these trends develop from the same premise: the Creator-God is not out of reach anymore. He is here, He has come, He has incarnated into humanity. What need is there to hope, to pray, or to wait for Him? Humanity has today replaced God.

In non-Christian contexts, the "search for the sacred cosmos" has found a spokesperson in the person of Vaclav Havel. In a recent lecture at Stanford University, the Czech president defended the thesis that all cultures—indeed, the whole of humanity—is united by a common spiritual dimension. Such appeals for "planetary democracy" echo that of the Marxist ideal of Internationalism. But after the fall of Marxism, this language takes on a new meaning. Humanist and anthropocentric concerns here unite with religious values.

The media all testify to such developments. From Nirvana's crucifixions to Madonna's Black Yeshua, from crystal jewels to pierced bodies, a new culture has been born. Egypt and Babylon seem to have come to an understanding. Of course, these are merely symptoms. The church and religion as a whole still antagonize secular and atheistic movements. But the ingredients are all present for the mixture predicted by the prophet. Soon Egypt and Babylon will merge into the melting pot of Babel.

Interlude: The Angel of Light, the Book, and the Two Witnesses

As with the sixth seal, the sixth shofar has a period of transition before the seventh shofar. And as with the seals, the interlude pauses for a look into God's camp.

The Angel of Light

In contrast to the fallen star, the angel of death and of chaos (Rev. 9:1, 2), we now behold a powerful angel of light, an angel of God (Rev. 10:1). The rainbow above his head is the sign of God's covenant with humankind (Gen. 1:12, 13). His feet, planted on both land and sea, evoke God's creation of the waters (verses 1-8) and of the earth (verse 9ff.).

The being resembles the Son of man in the first vision of the Apocalypse. Like Him, His face is "like the sun" (Rev. 10:1; cf. 1:16), his feet burn like fire (Rev. 10:1; cf.1:15), and his voice booms like thunder (Rev. 10:3; cf. 1:15). And like Him, clouds escort Him (Rev. 10:1; cf.1:7).

But taken as a whole, our passage is even more similar to the last vision of the prophet Daniel. In Daniel 12 he recounts this same vision of a being standing above both earth and sea, who raises his hands to the heaven swearing "by him who lives forever" (Dan. 12:7). The oath constitutes the answer to the question in the preceding verse: "How long?" (verse 6). But the response apparently does not satisfy Daniel—he does not understand (verse 8). The man draped in linen then answers him that these words are to be "sealed until the time of the end" (verse 9), adding: "Blessed is the one who waits for and reaches the end of the 1,335 days" (verse 12). It is only in those days that the complete answer to the question "How long?" shall be revealed. Only this period leads into the "time of the end." But a previous vision had already mentioned this "time of the end."

Daniel 8 records another vision of a dialogue between two heavenly beings. It also raised the question: "How long?" (Dan. 8:13). Again the answer led into the time of the end: "It will take 2,300 evenings and mornings; then the sanctuary will be reconsecrated" (verse 14). At the end of the book of Daniel the same question surfaces in relation to the 1,335 days, a time of intense expectation (Dan. 12:12). We thus should understand these two prophetic periods as leading to the same event, a heavenly Kippur.[20] Interestingly, the heavenly being that announces this Kippur of the end-time is draped in linen, like the high priest on duty at Kippur.

This time of judgment is the answer to the question of the martyrs: "How long?" It is also the response to the question of the weeping souls in the fifth seal (Rev. 6:10). The sixth seal, in fact, introduces this "time of the end," as anticipated by the prophet Daniel (Dan. 8:17, 19, 26). We now understand the meaning behind the attire of the mighty angel (Rev. 10:1). An angel had told the prophet Daniel that his vision was to be "sealed until the time of the end" (Dan. 12:9). The angel now declares that the "time of the end" has arrived, and that "there will be no more delay" (Rev. 10:6). The time of the sixth shofar marks the unsealing of Daniel's prophecy. It could now be understood.

The Book

Eagerly Yohanan takes the "scroll that lies open in the hand of the angel," and eats it (Rev. 10:8, 9). The word is thus assimilated and digested. "The scroll that lies open" represents the book of Daniel, previously sealed but now accessible to all. Yohanan's experience is similar to that of the prophet Ezekiel, who was also confronted with an angel of light and ordered to eat a scroll (Eze. 3:1). The next verses explain the strange command: the prophet upon assimilating the contents of the scroll now communicates its message to his contemporaries (verses 4-6).

But we notice yet another similarity between the two experiences. Like Yohanan, Ezekiel finds the contents of the scroll "sweet as honey" (verse 3; cf. Rev. 10:9, 10). But both experiences have a bitter aftertaste. The book contains "words of lament and mourning and woe" (Eze. 2:10), part of its dual message of judgment and restoration.

"The end! The end has come," the prophet declares (Eze. 7:2, 3, 6). Ezekiel, prophet in exile, announces God's impending judgment. The destruction of Jerusalem is at hand. The Lord chose the prophet to stand guard over Israel (Eze. 33:2) and warn His people of the nation's impending doom. Ezekiel's message is not limited to words and parables, but he lives it in the flesh: His wife, the "delight of [his] eyes" will be struck dead (Eze. 24:15-27). Then the prophet will be condemned to silent mourning for the three years of Jerusalem's siege, until its fall (Eze. 33:22).

But at the heart of the summons and threats of destruction lies the promise of hope. Ezekiel is also the prophet of restoration, because the captives are to be set free, the tribes reunited (Eze. 37:21), Jerusalem rebuilt (Eze. 40-48), and the land to prosper (Eze. 47:12). Men and women will receive a new heart (Eze. 36:24-28). The prophet foretells the event as a resurrection. The Word of God brings bones back to life (Eze. 37). The world once again witnesses the miracle of creation. As in Genesis 2:7, the Spirit changes dust into life (Eze. 37:9).

It is this bittersweet message of judgment and of creation that the book of the Apocalypse here alludes to through its reference to the book of Ezekiel—the message of Kippur.

The insights of Daniel and of the Apocalypse converge into a revelation of the "time of the end." Daniel compares it to Kippur, to a time of trembling expectation of judgment and recreation. The Apocalypse portrays this period through the vision of the "open scroll" with the bittersweet taste, evocative of the dual message of judgment and recreation that characterizes the nature of Kippur.

The books of Daniel and the Apocalypse complement each other. That the angel asks Yohanan to eat the book of Daniel further emphasizes their interdependence.

Once Yohanan has assimilated the message of the "open scroll," the angel tells him to prophesy to "many peoples, nations, languages and kings" (Rev. 10:11). We will hear a similar phrase later in chapter 14. The heavenly messenger must prophesy to "every nation, tribe, language and people" (Rev. 14:6). There again, the message is a dual one—a message of judgment but also of re-creation.[21] The

Apocalypse presents God's people in the time of the end as prophets commissioned to give the message of Daniel, "digested" by the Apocalypse itself.

The Two Witnesses

The next vision places us again in the prophetic context of Ezekiel. As did the prophet in the Hebrew Scriptures, Yohanan receives a rod to measure the temple of the future Jerusalem (Rev. 11:1; cf. Eze. 40:3ff.). The cycle of the seals explains this symbolic gesture. After the sixth seal the cycle had opened an aside on God's people, how they were marked by the seal of God and assured of salvation (Rev. 7:3). Likewise, after the blast of the sixth shofar, the prophet takes a moment to measure the temple of God and to announce its restoration (Rev. 11:1; cf. Zech. 2:2). More precisely, the angel asks Yohanan to measure the "altar, and count the worshipers." The vision speaks of God's people throughout history. They have received the mission to "prophesy" (Rev. 11:3). Their mission has been the same as that of the people at the time of the end: to testify of the revelation from above. But the mission now broadens. The oracle compares this nation of "prophets" to "two witnesses" (verse 3), explaining: "These are the two olive trees and the two lampstands that stand before the Lord of the earth" (verse 4).

The prophet Zechariah recounted a similar vision of two olive trees and a menorah (Zech. 4:1-6, 11-14). To his question "What are these?" (verse 4), the angel replies: "'Not by might nor by power, but by my Spirit,' says the Lord Almighty" (verse 6). The explanation of the angel proceeds from the image of the olive tree to that of the menorah: The menorah gives light in virtue of the oil poured from above, just as the Word of God gives light through the Spirit from above.

The Bible often compares the words of God to light: "Your word is a lamp to my feet and a light for my path" (Ps. 119:105). Proverbs relates the Torah to light, *"or,"* in a play on words. Both Hebrew words *(Torah* and *or)* have the same root. The New Testament depicts God as light (1 John 1:5), and when Yeshua identifies Himself with the light He does so in the dynamic context of the walk with God (John 8:12; 12:35; cf. Ps. 119:105), an indirect reference to the Torah.

Still another allusion joins the motifs of the olive tree and of the menorah as the miracles performed by the witnesses evoke two key figures from the Hebrew Scriptures—Moses and Elijah. The turning of water into blood and the plagues refer to Moses (Rev. 11:6; cf. Ex. 7:14-18). The fire that devours the enemy and the rain under supernatural control reminds us of Elijah (Rev. 11:5, 6; cf. 1 Kings 17:1). The only other text in the Old Testament that couples these two figures occurs in Malachi, the last prophet of the Hebrew Scriptures: "Remember the law of my servant Moses, the decrees and laws I gave him at Horeb for all Israel. See, I will send you the prophet Elijah before that great and dreadful day of the Lord comes. He will turn the hearts of the fathers to their children, and the hearts of the children to their fathers; or else I will come and strike the land with a curse" (Mal. 4:4-6).

This passage has a dual orientation. The first refers us back to Moses and the past. It is a call to remember and to remain faithful to the Old Covenant. Moses represents here the Old Testament. Christians during the time of Yohanan associated Moses with the revelation of the Old Testament.[22] According to Jewish tradition, the Torah originated with him. "Moses received the Torah at Sinai and transmitted it to Joshua. Joshua transmitted it to the elders, and the elders to the prophets and the prophets to the members of the Assembly."[23]

The second orientation, involving Elijah, looks to the future. It is the promise of the coming of the Messiah and the kindling of hope. Christians during the time of Yohanan associated the arrival of the Messiah with the prophet Elijah.[24] Likewise, Jewish tradition relates the person of Elijah to the messianic hope in much the same way. There Elijah is not only a precursor, but an active agent of the Messiah.[25] Legends, liturgical practices on the eve of the Seder, and nostalgic songs of the Shabbat all call upon Elijah in expectation of the Messiah.

Moses directs us back to the Torah while Elijah propels us forward in the Messianic hope of the New Testament.

When we consider the Judeo-Christian background of

Yohanan, we realize that the allusions to Moses and Elijah are no coincidence. It strongly evokes the two revelations of God received by the early Christians—the so-called Old and New Testaments. The two witnesses are both here present and play a part in the prophetic process. The dual reference brings out the relevance of the whole Bible, emphasizing the complementarity of, and the need for, the two testimonies.

But beyond the two documents, we have the reference to the two peoples who transmitted them. The prophet's main concern lies with the men and women who prophesy and who suffer (Rev. 11:3, 7).

We first think of the Jewish people, who have borne in their flesh and in their daily existence the testimony to the Torah from above and have taken great care to preserve the Hebrew Scriptures and their prophecies. And we also think of the Christians, who have brought to the world the news of the grace and love of God and have carried the name of the God of Israel to the ends of the earth. They carefully transmitted the writings of the New Testament, with its own prophecies.

Without these two peoples we would have no access to the Sacred Writings, either the Hebrew Scriptures or the New Testament—indeed, we would have no channel to truth from above. And without witnesses of flesh and blood the biblical documents would have remained voiceless and dead, left to molder in museum display cases.

In fact, it is precisely because one or the other of these testimonies has been neglected, rejected, or ignored (the Old Testament and the Torah by the church, the New Testament and the Messiah by Israel), that these two witnesses, Israel and the church, have to survive together; for they need each other. To leave out either one distorts God's purposes and destroys part of His revelation. Indeed, not only do the two testimonies shed light on each other, but they complete each other; each witness presenting a unique truth absent in the other, and that the other needs.

This principle of unity and complementarity of the two testimonies is all the more significant in that it constitutes the basis of how to interpret the Apocalypse. Without the book of Daniel, the

Apocalypse remains obscure, not only in virtue of its numerous allusions and references to Daniel, but also because it shares the same perspective and uses the same language, symbols, and accounts of the same prophetic events.

The passage we are discussing—Revelation 11:1-14—provides a striking example of this complementarity. The time periods announced by the Apocalypse reflect those in the prophetic calendar of the book of Daniel (verses 2, 3). Both speak of a period of oppression extending for 1,260 days, the equivalent of 42 months (42 times 30). Daniel predicts a time of persecution that is to last "a time, times and half a time" (Dan. 7:25). In the context of the book of Daniel, this expression means one year (360 days), two years (360 times 2), and half a year (360 divided by 2), amounting to a total of 1,260 days/years.[26] To describe the time of persecution, Yohanan uses a language reminiscent of Daniel's: "They will trample on the holy city" (Rev. 11:2) just as the little horn tramples the saints (Dan. 8:10).

Both prophecies have in mind the same event. History shows indeed that for 1,260 years—that is, from the time when the church became a political power (538 C.E.) to when events shook its political influence (1798 C.E.), the testimony of the Scriptures was muted. During this whole time, according to the Apocalypse, the two witnesses prophesy in "sackcloth" (Rev. 11:3), after which "the beast that comes up from the Abyss" strikes them dead (verse 7). The "spiritual" scene of our drama takes place in relation to three locations prominently associated with biblical history: the "great" city of Babylon (Rev. 14:8), personifying the usurpation of God; Egypt, representing the negation of God; and Sodom, incarnating moral depravation and ignorance of God. In essence God has been killed in them, either because He has been replaced, denied, or simply ignored. To murder God's witnesses is to murder God Himself. Persecution amounts to deicide. The Apocalypse sees in these locations another Golgotha "where also their Lord was crucified" (Rev. 11:8).

The French Revolution had devastating effects not only on the official religion, but also on its sources. The new cult of reason led to the destruction of the Scriptures and the denial of the God who inspired them. Mobs publicly burned both Jewish and Christian sacred books. A publication of the time, *Le Moniteur,* commented: "Yesterday, day of the decade, wiped out the last vestiges of superstition: a great fire ignited in the town square was garlanded with sacred portraits and pictures. The people threw more than five to six thousand volumes of pious works into the flames, singing Republican songs and proclaiming slogans of universal solidarity. Books were retrieved from everywhere. Even the Jews of the town brought their treasured manuscripts and renounced their hopes in this ridiculous messiah. The number of books burned was so high that the fire burned into the night until 10 a.m. this morning."[27]

Finally, in November 1793, the revolutionary convention made a decree abolishing all religious services. For the first time in the history of the church someone officially proclaimed the end of Christianity. "Reason has gained an important victory over fanaticism; a religion of error and bloodshed has been overthrown; for 18 centuries it has ravaged the earth in the name of heaven! . . . The crusades, the Waldensians, the Albigensians, the Sicilian vespers, the St. Barthelemy massacre, these are its works, these are its trophies, may it disappear from the face of the earth."[28]

History is full of irony. The church, which had subdued the testimony of the Scriptures, produced the reactionary outburst of the French Revolution, which then burned those Scriptures. By neglecting the revelation from above, the church became persecutor and engendered its own destroyer, who not only attacked its institutions, but speared it in the heart when it, too, rejected the Word of God. The prophecy contains a lesson that permeates the Apocalypse: iniquity gives birth to its own judgment.

But the Apocalypse sees more. A judgment from above joins the self-inflicted one. The impact of the divine judgment is double. First, a great earthquake shakes the "city" (Rev. 11:13), the great city of Babylon. The usurping power receives a terrible blow. We are in 1798, when the church encounters attacks from every side and the pope, its spiritual leader, is imprisoned. But the blow is not fatal. Only a "tenth" of the city collapses, and "seven thousand people" are killed (verse 13). These two casualties have a definite meaning in the biblical tradition. The tenth symbolizes the concept of a mini-

mum.[29] The quake affects only a small part of the city. The Bible relates the figure "seven thousand people" to the idea of "remnant,"[30]
thus signifying that the church will quickly recover from the blow.

The people of God and the witnesses will also come back to life.
The Apocalypse describes the event in language evocative of the resurrection. After the allusion to the crucifixion of Yeshua, the text
shifts to echo of His resurrection: "After the three and a half days a
breath of life from God entered them, and they stood on their feet"
(verse 11). Scripture uses the same language to describe the miracle
of resurrection in Ezekiel: "Breath entered them; they came to life
and stood up on their feet" (Eze. 37:10). The "three and a half
days"[31] evoke the length of time that Yeshua spent in the tomb
(Mark 9:31; John 2:19-22). What follows alludes to the ascension of
Yeshua after His resurrection: "And they went up to heaven in a
cloud" (Rev. 11:12; cf. Acts 1:9).

And indeed, right after the death decree against the Christian religion, France and other Western governments began to proclaim
tolerance and freedom of religion. We hear the intervention of the
writer and politician, Camille Jordan, one of the first legislators of
the Restoration in France, on May 1797, in the Council of Five
Hundred: "Faith in God is, for the state, the best guarantee of order
and stability, that even the best laws cannot replace. . . . Let all our
citizens be today fully reassured: let all, Catholics, Protestants, bap-
tized or non-baptized, know that it is the will of the legislator, as the
will of the law, that freedom of religion be assured. I wish to renew,
in your name, the sacred promise: all religions are free in France."[32]

For the Jews, the French Revolution and its heir, Napoleon, clearly
inaugurated a new era. The French legions liberated the Jews from the
ghettos everywhere they went, making them into full citizens. In
Spain, for example, French influence suppressed the Inquisition, and
the *marranos* could once again proclaim their Jewish faith.

The new era witnessed also a return to the Scriptures. Only a
few years before, Voltaire had predicted the disappearance of the
Bible, dismissing it as "last year's almanac." Yet the Bible again
found a place on book stands and in hearts.

The two witnesses have come back to life exactly three and a half prophetic days after their death. Resurrected from the dead, they live on today. The Bible is the number one best-seller. As for Israel and the church, they have more than survived, Israel in spite of the Holocaust and the church even in the face of Communism.

The Wrath of God

The seventh shofar announces a "third woe" (Rev. 11:14) to occur in the last moments of human history. The last vision anticipated the seventh shofar as the realization of the "mystery of God" (Rev. 10:7). The Apocalypse[33] often uses the term "mystery" to suggest a hidden meaning.[34] It is only at the end that the mystery makes any sense, when the prediction meets its fulfillment. The seventh shofar thus echoes the sixth seal. Both are concerned with the time of the end, when all prophecies reach their completion. And both announce this time in the same terms: the time of the wrath of God and of the judgment of the nations (Rev. 11:18; cf. 6:15-17). Contrasts, however, exist between the two visions. First, the sixth seal drew the curtain on an earthly scene while the seventh shofar does so on a heavenly scene. Second, they flow in different directions. In the sixth seal, the vision proceeds from the earth to the heavens, from the present to the future. But in the seventh shofar the vision proceeds back through time from the heavens to the earth in typical Hebrew fashion.[35]

The shofar vision goes through three stages in time. The first vibrates with "loud voices" proclaiming the end of all things: "The kingdom of the world has become the kingdom of our Lord and of his Christ" (Rev. 11:15). This part also shares themes with Revelation 4: the same ceremony of adoration, the same 24 elders seated on thrones (Rev. 11:16; cf. 4:4), and the same appellation of God—"Lord God Almighty, the One who is and who was" (Rev. 11:17; cf. 4:8). Our present passage lacks any mention of the God who "is to come" (cf. Rev. 4:8). The only explanation of this omission is that the Parousia has already occurred.

Moreover, in the liturgy of Revelation 4, the *Sanctus,* or praise, of the four living creatures precedes the intervention of the 24 elders. The loud voices that introduce the hymn of the 24 elders are those of the four living creatures (Rev. 11:15), who, as we have seen, represent the earthly creation. The moment has come when all creation proclaims God as its king, the final objective of God's plan. God can now reign completely and forever.

The 24 elders then go from adoration to remembrance as they recall both the negative and positive aspects of judgment (cf. Rev. 14:14-20).

a. The negative aspect includes the judgment of the dead and the destruction of the angry "nations" and "those who destroy the earth" (Rev. 11:18). The prophecy alludes here to later visions in the Apocalypse (Rev. 20:12-15) that place the completion of these events after the millennium.

b. The positive aspect involves the judgment of the "saints" and their reward (Rev. 11:18). This part of the vision materializes at the Parousia, when the Messiah shall take His own people home with Him before the millennium. Here again, the vision alludes to a later passage: "Behold I am coming soon! My reward is with me, and I will give to everyone according to what he has done" (Rev. 22:12).

In fact, the two judgments are interdependent. By eliminating "those who destroy the earth" God saves the earth.

Ecology is not the issue here. We must understand the reference to the earth in a spiritual sense. In the Apocalypse, particularly in the parallel text of the sixth seal, the earth represents the men and women threatened by the enemy (Rev. 7:3). And in the fifth shofar the "grass of the earth," the "plant," and the "tree" stand for those marked with God's seal (Rev. 9:4).

The destruction of the earth is a spiritual and religious one. Indeed, it results from the nations' being "angry" with God, a strange association already suggested through the word "angry" itself. It derives from Psalm 2, which describes the character of the Messiah when He returns to regain possession of His kingdom (Ps. 2:5). Our passage, on the other hand, speaks of the nations' anger. The nations, claiming the earth for themselves, display the wrath of the legitimate owner of the earth, God. Because they have rejected God as Lord of the earth and have taken His place, the nations have destroyed the earth. Again, we observe the same intolerance and oppression that has always characterized the usurper. People kill each other because they have forgotten God. The rejection of the absolute and transcendent God inevitably leads to the Crusades, to the Inquisition, and to the fascism of the fanatics and nationalists. That is why God's judgment against the nations saves the earth.

The prophetic vision of the seventh shofar looks back in time. Proceeding from the institution of the kingdom of God to the judgment of the nations, the prophetic eye ultimately rests on the event that triggered everything: the first coming of the Messiah (Rev. 12:1-6).

---

[1] See L. Ginzberg, "Tamid," *Journal of Jewish Lore and Philosophy* 1 (1919): 33, 38, 197, 263, 291.

[2] *Tamid* 5. 6.

[3] *Tamid* 3. 8.

[4] *Sukkah* 5. 6.

[5] See Doukhan, *Secrets of Daniel*, p. 128.

[6] *Ibid.*, pp. 13, 14.

[7] See Deut. 8:7, 9; Ps. 36:8, 9; Jer. 17:8, 13.

[8] See Deut. 29:17, 18; Jer. 9:15; 23:15.

[9] See Jacques B. Doukhan, *The Genesis Creation Story,* Andrews University Seminary Doctoral Dissertation Series (Berrien Springs, Mich.: Andrews University Press, 1978), vol. 5, pp. 64, 65.

[10] 1 Enoch 18:12-16; 19:1, 2, in a section written in the second century B.C.E.

[11] See Job 26:6; 28:22; 31:12; Prov. 15:11; 27:20.

[12] Prov. 10:28; 11:10; 19:9; 21:28; 29:3, etc.

[13] See Doukhan, *Secrets of Daniel*, pp. 108, 109, 143-145.

[14] See Jer. 51:14; Joel 1:4; Amos 7:1; Ps. 105:34.

[15] See Jer. 51:59-64; cf. Isa. 44:27, 28; Jer. 50:38.

[16] See 2 Sam. 18:3; 1 Cor. 4:15; 14:19.

[17] See Doukhan, *Secrets of Daniel*, pp. 171-175.

[18] See Isa. 31:1-3; 2 Kings 10:28; Jer. 46:8, 9, etc.

[19] See Doukhan, *Secrets of Daniel*, pp. 171-176.

[20] *Ibid.*, pp. 186-188.

[21] See section on Revelation 14:7-11.

[22] Matt. 23:2; John 1:17; Acts 15:21, etc.

[23] Mishnah, *Aboth* 1. 1.

[24] Luke 1:13-17; Matt. 17:10-13.

[25] Midrash Rabbah, *Leviticus* 34. 8; Midrash Rabbah, *Ruth* 5. 6.

[26] Doukhan, *Secrets of Daniel*, pp. 108, 109.

[27] *Le Moniteur,* 1er frimaire, An II.

[28] *Le Moniteur,* Nov. 14, 1793.

[29] See Isa. 6:13; Lev. 27:30; cf. Doukhan, *Secrets of Daniel*, pp. 23, 105, 106.

[30] 1 Kings 19:18; 20:15.

[31] According to ancient beliefs, the process of decomposition started only after the third day of death. Only then was the deceased officially dead. To speak of resurrection after the third day of death is to support the fact that the miracle of resurrection has occurred. Beyond the example of Yeshua, we have that of Lazarus, resurrected on the fourth day

(John 11:17, 39). Jonah emerges from the fish only after the third day, a time that he identifies with the abode of the dead (Jonah 2:2; cf. Hosea 6:1, 2).

[32] As quoted by J. Vuilleumier, *L'Apocalypse* (Dammarie-les-Lys, France: 1941), p. 177.

[33] Rev. 1:20; 17:5-7; cf. Dan. 2:22.

[34] Rom. 16:25, 26; cf. Col. 1:25, 26.

[35] See Doukhan, *Secrets of Daniel*, p. 155.

PART TWO

THE SKY IS RED

This last vision of the "God who comes" takes us to the very center of the Apocalypse and echoes the first vision of the book (Rev. 1:1-10). As with the book of Daniel, the structure of the Apocalypse has a central vision (Rev. 12-14) that focuses on the time of the end and judgment (Dan. 7).[1] After the heavy storms of church history, the clouds now dissipate to reveal the colors of hope (Matt. 16:2). The dragon of the earth who attacks the woman (first sign, Rev. 12) and calls upon the forces of the sea and of the earth (second and third signs, Rev. 13) is answered, from the midst of these heavens that still resonate with hymns of hope (interlude, Rev. 14:1-5), by three angels bearing a message of hope (fourth, fifth, and sixth signs, verses 6-13). At the completion of this triple outcry, God's presence invades the heavens (seventh sign, verses 14-20).

Kippur

Before entering this new series, the vision, as always, brings us back to the sanctuary: "Then God's temple in heaven was opened" (Rev. 11:19). The focus is the ark of the covenant in the Holy of Holies. We are thus in the context of the Day of Atonement (*Kippur,* in Hebrew), the only day of the year when the Holy of Holies was accessible to the priest. Yom Kippur is thus the Jewish festival that introduces the next vision.

The Day of Atonement followed 10 days after the Feast of Trumpets (Lev. 23:26-32). During those 10 days the people of Israel were to prepare for the great day of judgment (the tenth of Tishri, the seventh month). The allusion to the Feast of Trumpets clarified the mission of God's people as one of preparation for the judgment of God. Likewise, the imagery of the Day of Atonement now redefines their mission as proclaiming the coming judgment.

It is no coincidence that the ark takes up the whole space of the vision, considering its central role in the context of the Day of Atonement. On that day the priest sprinkled it with the sacrificial blood (Lev. 16:13-15). Placed in the back of the Holy of Holies and bearing two cherubim, the ark represented, in the mind of the Israelites, God's heavenly throne[2] and was identified with YHWH Himself (Num. 10:35, 36).

The sprinkling of the blood on the ark signified both God's judgment—the blood serving as a reminder that the animal died for the peoples' sins—and graciousness—that He had assumed the blame and that He forgave. Grace is here coupled with justice. The grace of forgiveness is welcomed only where the justice of the law is expected. Justice and grace are the two poles of the ark of the covenant.

Significantly, the ark contains the law, Aaron's rod that had blossomed, and a sample of manna.[3] On the one hand, the law symbolized justice, serving as the criteria for punishment. On the other hand, the rod of blossoms and the desert manna were signs of God's grace that creates life from dust. Jewish mysticism remembered the lesson of this association, interpreting the two cherubim of the ark as embodiments of God's attributes of justice and grace.[4]

That the blood of Yeshua the Messiah must be the prerequisite for forgiveness testifies to God's justice. That Yeshua consented to die testifies to God's love. And that His uncomparable act of love at the cross necessitates God's judgment shows that salvation depends on both divine love and justice. This message is the focus of the opening vision of the second part of the Apocalypse (Rev. 11:19). The open sky, which unveils the ark of the covenant and proclaims God's forgiveness, is also darkened by the "flashes of lightning, rumblings, peals of thunder, an earthquake and a great hailstorm" in a bittersweet reminder of the book's dual message of judgment and hope for earth's inhabitants.

---

[1] See Doukhan, *Daniel: The Vision of the End,* pp. 3-7; *Secrets of Daniel,* p. 100.
[2] Isa. 6:1-3; Eze. 1:4-28.
[3] Heb. 9:4; Ex. 16:33, 34; Deut. 10:5.
[4] Babylonian Talmud, *Baba Bathra* 93a; Babylonian Talmud, Yoma 54a.

CHAPTER 4

THE DEVIL AND THE WOMAN

(Revelation 12)

The Woman

It is from this background of hope and judgment that we must understand the vision in our passage. The same skies that rolled back to let us see the ark of the covenant now reveal a beautiful woman clothed with the sun, sandaled with moon rays, and crowned with 12 stars.

The vision weaves together a number of well-known biblical symbols. In the Bible the image of the woman has a dual interpretation. On the one hand, she represents the bride or beloved of God and by extension, the people of Israel He loves. The Song of Songs and the prophets Isaiah, Jeremiah, Ezekiel, Hosea, Amos, etc., all testify to the love affair between Israel and its God.

On the other hand, the woman represents the mother, the promise of life. Thus Adam names his wife Eve, "mother of all the living" (Gen. 3:20). For the first man, the woman represented the guarantee of survival. The seed of humanity must pass through the woman in order for life to come about. For the author of Genesis, the woman bears the seed that shall save the earth (Gen. 3:15). Both aspects of the image of the woman are in fact related, since through the conjugal relation the wife becomes a mother.

In our passage, the vision of the woman reminds us of Joseph's dream (Gen. 37:9-11). The sun, the moon, and the stars represented the family of Israel: Jacob, Rachel, and the 12 sons. Framed with their light, the woman depicts Israel, God's people.

Moreover, she now experiences the first pangs of childbirth. In biblical and Jewish traditions childbirth symbolizes the Messianic hope.[1] The impatience for the newborn struggles with the anguish of uncertainty and with the physical agony that tears through the flesh. There is but the promise. Only faith can imagine the seed of life that begets the promise. All of this is implied in the image of the suffering woman.

The Devil

Filled with the hope of God's sudden entrance into history, the prophet also witnesses the enemy of that hope: the dragon. Again the vision draws on Old Testament symbolism. From the very first pages of Genesis the serpent embodies evil (Gen. 3). He is the one that seduces the first man and the first woman into disobedience and death. The prophets later employ serpent imagery to illustrate the proud and evil empire of Egypt.[2] The book of Wisdom, dating from the first century before our era, also sees the serpent of the Garden of Eden as the devil in person.[3] Likewise, rabbinic exegesis has understood this "mythical" serpent as the representative of Satan himself. Among many others, Ibn Ezra, the famous Jewish commentator of the eleventh century, and later the Italian Jewish commentator Sforno, witness to that tradition.[4] Our passage follows these thoughts. Some verses later, the Apocalypse explicitly identifies the dragon as the "ancient serpent called the devil, or Satan" (Rev. 12:9).

All too often people have relegated the devil to ancient myths and tales until he has gradually vanished from the religious consciousness. The French poet Baudelaire spoke ironically of this skepticism: His majesty the devil told Baudelaire that he had feared but once for his power, the day that he heard a preacher, slightly more subtle than the others, preach: "My dear brothers, never forget, in hearing of the progress of this enlightened century, that the most treacherous trap of the devil is to dupe you into believing in his non-existence."[5] The piercing eye of the prophet penetrates reality and exposes the evil of he "who leads the whole world astray" (Rev. 12:9). It is not easy to detect the devil. His appearance is hardly that of the horned and tailed mythical figure. Indeed, Satan is a master of disguise. The most altruistic actions, the most noble aspirations, and the most sacred causes may camouflage his schemes. The devil is the one who clothes evil with goodness. Indeed, this is how he appears in the story of the Fall. There the serpent presents disobedience to God as a virtue (Gen. 3:5). For the Apocalypse, the devil exists as a historical and objective reality.

The book also describes Satan as an extraordinary 10-horned beast, one that recalls the fourth beast in Daniel 7. The number of heads (seven) is sacred and hints at the dragon-serpent's supernatural character. The beast embodies absolute evil. Its fiery red color adds to its aura of cruelty and violence.

The vulnerability of the woman giving birth contrasts with the heavy menace of the 10-horned beast. From this point on the dragon-serpent dedicates himself to oppressing the woman.

Cosmic Wars
Wars in Heaven

The conflict starts in heaven. The problem of evil is not a human one alone. It is a cosmic dilemma. The prophets Isaiah and Ezekiel testify to the same fact. In their oracles on Tyre and Babylon they allude to the ancient war in heaven and recount the same tragedy of the fall of the usurping angel: "You were anointed as a guardian cherub, for so I ordained you. You were on the holy mount of God; you walked among the fiery stones. You were blameless in your ways from the day you were created till wickedness was found in you. . . . Your heart became proud on account of your beauty, and you corrupted your wisdom because of your splendor. So I threw you to the earth. . . . I reduced you to ashes on the ground" (Eze. 28:14-18; cf. Isa. 14:13-15).

According to Revelation 12 this war broke out suddenly. The Apocalypse can give no cause or reason it happened. One may compare Ezekiel's simple statement of the situation: "Wickedness was found in you" (Eze. 28:15). The coming of evil is irrational. The absurdity that rules our existence is because of its invasion by Satan and his demons. God had to throw them out of heaven into the void and darkness that preceded the creation of the earth.

God's choice of precisely this devil-ridden location for the creation of the earth and of humanity may seem shocking. But, in fact, it contains a lesson with far-reaching implications. Paradoxically, God's salvation reveals itself in the very place that rejected Him—the world created out of darkness and the void.

Wars on Earth

As soon as he hits the earth, the devil attacks the woman. She is his first victim (Gen. 3:1ff.), and it is she that he pursues relentlessly, for she bears the seed of salvation. We see this truth recorded in the very first pages of the Bible. After the death of the child Abel, Eve receives instead Seth, a seed "put" by God to begin the genealogy of the Savior of the earth. The name of Seth, which means "God has put" or "God has granted" (Gen. 4:25), suggests His intervention in history. Within the name of Seth (in Hebrew, *Shet*) resonates the verb introduced in the first prophecy of the Bible: "I will put [in Hebrew, *shet*] enmity between you and the woman, between your offspring and hers" (Gen. 3:15).

The common themes of the woman, the serpent, childbirth, and conflict in Revelation 12 refer us back to this earlier prophecy. In spite of the troubles anticipated by our passage, hope remains. The two texts predict the victory of the woman's offspring over the serpent.

Beyond the allusion to Eve, "mother of all the living," we may also apply the prophecy to Israel, the woman of the covenant, who is to give birth to "a son, a male child, who will rule all the nations with an iron scepter" (Rev. 12:5). Behind these words we hear Psalm 2:9, which proclaims the coming of the Son of God (Ps. 2:7), king of the earth. According to our passage, the birth leads to the kingdom of God. The child is carried to the throne. "She gave birth to a son, a male child, who will rule all the nations with an iron scepter. And her child was snatched up to God and to his throne" (Rev. 12:5). Some verses later the prophet of the Apocalypse explains the mechanism of this victory: "Now have come the salvation and the power and the kingdom of our God, and the authority of his Christ. For the accuser of our brothers, who accuses them before our God day and night, has been hurled down. They overcame him by the blood of the Lamb" (Rev. 12:10, 11).

The death of the serpent necessitates the sacrifice of the child. Our passage speaks of the "blood of the Lamb" (Rev. 12:11). Genesis 3:15 hints at the same process. The death of the serpent, the crushing of his head, results in the death of the woman's offspring.[6] The imagery of the prophecy suggests that the deaths of the serpent and of the Messiah are simultaneous. While crushing the head, he is bitten at the heel. The Hebrew describes the crushing of the head and the bite of the heel by the same verb: *shuf.*

The victory of the Messiah and His enthronement are to be preceded by His death. The sacrifice of His life nullifies the accusations of the seducer. God is able to forgive and the kingdom is preserved, though it is a kingdom that does not yet belong to this world. Pure joy is still a heavenly privilege (Rev. 12:12). On earth, evil still rules.

Wars in the Desert

The incarnation of Yeshua, His death and resurrection, and His triumph over evil have not really changed the face of the earth. The serpent is still around. Death, suffering, and evil still strike human beings. God's people continue to wait for Him to establish His kingdom on earth.

In fact, the Apocalypse compares them to the Israel of the Exodus. Like the ancient Israelites, the church finds itself exiled in the desert and nourished by the hand of God (12:6, 14). The eagle's wings (Rev. 12:14; cf. Ex. 19:4) and the earth that engulfs the enemy (Rev. 12:16; cf. Ex. 15:12) both refer to the Exodus event, when the Israelites were still fleeing Egypt and were being tracked down by the Egyptian army.

Just as God freed the people of Israel from the Egyptian yoke and they made their way toward the Promised Land, He saves this people from the slavery of sin and they journey toward the New Jerusalem. The exile is difficult. The people of God shall have to endure it for 1,260 days (Rev. 12:6).

The Apocalypse mentions this period several times, as though to emphasize its historicity. Sometimes the book gives it in days.

Revelation 11:3 and 12:6 speak of "1,260 days." Other times it uses months: Revelation 11:2 and 13:5 talk of "forty-two months" (42 x 30 = 1,260 days). Or it may describe the period in terms of years. Revelation 12:14 (and Daniel 7:25 and 12:7) refer to "a time, times, and half a time" (360 + [360 x 2] + [360 ÷ 2] = 1,260).[7] And indeed, between 538 C.E., official date of the liberation of the church from Arian rule, to 1798, when the French Revolution and its philosophers jeopardized the church's sovereignty, we find a period of 1,260 years. The prophecy could not have been more precise.

Wars at the End

According to the Apocalypse, the 1,260 days/years lead into the time of the end, explaining the impatience and irritation of the serpent (Rev. 12:7), who feels that his rule is coming to an end. In these last days, the serpent will concentrate all his energies against the woman's offspring, throwing us once more into the context of Genesis 3:15. The moment has come to eliminate the woman forever.

But she is particularly resilient. The Apocalypse describes God's people as "those who obey God's commandments and hold to the testimony of Jesus" (Rev. 12:17). The remnant is characterized by its obedience and faithfulness—they "obey." They have not lost what God entrusted them with.

Furthermore, they are the last witnesses to a truth that comprehends all opposites, transcends all factions. It is a truth that appreciates the Torah of the Jews along with the Yeshua of the Christians, bringing together grace and law, love and justice, creation and judgment, and the New and the Old Testaments. This truth combines "God's commandments" with the "testimony of Jesus" the Messiah (Rev. 12:17).

Here is the profile of the last remnant (Rev. 14:2). Against them the dragon will focus all his evil. The serpent stands "on the shore of the sea" (Rev. 13:1), showing thereby his dual influence on both the sea and the earth.

---

[1] Isa. 13:8; Hosea 13:13.
[2] Isa. 51:9; cf. Eze. 29:3; 32:2.
[3] Wisdom of Solomon 2:24.

[4] See *Miqraoth Gdoloth* on Gen. 3:1.

[5] Charles Baudelaire, *Le spleen de Paris, œuvres complètes,* Bibliothèque de la Pléiade (Paris: 1961), p. 276.

[6] The interpretation that sees in the woman's offspring the image of a personal Messiah is ancient and already attested in the second century B.C.E. in the Septuagint, which translates the word "offspring" (seed) by the personal pronoun *(autos)* in the masculine singular form, instead of *(auto)* in the neuter form generally used for "seed." This Messianic reading appears in both Jewish tradition (see Jacques B. Doukhan, *Messianic Riddle* [forthcoming]) and Christian tradition (see Rom. 16:20; cf. Heb. 2:14, and the Church Fathers, particularly Irenaeus).

[7] See Doukhan, *Secrets of Daniel,* pp. 108-110.

CHAPTER 5

OF MEN AND BEASTS

(Revelation 13–14:5)

The Beast From the Sea

From the sea emerges a beast shockingly similar to the dragon. Like the dragon, the beast shows off its seven heads and 10 horns (Rev. 13:1). The Apocalypse declares the beast to have received its power from the dragon itself (verse 4). Its origin in the water already hints to its evil character. In both the Bible and in ancient Middle Eastern literature the dragon of the waters represents the enemies of the Creator,[1] the *goyim* who assault the people of God.[2] Its sea nature also alludes to the beast's geopolitical identity. The beast represents Rome, whose power the Middle Eastern nations experienced as coming from the sea. The visions of the fourth book of Ezra, an apocryphal work from around 100 C.E., depict Rome as a beast emerging from the sea (4 Ezra [2 Esdras] 11:1; 12:11).

But the new beast represents more than the dragon. Its features remind us of the four animals of Daniel 7—the leopard, the bear, the lion (Rev. 13:2; cf. Dan. 7:2, 3) and particularly the fourth, 10-horned beast (Rev. 13:1; cf. Dan. 7:7). The prophetic vision focuses on the distinguishing feature of this fourth beast: the little horn. Like the little horn, our beast receives a mouth that speaks with arrogance (Rev. 13:4; cf. Dan. 7:8). And like the little horn, our beast has usurping tendencies. It seeks to be worshiped and receives the praise, "Who is like the beast?" (Rev. 13:4). This expression echoes one traditionally spoken of the God of Israel: "Who is like God?" (cf. Ex.

15:11; Ps. 35:10), and it constitutes the very name of Michael (the Hebrew *mi-ka-el* means "who is like God?").

Moreover, like the little horn, the beast oppresses God's people during 42 months, after which it receives a fatal wound (Rev. 13:3). This sequence of events is hinted at by parallelism in our passage: ABC//A'B'C':

First paragraph:

    A. the beast receives authority from the dragon (Rev. 13:2)

    B. one of its heads is fatally wounded (verse 3)

    C. the wound is healed, the beast is worshiped (verses 3, 4)

Second paragraph:

    A.' the beast receives a mouth and authority (verse 5)

    B.' during 42 months (verse 5)

    C.' opens its mouth, worshiped by the world (verses 6-8).

This parallelism relates B to B'. In the first paragraph, the beast receives authority from the dragon (A) until one of its heads is wounded (B), after which the whole world admires it (C). Likewise, in the second paragraph, the beast receives authority from the dragon (A') during 42 months (B'), after which the whole world again worships it (C'). The beast therefore receives its wound upon the completion of the 42 months.

Until this point the prophecy only reformulates past revelations. Like the prophecy of Daniel, our passage describes the emergence of a power seeking to replace God that appears chronologically after the fall of Rome. According to the book of Daniel, this power would oppress the people of God during "a time, times and half a time" (Dan. 7:25), namely, 42 months or 1,260 prophetic days (years). Our passage further explains that after this period of oppression something would fatally wound the beast, but it would ultimately recover and "all inhabitants of the earth" would worship it (Rev. 13:8).

History confirms the prophecy. The 1,260 years begin in 538 when the church establishes itself as an institutional power and ends in 1798 when the sword of Napoleon stabs it.[3] Then the church quickly recovers and the Papacy reestablishes itself. The nineteenth century marks a revival in the Catholic Church. The first Vatican council (1870) inaugurated an era of renewed respect and devotion for the pope. The church had emerged from the period of the French Revolution stronger than ever and has increasingly received recognition as a political and moral authority. Jesuit teaching explained that when the pope mediates, it is God Himself who mediates through him. Catholic musicians composed hymns of praise to glorify Pius IX (pope from 1846 to 1878). Some church propagandists even called the holy father "the vice-God of humanity."[4] Finally, in 1870, church leadership pronounced the infallibility of the pope a dogma. From then on, the prestige of the Papacy has only grown. The fall of Marxism and other economic and social crises have reinforced its moral prerogative. *Time* magazine termed the pope its "Man of the Year" for 1994, devoting its cover story to him.[5]

To dare to identify the benign pope with a monstrous beast is hardly appropriate in our era of increasing tolerance, openness, and respect. The pope's immense popularity, his campaign for world peace, and his aid to the poor and the oppressed somehow contradict the prophecy.

Yet, interestingly enough, the prophecy predicts even this: "He was given authority over every tribe, people, language and nation. All inhabitants of the earth will worship the beast" (Rev. 13:7, 8). For the first time, the influence of the Papacy has exploded beyond the borders of the Catholic religion, beyond the territories of Italy or even France, the "eldest daughter of the church."

But the prophetic vision does not necessarily accuse the Catholic Church as such. The prophetic intention seeks less to condemn than to elucidate the meanders of history, so that we may know that behind them a divine providence is working to strengthen faith and support hope. This is the lesson of our passage: "This calls for patient endurance and faithfulness on the part of the saints" (Rev. 13:10).

The Beast From the Land

Just after the world begins to admire the healed sea beast, the prophet of the Apocalypse sees another beast, this time of earthly origin. The beast from the land then stepped into the camp of the first beast and "he spoke like a dragon" (verse 11). The land beast thus allied itself to the sea beast, and shared that same power dispensed by the dragon (verse 4): "He exercised all the authority of the first beast on his behalf" (verse 12).

Furthermore, the land beast does everything in its power to incite "the earth and its inhabitants" to "worship the first beast" (verse 12). Seducing the world with great wonders (verses 13, 14), it campaigns for the first beast, setting up a great statue of it (verse 14). It even animates this statue, complete with sound effects, like some of those new toys that a push of a button brings to life. We would be inclined to smile were it not for the ensuing violence.

Our passage reminds us of the incident recounted in Daniel 3. Nebuchadnezzar erects a great statue—the replica of the image of his dreams (Dan. 2)—and orders his subjects, "peoples, nations and men of every language" (Dan. 3:4; cf. 3:7), to worship it on penalty of death (Dan. 3:6). The land beast now seeks to "cause all who refused to worship the image to be killed" (Rev. 13:15).

The Apocalypse depicts the mark of worship as being stamped on the right hand or on the forehead (verse 16), imagery borrowed from the book of Deuteronomy, in which it applies to faithfulness to God's law: "Tie them as symbols on your hands and bind them on your foreheads" (Deut. 6:8; cf. Ex.13:9). For Jews such language is particularly meaningful, since it evokes their daily habit of binding the *Tefillin* on the hand and forehead to remind themselves of their total submission to the law, involving both actions (the hand) and thinking (the forehead).

The intention of the land beast is crystal clear. He wants to force all people to submit to the law of the sea beast just as God expected the Israelites to submit themselves to the law of Moses—on the forehead and on the hand, that is, in thought and in actions—totally. The land beast thus helps the sea beast reach divine status. Its law replaces God's in human hearts and actions. "The mark of the beast" is thus more than a superficial tattoo, since it acts as a sign that the sea beast's law is inscribed deeply in people's hearts and manifests itself through their actions.

The number of the beast also betrays its character and vocation: 666. It is a "man's number," the Apocalypse explains (Rev. 13:18).

Biblical tradition associates the number 6 with humans, since they were created on the sixth day. The number 6 symbolizes the self-sufficiency and pride of the person who does not need God. And the number 6 is also a key figure in the construction of Nebuchadnezzar's statue (Dan. 3:1).[6] Nebuchadnezzar erected it to promote the unity of the peoples of the earth and to replace divine authority. The triple repetition of the number 6 alludes to the creature's desire to usurp God's role. Indeed, the number 3 is the number of God. To repeat the human number three times amounts to promoting the human to the level of the divine, who is three times holy (Isa. 6:3; Rev. 4:8).

By naming this power 666, the Apocalypse reveals the true nature of the sea beast. Behind its mask of religiosity lurks the all-too-human aspiration for power. God is of no concern to the church. It is all a political game. Ever since Constantine and Clovis the church has lusted after political power. At times the church has had no other concern than to regain a foothold in the political arena. It has traded its soul for worldly recognition and is now backed by the land beast. Several clues help us identify this last power:

Its nature: it is different from that of the sea beast. Not a religious power, it receives no worship (Rev. 13:12, 15). But the Apocalypse defines its nature as one of economics—it determines who can "buy or sell" (verse 17)—and as political—it can kill (verse 15).

Its time: it emerges after the first beast appears, and its actions begin after the first beast recovers from its wound (verse 12); therefore, this power starts to manifest itself only at the end of the eighteenth century.

Its space: in contrast to the sea beast, this one comes from the earth. The difference in origins has great meaning for the Hebrew reader. Whereas the sea is threatening, the earth is familiar and reassuring. The Hebrew word *erets* (earth) denotes the country, the motherland, or the home.[7] Coming from *erets,* the beast presents itself in soothing tones as an ally. In fact, a few verses earlier, the Apocalypse shows the earth as saving the woman (Rev. 12:16).

Its character: the appearance of the beast confirms this first impression of harmlessness. With its two little horns, the beast resembles a lamb (Rev. 13:11)—it can be trusted. The sea beast, with its 10 horns and savage features, was impure and terrifying. The land beast, on the other hand, seems tame and domesticated. Moreover, for the Christian Yohanan, its lamblike features recall those of the gentle Yeshua (Rev. 14:1).

Yet we must not let it fool us. The lamb speaks like a dragon (Rev. 13:11). Such contradictory traits should shock us. Shattering its innocent and comforting image, the lamb suddenly roars like a dragon.

The pieces of the puzzle come together to form an unexpected portrait. An economic and political superpower originating in the late eighteenth century, a haven for the religiously oppressed, the United States of America roars on the international scene like a dragon, yet displays the face of a lamb.

The beast's dual nature manifests itself on both the political and psychological levels. The naive idealism of America goes hand in hand with strong military, economic, and political power. Indeed, often the roaring threats of the American dragon sound out of place coming from this lamb-faced beast.

History confirms the prophetic vision. According to our passage, this beast also has a dual influence. It interacts with both the inhabitants of the earth and the first beast. On the one hand, it seduces the inhabitants of the earth with its wonders and its power to make fire fall from heaven. For the Hebrew, this image evokes the power of the prophet Elijah (1 Kings 18:17-39). And in the Apocalypse it characterizes the power of the two witnesses of God (Rev. 11:5). The land beast thus imitates divine wonders. Whether on the military and diplomatic scene, or on the big screen, the United States always ends up saving the world. Its influence shows up everywhere. The dollar has become a global monetary standard. American productions and commercials saturate international media. Rock music, blue jeans, McDonald's, and Coca-Cola are universal commodities. Indeed, the United States has seduced the world.

On the other hand, it plays a central role in the success of the other beast. And indeed, the Vatican holds a privileged relationship with the United States. Both have often worked together in the past, and more recently they played an important role in the fall of

Marxism. The first historical moves anticipated by the prophecy are beginning to surface on the international scene.

Indeed, the totalitarian overtones of the beast's regime are quite unexpected from a free country such as the United States. Our passage specifies that those who refuse the mark of the beast will find themselves eliminated from the business world. The identity of all will be molded into the number 666. If the prophecy speaks the truth, we may expect that one day the United States, the land of the free, will become the center of religious oppression. The "mark of the beast" will work hard to stamp out individuality. Human authority will replace God's in people's hearts and actions.

We can see the fulfillment of the prophecy in current religious developments. Sociological, psychological, or even entertainment concerns are increasingly replacing the worship of God. And we even see efforts to standardize the day of worship[8] for reasons of practicality, or in an ecumenical stance of universal love and unity.

But these are just symptoms. The "mark of the beast" implies more than a day or a form of worship—it involves also allegiance to the beast, to the power of Babel, with all its potential for repression, conformity, and alienation from God. Such accusations are incredible. Yet certain developments seem to point in the direction of the prophecy, especially the rise of the Christian Right, with its passionate fight against the separation of state and church.

The prophecy closes with the cold clamp of totalitarianism. The number 666 makes the last words of the prophecy cold and unfeeling—as though hope and humaneness were no longer an option.

Interlude: The Men in Heaven

Suddenly a new vision grasps the prophet as he sees a triumphant crowd singing praises of hope and joy. The scene is in direct contrast with what we have just heard and feared. To those crushed by the power of Babel, the vision brings tidings of hope. Above the sea and the earth rises the "Mount Zion" (Rev. 14:1) of the future. The only mention of Zion in the Apocalypse, it is the heavenly Zion.

The voice that the prophet hears comes from heaven (verse 2), and the 144,000 stand assembled before the heavenly throne.

On the basis of His presence on the earthly mount of Zion, the people of Israel had come to refer to God's dwelling place in heaven by the same name: "Mount Zion."[9] Thus when in Psalm 48:2 the sons of Korah link Zion, the holy mountain of God, to "the utmost heights of Zaphon" *(yarketey tsafon),* they are alluding to heaven. The prophet Isaiah confirms this by identifying the "utmost heights" with "heaven . . . above the stars of God" (Isa. 14:13). As opposed to the beasts that "come out" of the sea and of the earth, the Lamb "stands" on the heavenly Mount of Zion. Stability and order confront the confusion and chaos brought about by the dragon. Even the seal of ownership, which in the case of the dragon is stamped sometimes on the hand and sometimes on the forehead, is now firmly inscribed on the foreheads of the redeemed (Rev. 14:1). Likewise, the number 144,000 symbolizes the covenant with God (12 x 12,000) and contrasts with the number 666, which symbolizes God's absence.

The "pure" (the Greek has the word for "virgins") contrast with those who let themselves be "deceived" by the beast (Rev. 13:14; cf. 13:3, 8). Again Scripture employs the conjugal metaphor to indicate the intimate relationship between God and His people. The Hebrew Scriptures often call the people of God the "Virgin daughter of Zion."[10] In the Song of Songs the longing of the Shulammite for Solomon her beloved represents Israel's desire for God its beloved.[11] The prophet Hosea wept nostalgically at the thought of Israel's days of betrothal in the desert (Hosea 2:16).

The Apocalypse obviously does not use this imagery of the virginity of the people of God to encourage sexual abstinence, but as an exaltation of the virtue of patience. Israel shall remain forever pure because it always awaits its beloved. The kingdom is not of this world. In contrast to those who have joined with the earthly kingdom, the "pure" of Zion preserve themselves for the kingdom of God. By describing them as "virgins," the prophet of the Apocalypse means a consecrated people, one set apart for God.

The other title that characterizes them—the "firstfruits to God" (Rev. 14:4)—implies the same concept. Again, the Apocalypse has borrowed language from the Hebrew Scriptures. It evokes the ritual during which Israel reserved the firstfruits of the harvest for God.[12] Scripture considered Israel the firstborn of God[13] and, in the same line of thought, the firstfruits of the harvest (Jer. 2:3), a holy people set apart for God.

The Apocalypse sets the 144,000 apart from the rest of the human race. God's people and the dragon's people differ by their actions and attitudes. The followers of the dragon are like robots. They do not even speak. The beast speaks for them. Their main concern is material and economic, their goal worldly success and recognition.

On the other hand, the disciples of the Lamb follow him spontaneously (Rev. 14:4) and sing "a new song" (verse 3). The creativity of these poets/musicians is opposed to the twisted calculations of the dragon's technicians of commercial and economic success. Life, imagination, and quest for adventure and discovery confront the death and boredom of the plotters of material success.

The expression "new song" is fundamental to the book of Psalms, in which it celebrates the rebirth of salvation.[14] In this instance, the 144,000, overwhelmed by the miracle of resurrection, burst forth in harmonies of praise only they can express.

The prophetic vision anticipates the final judgment. The prophet hears in the background thunder and the roar of rushing water "like that of harpists" (verse 2). The moment has come for the justice and the love of God to come together again and put an end to evil.

[1] Isa. 27:1; Eze. 29:3-5; 31; 32; cf. Ps. 69:1, 2; 74:12-17; 124:1-5.
[2] Isa. 17:12; Jer. 46:7; Rev. 17:1, 18.
[3] See Doukhan, *Secrets of Daniel*, pp. 108-110.
[4] Bruce L. Shelley, *Church History in Plain Language* (Waco, Tex.: 1982), p. 381.
[5] *Time,* Dec. 26, 1994.
[6] Doukhan, *Secrets of Daniel*, p. 46.
[7] Gen. 11:31; 12:1, 5-7; Lev. 14:34; Deut. 18:9; 2 Kings 5:2; cf. Matt. 2:20, 21; Eph. 6:3.
[8] See "Lord's Day Alliance Officials Have Audience With Pope John Paul II and Others in Europe," *Sunday: The Magazine of the Lord's Day Alliance in the United States,* October/December 1986, pp. 8, 9; cf. James P. Wesberry, ed., *The Lord's Day* (Nashville: 1986), p. 123.
[9] Ps. 2:6; 68:18; 87:1; 99:9.
[10] Cf. 2 Kings 19:21; Isa. 37:22; Jer. 14:17; Amos 5:2; etc.
[11] S. of Sol. 2:8, 9; 5:2; 8:14.
[12] Deut. 26:1-11; Lev. 23:9-21.
[13] Ex. 4:22; Jer. 31:9.
[14] Ps. 33:3; 40:3; 96:1; 98:1; 144:9; 149:1.

CHAPTER 6

SCREAMING ANGELS

(Revelation 14:6-20)

Three angels racing for the earth now shatter the skies. We are now back in history. The people of the earth are again present. The heavenly messengers bear news concerning the destiny of the world. They directly precede the coming of the Son of man on the clouds (Rev. 14:14) and follow the four beasts of Daniel 7 (Rev. 13:2ff.) The parallel between the two passages suggests that the message of the three angels corresponds in Daniel 7 to the time of judgment (Dan. 7:9-12), or of Kippur (Dan. 8:14). We are now in "the time of the end" (Dan. 8:17).

Daniel 7	Revelation 13 and 14
1. Four beasts (lion, bear, leopard, 10-horned beast)	1. Ten-horned beast (features of the lion, leopard, and bear)
2. Usurping and oppressive power (1,260 days)	2. Usurping and oppressive power (42 months)
3. Heavenly judgment	3. Proclamation of the three angels
4. Coming of the Son of man	4. Coming of the Son of man

According to the Apocalypse, the earth will then resonate with three proclamations.

The First Angel

The first angel of Revelation 14 has as its mission to proclaim the

123

"eternal gospel" (Rev. 14:6). The Greek term *euangelion,* translated here by "gospel," literally means "good news." Classical Greek literature used the word to express the news of victory. It concerns either the death of the enemy or the arrival of the Roman emperor[2] who saves the nations from trouble and brings the *Pax Romana* (Roman peace).

This message of the first angel is one of hope—the end of human tragedy is near. The angel's message is a dual one—fear the Judge and worship the Creator: "Fear God and give him glory, because the hour of his judgment has come. Worship him who made the heavens, the earth, the sea and the springs of water" (verse 7).

Fear the Judge

In the ancient Near East a king was also the judge. The Bible also associates both functions (Ex. 18:13; 2 Kings 15:5; 2 Chron. 1:10; Ps. 72:2). It is in the context of this glorious vision of a God who rules and judges that we must interpret the call to fear Him.

The fear of God is an often misunderstood concept. True fear of God is an awareness of His eyes upon us. The Hebrew word for this concept *(yr')* probably comes from the same root as the verb "to see" *(r'h).* To fear God is to know that He is watching us wherever we are, whatever we do. Thus the Bible relates the fear of God to His law: "So that you, your children and their children after them may fear the Lord your God as long as you live by keeping all his decrees and commands" (Deut. 6:2). The fear of God is the beginning of the moral life: "Fear God and keep his commandments" (Eccl. 12:13). In this last passage the syntax of the Hebrew phrase suggests that we should not understand the conjunction of coordination "and" in an additive sense but in an explicative sense: "Fear God, in other words, observe His commandments." The author of the book of Ecclesiastes considers "man" *(kol haadam)* to be bound by the commandments in the perspective of the judgment: "For God will bring every deed into judgment, including every hidden thing, whether it is good or evil" (verse 14).

To fear God means to concern ourselves with that which is good, just, and right; to observe the commandments not only in public, but also in the privacy of the home. Religion is not relegated to the Lord's Day or prayer or to the sacred places in church or the synagogue. Every moment, every act, every thought at any time or anywhere is under God's scrutiny. That is why the fear of God is such an important recurring theme in biblical wisdom literature. In the midst of profound and challenging reflections on human existence—*there* is the fear of God: "The fear of the Lord is the beginning of wisdom" (Prov. 9:10; cf. 1:7ff.).

The fear of God has nothing to do with superstitious beliefs that paralyze and lead to a mechanical and magical religion. The Bible often associates the fear of God with love. Immediately following the exhortation to fear God and to obey His commandments we find the command to love: "Love the Lord your God with all your heart and with all your soul and with all your strength" (Deut. 6:5). To fear God is to love Him and to be loved by Him. It is also the assurance that God is watching *over* us: "But the eyes of the Lord are on those who fear him" (Ps. 33:18). Obedience to the law is the visible sign of our love for God. To live in the sight of God is to live with God. Inversely, because we live with God, we live according to His will. True religion takes God consistently and seriously.

Revelation 14:7 follows the call to fear God with a summons to praise Him. The Hebrew word *kabod*, "glory," contains the idea of weight. We give God weight in our thoughts and actions; we take Him into consideration. The message of the Apocalypse strikes at the heart of hypocritical and superficial religions that fail to inspire an awe of God precisely because they have no concept of the fear of God. People may invoke God's name, build temples and cathedrals to His glory, and debate theology about Him, but the human heart remains closed, crippled by its own lies and crimes. At the heart of the past century the event of the Holocaust proclaimed the failure of religion, particularly that of Christianity.

Humanity no longer takes God seriously. He has become the good, harmless old father that we can manipulate or the sweet baby Jesus who is too cute to be real. And the world has turned away in a bitter sneer. "God is dead" some have proclaimed in response, a belief that at times has spread even to religious circles. Religion is but a spiritual experience, a moral code, or simply a tradition. Who believes in the God of heaven and in His kingdom?

Because we have lost the fear of God, we cannot imagine it, let alone wish for it. As a result, the Apocalypse is all too relevant today. The first angel calls for the fear of God to awaken us to His presence, to kindle in the hearts of men and women too busy building a worldly city their need for the return of God in His glory.

Worship of the Creator

From the idea of a God that we fear, the angel leads us to the God that we worship. And from obedience to the law of a just God we move to the loving worship of the God that gave us life. Awed by the infinity and beauty of the universe, the human creature can but worship its Creator. Interestingly, the psalms and the prayers of Israel directly associate worship with creation (Ps. 95:6; 102:18; Neh. 9:6). It is by creating that God has demonstrated His grace and power. His infinite goodness invites us to worship Him, and His proximity enables us to encounter and love Him. Worship is the only response to Creation. Indeed, worship is the dual awareness of God's infinite distance—as the great Creator—and of His proximity—in guiding the very breath of His creatures.

The very first pages of the Bible—the two accounts of Creation—hint at this dual manifestation. In the first account (Gen. 1:1–2:4), God, *Elohim*, is the transcendent and omnipotent deity, master of the universe. In the second account (Gen. 2:4-24), God, YHWH, is the immanent and personal God, the deity of history and of existence, the God of the Creation.

The Bible opens with the story of Creation not only in virtue of its chronological precedence, but also as to situate the creature relative to its Creator. The Bible begins with Creation to provide a basis for worship.

But our passage in the Apocalypse alludes to more than Creation. The unexpected mention of the "springs of water" in addition to the three traditional components of Creation (heavens, earth, and sea) is particularly meaningful. In the desert home of Israel water was life. Thus in our passage the "springs of water" contrast

126

with the desert of death and evil (Rev. 12:6, 14; 17:3).

The Lamb leads His people to the springs of water (Rev. 7:17; 22:17). Likewise, the book of Ezekiel envisions the Jerusalem of hope abounding with springs of water (Eze. 47:1-12) as had the Garden of Eden (Gen. 2:10-14).[3] The springs of water thus have a futuristic ring. They allude to the ideal Jerusalem, portrayed as the Garden of Eden. Worship of the Creator lends to hope in a future creation.

The Second Angel

Suddenly the tone changes. The second angel looks to the oppressor's camp and inverts its message. Instead of the good news of hope, we now hear a judgment predicting the fall of Babylon: "Fallen! Fallen is Babylon the Great, which made all the nations drink the maddening wine of her adulteries" (Rev. 14:8).

The verb is conjugated in the past tense so as to indicate its inevitability. The Hebrew prophets considered a predicted event so certain that they announced it in the past tense. Thus the prophet Isaiah proclaimed: "Babylon has fallen, has fallen!" (Isa. 21:9). Likewise, the prophet Jeremiah declared: "Babylon was a gold cup in the Lord's hand; she made the whole earth drunk. The nations drank her wine; therefore they have now gone mad. Babylon will suddenly fall and be broken" (Jer. 51:7, 8).

The disciples of Babel, intoxicated by her wine, have lost all sense of reality. They have been fooled. Babel masqueraded as the city of God and they fell for it. According to the book of Proverbs, that is the inevitable fate of the drunkard: "Do not gaze at wine when it is red, when it sparkles in the cup, when it goes down smoothly! In the end it bites like a snake and poisons like a viper. Your eyes will see strange sights and your mind imagine confusing things. You will be like one sleeping on the high seas, lying on top of the rigging" (Prov. 23:31-34).

In contrast to the 144,000 virgins, the Apocalypse portrays the disciples of Babel as adulterers. The camp of the Lamb has as its prime characteristic the fear of God, which they experience in a relationship of love and faithfulness. But the camp of Babel replaces God with a worldly institution, and religion becomes adulterous.

127

The mission of the second angel consists in revealing this fraud to humanity. The Apocalypse and the book of Daniel have described the power of Babel as a human one. The little horn with the human face acting as an usurper (Dan. 7:24, 25; 8:9-11, 25) or the beast posing as God (Rev. 13:4) both represent a human institution.

The angel's intention is less to accuse than to warn. The fall of Babylon is the paradigm of all falls. The collapse of the historical Babylon to the invading army of Cyrus in 539 B.C.E. became the biblical archetype for the eventual outcome of all pride and self-sufficiency. Pride and the pretension to infallibility lead to confusion and later to a fall. No political ideal, no religious ideal, no man, and no woman can escape this possibility. Babylon is also a mentality that can manifest itself beyond the ramparts of Nebuchadnezzar or the cathedrals of the medieval church. The fall of Babylon should warn each of us of the downfall that our own pride can cause.

The Third Angel

The third angel draws out the implications of the fall of Babylon for both camps. For the camp of Babel, whoever "worships the beast and his image" shall end up like the beast. The verb "worship" is significant. The first angel just used it in the context of Creation (Rev. 14:7). Now the beast misappropriates it by being "worshiped" in place of the Creator.

The Apocalypse portrays the disciples of the beast like the 144,000. Also sealed (Rev. 14:9, 11; cf. 7:3), their seal is the outward sign of their internal allegiance to the beast as indicated by the mark on the forehead, or through their actions, as revealed by the mark on their hand.

Ironically, the followers of the beast will become the victims of their own illusions. They will drink of yet another wine—that of God's wrath (Rev. 14:10). The wine of Babylon will mix with the wine of His wrath. Their flaw contains their punishment. The more they drink, the more control they lose, and the more they lose control, the more they drink.

Tragic. Babylon's lovers will have no respite. It is the same obsession with success that consumed the builders of Babel (Gen. 11:3,

4), the satraps of Darius (Dan. 6:6),[4] and now the followers of the beast. Born of a spirit of self-reliance, the fatal flaw refuses to acknowledge any external Creator.

But all their work, all their efforts will go up in smoke: "He will be tormented with burning sulfur. . . . And the smoke of their torment rises for ever and ever" (Rev. 14:10, 11). The language is ironic, evocative of the famous Valley of Hinnom *(Gey Hinnom),* from which we derive the word "Gehenna." It was a sacrificial place to the south of Jerusalem where Israel burned children and infants to Molech.[5] The Bible recounts that eventually King Josiah desecrated and abolished it (2 Kings 23:10). The people of Jerusalem later converted the area into a site for burning the city's trash. This dumping ground, with its garbage that never ceased to burn and its past association with the abominations of Molech, constitutes the final destination of the proud followers of Babel.

The Apocalypse is not referring here to an eternal hell. Rather, the image seeks to reveal the idolatrous nature of the cult of Babel. Moreover, the expression "for ever and ever" hints less to an eternal duration than to a definitive ending. They are burned forever. We see the same way of thinking attested in the book of Isaiah (Isa. 33:14), in which the expression "consuming fire" parallels "everlasting burning" to mean that this fire has an eternal effect on the object—it destroys it forever. The prophet portrays the fall of Babylon and of its disciples then as the shameful death of the scum of the earth—an absolute and definitive death.

But for the camp of the Lamb, the fall of Babylon has totally different implications. When the angel breaks the news, Babel is at the height of its success. The human institution seems overwhelmingly successful. The God of heaven seems to be absent. The followers of the Lamb seem doomed to failure.

In this context, the news of the fall of Babel encourages perseverance. "This calls for patient endurance on the part of the saints" (Rev. 14:12). Too many have misunderstood the last word in the passage. The "saint" in the Bible *(qadosh)* has nothing to do with the goodie-goodies of our childhood who informed on us and always got the best grades. The saints envisioned by the prophets are more like nightmare material: they trouble and disturb the established order of things and always go against the social and cultural flow. The saints of the end of times are revolutionaries. Because they feel the end coming, they are already in tune with another world.

Such is the character of these last saints, those who "obey God's commandments and remain faithful to Jesus" (verse 12). Against the majority who follow the prescribed norm, the saints make up the minority who live in the fear of God and remain faithful to the ancient commandments of the God of Israel and of Yeshua. Contrary to those who believe only in their own works, these refugees of history have remained true to the faith of their forebears. They believe in spite of spiritual darkness and divine silence. And they hope in spite of hopelessness.

But beyond the person of the saint is the reference to the document that constitutes the basis of their identity. Through the double reference to the "commandments" and to faith in the Messiah, the Apocalypse alludes to the two main events of God's revelation in history: on the one hand, the Torah, the law of God; and on the other hand, the incarnation and death of Yeshua the Messiah.

The Apocalypse again reconciles the two "witnesses" (cf. Rev. 11) and opposes the rift played out in the tension between Judaism and Christianity that has artificially separated Moses from Yeshua, the Old Testament from the New Testament, law from grace. The Apocalypse reminds the Christian of the law's relevance. The New Covenant is not a rejection or a modification of the Old, but constitutes a renewed and deeper commitment to the Old Covenant. Faith in Yeshua does not exclude the fear of God. Trust in God implies the passion to serve Him and the desire to live according to His will.

It is not a coincidence that the key message of the three angels revolves around the two themes of judgment and Creation. On the one hand, the judgment implies the law and fear of God. Judgment is based on the verdict of the law. The Bible often identifies the two. In fact, the Hebrew word for judgment, *mishpat,* also means law or commandment.[6] It is the perspective of the judgment that inspires the fear of God and the desire to obey Him. On the other hand, the miracle of Creation motivates faith and worship of God.

Significantly, the only biblical definition of faith appears in a context of Creation: "Now faith is being sure of what we hope for and certain of what we do not see. . . . By faith we understand that the universe was formed at God's command, so that what is seen was not made out of what was visible" (Heb. 11:1-3).

To believe that God was and is capable of creating from nothing is to base one's faith and one's existence on the invisible. It is to take a risk. Creation is the miracle that necessitates the greatest faith. The evolutionist does not have the audacity to envision such a possibility and prefers to have life originate "naturally" from within preexisting matter. As such, it constitutes the antithesis of faith and Creation.

Not only do the saints obey the commandments of a God they do not see, but they believe in a Creator God, one who remains forever external to them. The saints express their faith in the existence of the true God who exists outside of themselves—the God who judges and creates. Such a message strikes a dissonant chord in a civilization searching for its inner gods. Never have spiritualist and pantheist theories been so popular. The ancient beliefs, reminiscent of paganism—such as reincarnation, the spirituality of nature, and even the immortality of the soul—find great favor today. The influence of the Orient, through the New Age movement, is becoming ever more prominent.

Indeed, the immortality of the soul has been long instilled in the Judeo-Christian psyche. This belief, according to which a spark of life remains after death, exemplifies our civilization's denial of the transcendent—of an external God. But faith in Creation rejects belief in the immortality of the soul. According to the Bible, God created humanity from dust, and it remains totally dependent on the breath of its Creator (Gen. 2:7). God clearly stated our mortality: "You will surely die" (Gen. 2:17). Because we are created beings, we are not immortal by nature. Faith in Creation makes faith in resurrection possible.

In contrast to those who love Babel and anguish at the thought of death, the Apocalypse portrays the disciples of the Lamb as "blessed" (Rev. 14:13). For them, there is life beyond death: "Their deeds will follow them" (verse 13). The Jews of the time used the word for "deeds" (in Greek *erga*) in the context of the final judgment.[7] It is the equivalent of the Hebrew *mitswot* of Jewish life and the technical term for the good deeds of the Christian life (Rev. 2:2, 19). In the letters of the apostle Paul such "deeds" survive trial by fire: "His work will be shown for what it is, because the Day will bring it to light. It will be revealed by fire, and the fire will test the quality of each man's work" (1 Cor. 3:13). Likewise, the ancient rabbis stated: "All the *mitswot,* which the Children of Israel perform in this world, come and testify in their favor in the World-to-come."[8] In the Epistle to the Hebrews, the "work" of the faithful remains in the memory of God in view of "what has been promised" (Heb. 6:10-12).

The reference to "deeds" is not a legalistic one. Significantly, God's people do not perform such deeds as a means to salvation. On the contrary, the deeds "follow." We discover them only when the saint is not around anymore to exhibit them and promote himself or herself as a saint. The true "deed," the true *mitswah,* remains even after the believer's death. It survives beyond the boasts and the politics. The "deed" is what remains in God's memory, not in humanity's.

The proclamation of judgment and Creation by the three angels is thus more than the objective reference to the two framing events of human history—its beginning and its end. The angels are also calling for a change in perspective, a transformation in life.

The pairing of judgment and Creation forms a tension that is rich in meaning. On the one hand, the reference to Creation is the celebration of life that says yes to God, to nature, to joy, to love, and to life. On the other hand, pleasure is measured with law, discipline, and judgment. The Bible introduced this tension in the very first commandment: "And the Lord God commanded the man, 'You are free to eat from any tree in the garden; but you must not eat from the tree of the knowledge of good and evil, for when you eat of it you will surely die'" (Gen. 2:16, 17).

This same tension appears in the book of Ecclesiastes: "Be happy, young man, while you are young, and let your heart give you joy in the days of your youth. Follow the ways of your heart and whatever your eyes see, but know that for all these things God will bring you to judgment" (Eccl. 11:9).

We have not yet understood the importance and the necessity of such a tension. Religious communities too often divide between the two poles. On the one hand, we have the holy and the firm, who threaten others with the judgment and the law of God. They promote as virtues rigor and perfection, proclaiming there can be no salvation without them. On the other, we have the generous liberals who smile and point to the grace of God, to the love of the human God of the cross. Often they reduce religion to good feelings and make salvation something easily and cheaply acquired.

The dual proclamation of judgment and Creation maintains the tension between the two. The Jewish philosopher Abraham Heschel found the ideal to reside in being both "holy and human."[9] He based his understanding on the Bible that portrays an Israel who wrestles both with God and with humanity. Christians add to this a Yeshua who resides, eats, laughs, and sings with men and women. We see it embodied in the prayer: "My prayer is not that you take them out of the world but that you protect them from the evil one" (John 17:15); and in the image of salt that must keep its flavor while mingling with the food (Matt. 5:13).

But beyond this lesson and this ideal, the proclamation of judgment and Creation points to a cosmic and historical reality.

The association of judgment and creation constitutes the essence of the Day of Atonement. Both the rituals of Kippur, as prescribed by Leviticus 16, and the traditional Jewish prayers testify to this dual concern with judgment and Creation. The biblical symbolism of the ritual of Kippur has implications that extend beyond individual destiny. Not only are the people of Israel forgiven of "all their sins" (Lev. 16:21, 22), but the sanctuary itself is purged of all the sins and declared atoned (verses 16, 33). For the ancient Israelites, this "atonement" of the sanctuary was more than a spring cleaning. Rather it symbolized, in biblical thought, the atonement of the whole earth, because the ancient Israelites understood the Temple and the tabernacle as the "microcosm" of Creation.[10]

The explicit link between Creation and the sanctuary appears in the psalms: "He built his sanctuary like the heights, like the earth that he established forever" (Ps. 78:69).[11] It is also developed in the account of the construction of the sanctuary, told in a way that mirrors the Creation story. Like the Creation account (Gen. 1:1–2:4), the passage about the sanctuary follows the same seven-step progression and concludes the seventh step with the same Hebrew expression: "finished the work" (Ex. 40:33; cf. Gen. 2:2).[12] Significantly, the account of the construction of Solomon's Temple also has the same seven-step progression, employs a period of seven years, and concludes with the same language: "finished . . . the work" (1 Kings 7:40). It is highly significant that, in the whole Bible, this expression occurs only in these three passages, thereby linking the sanctuary to Creation.

Reversely, Scripture also describes Creation itself in terms evocative of the Israelite sanctuary: "He stretches out the heavens like a canopy, and spreads them out like a tent to live in" (Isa. 40:22).[13] The gospel of Matthew identifies the destruction of the Temple of Jerusalem with the destruction of the cosmos (Matt. 24:1-39), and the tear in the veil of the Temple corresponds to the ripping open of the earth (Matt. 27:51).

The ritual of Kippur, by symbolizing the purification of the whole earth, points to the re-creation of the world. That is why Scripture ties the creation to come of "new heavens and a new earth" with the creation of the "new Jerusalem" (Rev. 21:2; cf. Isa. 65:17, 18). The prophet Daniel also describes the cosmic Kippur in Daniel 8 in terms reminiscent of the Creation account: "evenings and mornings" (Dan. 8:14), an expression found elsewhere only in the context of the Creation account (Gen. 1:5, 8, 13, 19, 23, 31).

Jewish tradition also assimilates the judgment of Kippur to Creation. In one of the most ancient Jewish commentaries on Genesis, the birth of Kippur coincides with that of the universe: "There was an evening, there was a morning, one day, this means that the Holy One, Blessed be He, gave them (Israel) one day, which is none other than the day of *Kippur*."[14]

The prayers spoken on this day and the theological reflections that inspired them, all point to the same association of judgment and Creation. "Blessed art Thou, O Lord our God, King of the Universe, who opens the doors of Your grace and opens the eyes of those who wait for the forgiveness of Him who has created light and darkness, and all things." [15]

"How is the human to be just before his Creator, when he stands naked before Him?" [16]

"We must give all holiness to this day, for it is a day of fear and trembling. On this day, Your reign shall be established, and Your throne affirmed. . . . For You are the *judge,* the prosecutor, and the witness, He who writes and seals. And You will remember the things long-forgotten and open the book of memory. . . . Then shall sound the great shofar, and the voice of silence shall be heard, the angels shall be gripped by fear and trembling and shall say: 'Behold, the day of Judgment!' " [17]

"Spread the fear of Your name, O Lord our God, on all Your creatures so that all humans may *fear* You and bow down before all whom You have *created.* . . . For we are aware, O Lord our God, that sovereignty and power are in Your hands. May Your fearsome name be proclaimed to all Your creatures." [18]

This concept, as seen both from the Bible and Jewish liturgy, constitutes the background of the words of the first angel in Revelation 14.

This prophecy applies historically to a great movement that from the nineteenth century onward defined itself precisely in terms of judgment and Creation. The religious movement not only testifies to the heavenly Kippur; it also warns the inhabitants of the earth of the soon return of the Son of man and prepares them for a new world.

The Son of Man

The prophet had started his series of seven signs with a vision of a woman draped in the sun and the moon and crowned with stars. Now Yohanan closes it with a vision of the Son of man adorned with the clouds and crowned with a golden crown. The vision of the Son answers that of the woman.

The coming of the Messiah responds to the sigh of the woman exiled in the desert, who lives by and for this event. It is the culmination of biblical hope, a hope that even came to inspire the traditional greeting of the early Christians: *Marana tha,* "Come, O Lord"

135

(cf. 1 Cor. 16:22). The Aramaic word *tha* is the same verb that in Daniel 7 describes the coming of the Son of man (Dan. 7:13).

The end has arrived. To understand his message of the "end," the prophet Amos received a vision featuring a basket full of ripe fruit (Amos 8:2). It compares the end to ripe fruit, the culmination of the process of growth. The words of the vision themselves hint at the correlation between the end and the fruit. In Hebrew, the word "end" *(qets)* echoes the word "ripe fruit" *(qayits)*.[19]

For the ancient prophets of Israel the end was not a return to nothingness but a new beginning, a new hope. To render the dual character of the end, the prophets used the metaphor of the harvest (Joel 3:13). The harvest implies both the violence of the reaper who slashes through the stalks as well as the gathering of the sheaves themselves. It suggests both death and life.

The prophet of the Apocalypse brings up the same image of the harvest to portray the end (Rev. 14:14-19). But to better render the ambivalent character of that end, the prophet describes it in terms of the two principal harvests of Palestine: the harvest of grain at spring-time and the grapes in the autumn.

The harvest of the grain represents the gathering together of the faithful (verses 14-16). The image has sacrificial overtones—they are the "firstfruits" of God (verse 4). Yohanan directly relates the harvest to the coming of the Son of man.

The vision of the Apocalypse coincides here with that of the prophet Daniel. He too announced the judgment as the last event of human history in the perspective of the coming of the Son of man. Daniel 7 directly involves the Son of man in the event of the judgment. He approached the "Ancient of Days" and was led into His presence before receiving the throne (Dan. 7:13, 14; cf. 7:26, 27).

Our passage follows the same development. The Son of man comes first as a reaper, who separates and gathers His people to Himself. It is a positive judgment, one in favor of the accused (Dan. 7:22).[20] The harvest brings a message of life. Scripture's word choice here is particularly significant. The Greek words used by our passage for a "harvest" *(therismos)* and for "reaping" *(therizo)* specifically allude to the gathering of the sheaves and not to their cutting. The sheaves are laden with grain. The image evokes the idea of storage, hence of security. The harvester has safely collected the grain to its final destination.

On the other hand, the gathering of the grapes represents the punishment of the wicked. This time the vision associates the reaper with fire (Rev. 14:18), which, as in Daniel 7, is the instrument of negative judgment (Dan. 7:11). Moreover, we see the angel who executes the judgment emerging from the altar of the martyrs (Rev. 6:9; cf. 8:3-5). This judgment constitutes an act of avenging justice—a manifestation of God's wrath. The pressed grapes drip like blood.[21] Indeed, the prophet sees blood flowing out of the winepress (Rev. 14:20). The imagery then develops into that of a battlefield with horses plunged up to their bridles in a sea of blood.

The geographical dimensions hint at the scope of the massacre— 1,600 stadia, roughly 200 miles. The number is of course symbolic and plays on the number 4 (4 x 4 x 100), suggesting geographic universality, "the whole earth."[22] The divine punishment reaches cosmic proportions. Moreover, this number is squared (4 x 4), just as with the 144,000 (12 x 12), alluding to a certain correspondence between the two entities symbolized by the numbers: the earthly camp (number 4) versus the camp of the covenant with God (number 12 = 4 x 3).

The harvest takes place "outside the city" (verse 20). The language is again symbolic and alludes to the traditional location of the judgment of the nations, the *goyim*,[23] those who belong to the camp of the enemy.

This is the most shocking passage of the Apocalypse. Many Christians have looked away in disgust. The great Reformer Martin Luther decanonized the Apocalypse for this reason. To him a God of wrath, a God of justice, who turns wine into blood, has nothing to do with the God of love who saves.

Such hyperbolic language is a natural feature of ancient Near Eastern expression—a way to render the intensity of emotion at the event's extraordinary nature. But beyond this cultural observation the fantastic vision conveys an important lesson that Martin Luther failed to understand—namely that love cannot operate without justice. The sentimental theorists of love who ignore the rigor and the requirements of justice are for the most part well-to-do altruists who have never tasted the humiliation of oppression or the bitterness of injustice. Love without justice is not true love. This is why the Bible associates justice *(tsedek)* with grace *(hesed).*[24]

God's love is more than good feelings, soft-spoken words, and tender smiles that glide over the wretchedness of reality. The love of God is also action that saves His people from such a condition. It accepts no compromise with the enemy. There can be no salvation from death and suffering without the total destruction of evil. Such is the message behind the horrifying scene depicted by our passage. The judgment is therefore thorough and comprehensive and, like a sea of blood, covers the whole earth.

Paradoxically, the image seeks not to cause fear, but to reassure. It proclaims the good news of the final and total victory and gives a war cry of hope.

To save His people, God will face the enemy. He will fight and grasp for the sheep caught in the clutches of the raging lion, and will at last shake and orient history in the right direction—that of life and of justice.

---

[1] Kittel, ed., *Theological Dictionary of the New Testament,* vol. 2, p. 722.

[2] Josephus *Antiquities* 18. 228, 229.

[3] Cf. Joel 3:18; Zech. 13:1; Ps. 46:4; Rev. 22:1, 2.

[4] Doukhan, *Secrets of Daniel,* p. 90.

[5] Ps. 106:38; Jer. 7:31; Isa. 30:33; 2 Chron. 28:3.

[6] Deut. 1:17; Mal. 2:17; Ps. 1:5, etc.

[7] 2 Baruch 14:12; 24:1; 4 Ezra (2 Esdras) 7:77; Psalms of Solomon 9:9, etc.

[8] Babylonian Talmud, *Avodah Zarah* 2a-b.

[9] Abraham J. Heschel, *God in Search of Man* (New York: 1955), p. 238.

[10] This association between the Temple of Jerusalem and the "heavens and the earth" has other parallels in the Middle East. Ancient Sumeria called the temple *Duranki,* "place of the heaven and of the earth," and in Babylon we find evidence of an altar named *Etenanki,* "house of the foundation of the heaven and of the earth" (see J. Levenson, *Creation and the Persistence of Evil* [New York: 1988], pp. 78-99; cf. G. W. Ahlstrom, "Heaven of Earth—at Hazor and Arad," in *Religious Syncretism in Antiquity,* ed. B.A. Pearson [Missoula, Mont.: 1975], p. 68).

[11] Cf. Ps. 134:3; 150:1, 6.

[12] See P. J. Kearney, "Creation and Liturgy: The P Redaction of Ex 25-30," *Zeitschrift für altestamentliche Wissenschaft* 89 (1977): 375; cf. J. Blenkinsopp, "The Structure of P," *Catholic Biblical Quarterly* 38 (1976): 276-278.

[13] Cf. Isa. 44:24; Job 9:8; Ps. 104:2; Jer. 10:12.

[14] Midrash Rabbah, *Genesis* 4. 10.

[15] *Yotser leyom Kippur.*

[16] *Mosaf leyom Kippur.*

[17] Author's translation from the prayer book, *Mahzor min rosh hashana weyom hakippurim,* first part, p. 31.

[18] *Shulkhan Arukh,* p. 514.

[19] The NIV has "the time is ripe" for the clause "the end has come."

[20] Doukhan, *Secrets of Daniel,* pp. 112, 113.

[21] See Isa. 63:1-6; Lam. 1:15.

[22] See Doukhan, *Secrets of Daniel,* pp. 84, 85.

[23] See Joel 4:2, 12; Zech. 14:2-12.

[24] See, for example, Ps. 36:11; 103:17; and on the relationship between love and justice, see particularly H. Baruk, *Tsedek, droit hébraïque et science de la paix* (Paris: 1970), pp. 15, 23ff.

PART THREE

NEWS FROM THE EAST

Beginning with chapter 15, the Apocalypse takes on a new tone. In the first part (Rev. 1-11) the prophecy covered historical events (from the time of Yeshua the Messiah to that of the judgment). Then in the second part (Revelation 12-14) the vision focused on the time of the end (the time of the judgment), the last days of history preceding God's return.

Now in this third part (Rev. 15-22) the prophetic vision sees beyond the end of fallen earthly time (from the judgment to the new Jerusalem). For the first time God will directly and uniquely propel history. The experience is absolutely new for Babylon as well as for Jerusalem.

The wrath of God reaches unimaginable proportions. Destruction has never been so complete and drastic. The Apocalypse speaks of an earthquake such as has never "occurred since man has been on earth" (Rev. 16:18). Nor has God's creative power ever been so intense, or the transformation so deep. "I am making everything new," the God of the Apocalypse promises (Rev. 21:5).

This divine breakthrough into human history will erupt from the East (Rev. 16:12), in many ways like the harmful Middle East wind, the *khamsin,* that devours everything (Eze. 17:10), or the sunrise that illuminates the new day.

CHAPTER 7

THE WORLD CUPS

(Revelation 15–18)

End Kippur

But before any of this occurs, the author brings us back to the liturgical context of the heavenly temple. The prophetic vision extends beyond the seven cups to God's final victory. He first sees a sea smooth as glass (Rev. 15:2), an image already encountered in the context of the temple (Rev. 4:6) and representing the primal waters defeated in the process of creation.[1]

The next scene takes us to the immense crowd of the redeemed (Rev. 15:2-4). The prophet sees them, like the ancient Israelites of the Exodus, standing near the waters, singing the song of Moses (Ex. 15) and celebrating God's victory over Israel's enemies.

After this vision of victory, the prophet looks back to the seven angels before they start their task of devastation. The prophet sees them emerging from the temple clad in the priestly garb traditionally worn during the Day of Atonement: the robe of fine linen (Rev. 15:6; cf. Lev. 16:4). The scene reminds us of the ritual marking the end of the ceremony of Kippur: "No one is to be in the Tent of Meeting from the time Aaron goes in to make atonement in the Most Holy Place until he comes out, having made atonement for himself, his household and the whole community of Israel" (Lev. 16:17).

And indeed, the temple is "filled with smoke from the glory of God" (Rev. 15:8). No one may penetrate its realm as the service of atonement is completed. The same phenomenon occurred when the building of the tabernacle had finished in Exodus. The cloud of God's presence filled the sanctuary, and no one could enter it (Ex. 40:35). This passage in Exodus echoes the language of the Creation account. The same expression, "finished the work," that concluded the Creation account (Gen. 2:2) appears in Exodus 40:33.

The end of the construction of the sanctuary parallels the end of the world's creation. God honors both moments with His presence. The apocalyptic event points then to the finishing of God's work of Creation, another way of suggesting the conclusion of the cleansing process that characterizes Kippur. In fact, we have come to the end of judgment. The sentence is sealed, a truth retained in the liturgy of Kippur. The closing prayer of Kippur recited at sunset, the *ne'ilah* (which means "closing") the Talmud of Jerusalem associates with the closing of the heavenly temple. In Jewish tradition, since Kippur is the fulfillment of a 10-day probationary period, it is during the *ne'ilah* that "our conceptions, our destinies, and our judgments are sealed."[2] Interestingly, the word *hotmenu* (seal us), taken from the *ne'ilah,* later developed into the traditional Kippur greeting, *hatimah tovah,* "May you be well sealed!"

The Apocalypse also alludes to this tradition of the moment when the destiny of each person is sealed. God cannot forgive anymore. Even the intervention of the Messiah and the evocation of His sacrifice is of no more use.

For many Christians, the notion of a God of love has been diluted to a form of sentimentalism that has lost touch with historical reality. But, as pointed out before, because salvation is real, because it is an event, it finds itself limited in what it can do. Were it otherwise, biblical hope would be no more than a meaningless idea or an emotion. But God's refusal to intervene after a certain point indicates the reality of His existence and action in history. All historical events are finite and limited by time and circumstance.

We can also explain on a human level God's refusal to intervene after a certain point. The pattern of our actions and thoughts eventually cement our destiny. The seal from above is but the recognition that there is no turning back. By consistently sinning, we reach a point of no return at which repentance is no longer possible. We can no longer change who we are. The process will reach its ultimate fulfillment at the time of the end, when everyone will determine their fate by the deliberate repetition of their own choices.

This same principle appears later in the Apocalypse in proverbial form: "Let him who does wrong continue to do wrong; let him who is vile continue to be vile; let him who does right continue to do right; and let him who is holy continue to be holy" (Rev. 22:11). Some of the approaching seven plagues conclude with the prophet's desolate observation: "But they refused to repent and glorify him" (Rev. 16:9; cf. verses 11, 21).

Any fear or any speculation on our part about the time of this sealing is out of place. We are not yet there. And the very fact that we may worry about it shows that we still have time to repent. The day when there will no longer be any hope will be the day when we will choose not to hope anymore.

The Apocalypse has just portrayed God's wrath as the great winepress that pulverizes grapes to blood. Our passage now fulfills the vision. The wine of God's wrath now pours from the great winepress into the cups of the world. The language is again symbolic. The image of the cup derives from the Hebrew Scriptures. Joseph used a cup to predict the future (Gen. 44:5). Jeremiah saw in the cup the future destiny of the nations: "This is what the Lord, the God of Israel, said to me: 'Take from my hand this cup filled with the wine of my wrath and make all the nations to whom I send you drink it. When they drink it, they will stagger and go mad because of the sword I will send among them'" (Jer. 25:15, 16).[3]

Another clue for when the sealing time has come is God's manifestation of His wrath—He pours the seven cups of wrath onto the earth. The closing of the temple coincides with the devastations of the cups (Rev. 15:8). The wrath of God, already anticipated by the sixth seal and the seventh shofar (Rev. 6:12; 11:15), was announced by the third angel: "If anyone worships the beast and his image and receives his mark on the forehead or on the hand, he, too, will drink of the wine of God's fury, which has been poured full strength into the cup of his wrath" (Rev. 14:9, 10).

The seven cups of wrath thus follow the proclamation of the

three angels and begin to be poured at the time when the beast is fully established. With the first cup, the prophet informs us that the judgment concerns those who "had the mark of the beast and worshiped his image" (Rev. 16:2).

The seven cups are in fact but a rerun of the judgment of the seven shofars:

First Shofar Earth	**First Cup** Earth
Second Shofar Bloody sea	**Second Cup** Bloody sea
Third Shofar Rivers and springs of water	**Third Cup** Rivers and springs of water
Fourth Shofar Sun	**Fourth Cup** Sun
Fifth Shofar Darkness	**Fifth Cup** Darkness
Sixth Shofar The Euphrates	**Sixth Cup** The Euphrates
Seventh Shofar Divine wrath: hail Repossession of the kingdom	**Seventh Cup** Divine wrath: hail Repossession of the kingdom

Like the shofars, the seven cups follow a sequence that recalls that of the Creation story in Genesis 1 (earth, sea, rivers, sun). The judgment is here also cosmic.

But whereas the shofars devastated only the third part of anything, the cups now destroy everything—"the earth," the "sea," and the "sun." The judgment of the cups completes that of the shofars. It is God's last judgment. Whereas the seven shofars dealt with the church's

146

iniquities, the seven cups focus now on the last days of history.

Divine judgment takes place in two phases:

The first five cups comprise the first phase (Rev. 16:1-11). It must be an extremely brief one since we find the victims of the fifth cup still recovering from the ulcers of the first. Characterized by a judgment inherent to the sinful condition, it operates according to the "law of reciprocity."[4] The sixth and seventh cups cover the second phase (Rev. 16:12-21). The period of Armageddon, it involves a judgment that necessitates a divine intervention to counter the gathering of the nations.

The Phase of the Ulcer

The first cup identifies those who have been marked by the foreign god (Rev. 16:2). The ulcer emerges from the iniquity that produced it. Thus the mark of the beast becomes an ulcer recalling the leprosy curse of the Old Testament (see Deut. 28:27; cf. Lev. 13) and acts as the external sign of inner corruption.

The lesson behind this symbolic language is that punishment is implied in the very sin that caused it. The worship of the beast and the resulting subjugation and the alienation of its worshipers carries in itself the seeds of death.

The irony of this first plague is that it recalls that of the sixth Egyptian plague, which afflicted both the Egyptian people and their priests (Ex. 9:11). The ulcers break out on the worshipers of the beast as well as on the beast itself. It unmasks the god of Babel just as its ancient counterpart revealed the gods of Egypt as frauds. The ulcers spare no one—they all itch. The god of the beast simply does not exist. Even the priests are victimized by their own religion.

This first cup, like the first shofar, concerns the earth. But this time the plague strikes the human population. That which had hereto devastated only the earth now burns deep into people's bodies. The destruction of the first shofar now reaches its fullness in the first cup.

The ulcer announced by the first shofar represented the state of desolation in the aftermath of the wars between the church and the barbarians, when the church fought for supremacy. The prophet of

147

the Apocalypse portrays the last moments of human history as a power struggle similar to that of the early church's. But what remained on a local level in the history of Christianity will take on global proportions at the time of the first cup. Evil has now reached alarming proportions and has spread to the totality of the earth. Since the ulcer is still mentioned by the fifth cup, we assume it will last until then.

During the first phase of the cups the church oppresses the whole earth. The prophet Daniel had already foreseen this. At the end of chapter 11 of his book (Dan. 11:42, 43) he predicted that during the end-time the religious power represented by Babylon would rule the planet.[5]

The church has not lost its ambition, as we see in both religious and secular contexts.[6] In the light of such events, the prophecies of Daniel and of the Apocalypse begin to make even more sense.

The next two cups the angel pours on the waters of the earth. The second cup drenches the sea, while the third touches the rivers and springs. The ensuing plague is similar to the first plague of Egypt. Water turns to blood (Ex. 7:17-21). In the context of ancient Egypt, the plague had great meaning. Pharaoh, whom the Egyptians considered as a god on earth, was responsible for making sure that the Nile watered the land and that Egypt remained fertile. Egypt was almost completely desert, and life existed only because of the water of the Nile. To attack the river was to challenge his divinity and the whole Egyptian order of creation.

The experience of the last enemies of God resembles that of the Egyptians at the dawn of the Exodus. They realize then that the god they had worshiped and trusted, whom they thought had given them life, was in fact a god of death. Here again, the apocalyptic plague follows the law of reciprocity. "They have shed the blood"; therefore, they are now "given . . . blood to drink" (Rev. 16:6). The punishment is again inherent in the sin. The very death they had previously caused now in turn poisons them.

Their punishment is proportionate to their crime: "as they deserve" (verse 6). The angel of the altar, associated with the victims crying out for justice, echoes the angel of the waters: "Yes, Lord

God Almighty, true and just are your judgments" (verse 7).

The second and third shofars also announced plagues that would befall the waters (Rev. 8:8-11). At the time, the curse was a spiritual one. The church had become too preoccupied with material success to care for the essential needs of its believers. The spiritual life, symbolized by the waters,[7] had dried up.

Whereas the shofars cursed only a third of the waters, the cup of wrath mixes with all the waters of the earth. And this time the transformation to blood is not limited to the sea (Rev. 16:3) as had been the case with the shofars (Rev. 8:8), but the springs and the rivers within the land also turn to blood (Rev. 16:4).

The spiritual condition of the citizens of Babel is tragic. For the exiled prophet of Patmos, the bloodied waters are particularly suggestive. From the shores of his island surrounded by the sea, the prophet sees the horizon smeared with future death. The people of Babel have no reason to hope anymore—they no longer even know the taste of water.

The fourth cup only worsens the curse of the third. Scorching heat now accompanies the lack of water. The skies are empty of rain or even clouds. The spiritual drought becomes almost unbearable.

Again the punishment derives from the crime. The fourth shofar had predicted an eclipse of the sun. Now the sun has become a deadly blaze. The people suffer as victims of the very god they had worshiped as the source of life.

The fifth cup hits at the heart of the problem as it strikes the throne of the beast (Rev. 16:10). The resulting plague reminds us of the fifth shofar. Darkness covers the scene. In the fifth shofar the darkness came from the abyss—the *tehom*, symbol of the rejection of God that accompanied the secular humanism of the French Revolution (Rev. 9:1, 2). Back then the darkness covered but one third of the territory (Rev. 8:12). Now darkness shrouds the entire kingdom (Rev. 16:10). Then an antireligious power had usurped God. Now the negation of God lies at the very heart of religion. To quote the prophet Daniel, the north has now overtaken the south (Dan. 11:43).[8] Babel establishes its sovereignty on the negation, the rejecting, of God that had characterized its opponent, Egypt.

Again the judgment is proportional to the sin. Because the people worshiped the beast and its throne of darkness, they now find themselves invaded by that same darkness. They are once more victims of their own religion of death.

The plague is similar to the ninth plague of Egypt, the one preceding God's deadly intervention against Egypt's firstborn. The so-called Wisdom of Solomon, an apocryphal work of the first century B.C.E., gave the plague of darkness a cosmic dimension. The darkness rising from the abode of the dead represents the ultimate punishment, which contains and concludes all others.[9]

Likewise, the fifth cup contains all the curses that preceded it. The ulcers are still open, the sea is as blood, and the people continue to grope in darkness. The hatred of God has grown with the pain. Idolatry (Rev. 16:2) led the people to curse the "name of God, who had control over these plagues" (verse 9) and finally to blaspheme against the "God of heaven" (verse 11).

Moreover, the people realize that their spiritual leaders have lied to them. But instead of changing their ways, they rush even deeper into error and turn brutally against the One they should have recognized. What was once religious confusion becomes conscious and deliberate hatred of God. Their behavior is similar to that of the Egyptian pharaoh. Faced with overwhelming evidence of the Lord's existence, he was too proud to admit defeat but continued blindly to deny Him. From then on, conflict was unavoidable.

The Phase of Armageddon

The sixth cup, as with that of the sixth shofar, affects the Euphrates (verse 12; cf. Rev. 9:14). The waters of the river dry up "to prepare the way for the kings from the East" (Rev. 16:12). Biblical tradition associates the drying up of the Euphrates with the conquest of Babylon by Cyrus in 539 B.C.E.: "[I am the Lord,] who says to the watery deep, 'Be dry, and I will dry up your streams,' who says of Cyrus, 'He is my shepherd and will accomplish all that I please'" (Isa. 44:27, 28; cf. Jer. 50:38).

The historian Herodotus (484-425 B.C.E.) recounted the Persian king's strategy. "[Cyrus] posted his army at the place where the river goes into the city, and another part of it behind the city, where the river comes out of the city, and told his men to enter the city by the channel of the Euphrates when they saw it to be fordable. Having disposed them and given this command, he himself marched away with those of his army who could not fight; and when he came to the lake, Cyrus dealt with it and with the river just as had the Babylonian queen: drawing off the river by a canal into the lake, which was a marsh, he made the stream sink until its former channel could be forded. When this happened, the Persians who were posted with this objective made their way into Babylon by the channel of the Euphrates, which had now sunk to a depth of about the middle of a man's thigh." [10]

This reference to "the kings from the East" (Rev. 16:12) alludes to Cyrus, whose prophesied coming Israel had preserved in its memory as a channel of approaching salvation. "I will raise up Cyrus in my righteousness: I will make all his ways straight. He will rebuild my city and set my exiles free" (Isa. 45:13); "Who has stirred up one from the east, calling him in righteousness to his service? He hands the nations over to him and subdues kings before him" (Isa. 41:2; cf. verse 25).

The fall of Babylon is an event of supreme importance in Israel's history. The book of Daniel molds its entire structure around it (Dan. 1:21; 6:28; 10:1).[11] Significantly, the canon of the Hebrew Bible ends with a reference to Cyrus (2 Chron. 36:22, 23). His conquest of Babylon liberated the Hebrew exiles. It is his decree that allows them to rebuild Jerusalem. Scripture sees their return from the exile as a new creation. Just before he mentions Cyrus, Isaiah evokes the act of Creation: "This is what the Lord says—your Redeemer, who formed you in the womb: I am the Lord, who has made all things, who alone stretched out the heavens, who spread out the earth by myself, . . . who says of Cyrus, 'He is my shepherd and will accomplish all that I please; he will say of Jerusalem, "Let it be rebuilt," and of the temple, "Let its foundations be laid"'" (Isa. 44:24-28; cf. 45:18; 43:15).

Basing it on the memory of Cyrus and the return from the Babylonian exile, with the prospect of a rebuilt or new Jerusalem, the prophet Yohanan sets up his vision of the sixth cup. Here, also, the fall of the mythical Babylon and the battle that ensues pave the way for final deliverance and the creation of a new Jerusalem.

Two opposing camps form. On the one hand, the "kings from the East" (Rev. 16:12) represent the forces of the saving God, the God of Jerusalem. On the other hand, the "kings of the whole world" (verse 14) stand for the forces of evil—for Babylon. All God's enemies assemble in the latter camp, particularly the demonic powers symbolized by the frogs.

The sixth cup evokes the second plague of Egypt (Ex. 8). The frog was the Egyptian deity of fertility *(Hiqit)*. During the plague, they invaded the most intimate places—the bedroom and the bed (verse 3). Again, the judgment of God had an ironic twist. The goddess of fertility and childbirth became an obstacle to fertility. The magicians, eager to demonstrate their powers, only added to the problem when they produced more frogs (verse 7).

The Jews of the first century C.E. came to associate frogs with charlatans and demonic water spirits.[12] The Apocalypse identifies them as the "spirits of demons" (Rev. 16:14) who emerge from the mouth of the three enemy beasts of God: (1) the dragon who represents the devil (Rev. 12); (2) the sea beast who symbolized the institution of Babel (Rev. 13:1-10); and (3) the land beast called by our passage the "false prophet." Of the three, the last beast is the only one to receive a new name, one charged with a religious connotation. Once a political power, this beast now assumes the role of a false prophet. The prophet Jeremiah more than any other biblical prophet earned the reputation as an opponent of false prophecy. Significantly, he repeatedly uses the key word *sheqer* (false) to characterize false prophecy (Jer. 28:15; 29:31; 37:19; 40:16; Lam. 2:14). He depicts the false prophet as the kind that works for earthly institutions and powers (Jer. 5:30, 31; 23:14), deceiving people, and pretending to be inspired by the spirit but who does not in fact speak the word of God (Jer. 5:13; 23:16).

The false prophet thus represents the United States in its religious campaign to support the power of Babel. Such efforts, be they political, economic, or religious, all lead to the same goal: the worship of the first beast (Rev. 13:12). Interestingly, the methods used

all derive from the realm of the paranormal. It calls upon the supernatural, the "spirits of demons," who perform miraculous signs
(Rev. 16:14; cf. 13:14).

Current events increasingly support the prophecy, with access to
the supernatural today only a phone call away. The miracles once reserved to an obscure religious fringe the main church now increasingly exploits and promotes. Apparitions of the virgin Mary and of
other dead relatives are but the warning signs. Such events seem to
defy reason, yet they make the headlines of even respected publica-
tions. The biblical prediction of the Apocalypse seems more and
more plausible.

Whether the frogs represent paranormal power or political
rhetorical tricks as suggested by their origin (they come out of the
mouths of the three beasts), their objective is still clear-cut: to seduce
and assemble "the kings of the whole world" (Rev. 16:14) to fight
against the God who comes.

This is nothing new. Already in the days of ancient Babel the
people had proclaimed: "Come, let us build ourselves a city, with a
tower that reaches to the heavens, so that we may make a name for
ourselves and not be scattered over the face of the whole earth" (Gen.
11:4). Since then this same ambition has obsessed Babel's disciples—
to unite and to take over the divine prerogative of world dominion;
to reach heaven and the "door of God" (Babel). For the first time,
however, since ancient Babel, the preoccupation is worldwide. "The
whole world" now participates in the project of divine usurpation.

The book of Daniel also predicted such a gathering. The last
conflict, according to the Old Testament prophet, would be fought
between the united camps of the north and south, and the "beautiful holy mountain" (Dan. 11:45), the mountain of Zion, the heavenly Jerusalem.[13] And also "reports from the east" will bring an end
to the conflict (verse 44).

This shall be the last world war, one not fought among humanity, but between it and God. This last conflict shall unite the human
race in a cosmic struggle against the holy mountain of God.

The Apocalypse gives the Hebrew name of "Armageddon" to
this last battle (Rev. 16:16). "Armageddon" means "the mountain of

Megiddon." The parallels between the prophetic war in Daniel and that of the Apocalypse suggests a connection between this mountain of Megiddon and what Daniel calls the "beautiful holy mountain" (Dan. 11:45).

The only passage in the Bible combining the three motifs (mountain, Megiddo, and Jerusalem) appears in the book of Zechariah. It is also the only passage employing the word "Megiddo" in this particular form (ending in "on"): "On that day the weeping in Jerusalem will be great, like the weeping of Hadad Rimmon in the plain of Megiddo(n)" (Zech. 12:11; in the NIV, "Megiddo").[14]

The passage uses "Megiddon" instead of "Megiddo" for two reasons.[15]

1. The first reason is poetic—to rhyme "Megiddon" with "Hadad Rimmon," a common procedure in biblical names.[16]

2. The second reason is rhetorical—a desire to use the more ancient form of "Megiddon" instead of the more recent version, "Megiddo," in order to allude to a past history.[17]

The prophet of the Apocalypse associates the fate of the holy mountain (har) with that of the valley of Megiddon, producing thereby the composite *Har Megiddon,* mountain of Megiddon. The expression *Har Megiddon* is in the qualitative genitive form, a function similar to our qualitative adjective. Thus, for example, literal Hebrew renders the expression "holy mountain" as "mountain of holiness" (Dan. 11:45); likewise, Hebrew expresses the concept "just balances" (KJV) by "balance of justice" (Lev. 19:36), etc.

Moreover, the Apocalyptic expression *Armageddon* alludes to the passage in Zechariah in a game of assonances (paronomasia), a frequent form of association in the Bible:[18]

Har	*Megiddon*
*Ha*dad Rimmon	*Megiddon*

The expression "mountain of Megiddon" (Armageddon) already alludes to the battlefield. It is a "mountain," and therefore it cannot apply to the valley of Jezreel and its battles, such as that of Barak against Sisera (Judges 5:19) or of Jehu against Ahaziah (2 Kings 9:27). Nor can it intend Mount Carmel, or by extension to the conflict between Elijah and the prophets of Baal (1 Kings 18:20-40); Mount Carmel is more than eight miles away from Megiddo.

The prophet speaks of a "mountain" of Megiddo (Armageddon) while thinking specifically of Jerusalem. The location of the battle is not the valley of Jezreel, but, as predicted by the prophet Daniel, the "beautiful holy mountain" (Dan. 11:45). The kings of the earth—the assembled powers—have no other objective but the control of Jerusalem.

We are not dealing here with the Jerusalem of the present state of Israel. As we read the Apocalypse we must understand "Jerusalem" in a symbolic sense. The book of Daniel often identifies the beautiful holy mountain as the heavenly kingdom of God. In Daniel 2 a huge mountain representing the heavenly kingdom of God (Dan. 2:35, 44, 45) invades the earthly kingdoms. Furthermore, Daniel 11:45 speaks of the "beautiful holy mountain," clearly meaning Jerusalem.

Jerusalem and the mountain of Zion are key motifs in the biblical formulation of hope. Scripture places the Zion of hope high in the heavens (Ps. 48:2; cf. Isa. 14:13), calls it the dwelling of God (Ps. 78:68; 132:13), and states that it resembles the Garden of Eden (Eze. 47:1, 2; Joel 3:18; Zech. 13:1; Rev. 22:1, 2). In the Old Testament as in the New Testament, Jerusalem has become the name of the city of God (Gal. 4:26), the promise of joy and of the everlasting presence of God (Heb. 12:22).

It is this symbolic Jerusalem that the forces of the world seek to conquer. Like the ancient builders of Babel, they hope to manufacture the kingdom of heaven here on earth. Humanity has switched its hope to the humanly possible, and the god of Babel has replaced the God of the heavens.

Such a mind-set does not spring out of nowhere. The rejection of the kingdom of heaven necessitates, as it did for the Egyptian pharaoh, a long sequence of "hardened, toughened, stiff-necked" refusals. We are all candidates for this type of attitude, and must take heed that we do not gradually forget that our hope lies beyond this world.

For that reason, Yohanan then changes his tone. The prophecy becomes a lesson that concerns each one of us, now: "Behold, I come like a thief! Blessed is he who stays awake and keeps his clothes with him, so that he may not go naked and be shamefully exposed" (Rev. 16:15). It is a message for those who have come to put their trust and hope in the visible god of Babel. But the prophet's message has not only the atheist and materialist in mind—it also concerns the community of the "saints," the last link to the God of heaven, the church of the last days. Significantly, the beatitude echoes the last words of the letter to the Laodiceans (Rev. 3:18).

Even the evangelists of hope, those who proclaim God's kingdom, find themselves exposed to the Babel syndrome. Babel's insidious infection manifests itself when the institution—the structures of the church—take precedence over message and content. It also reveals itself when numbers of converts become more important than the depth of their conversion, or when church members are more interested in happiness and immediate success than in patiently waiting for God's future kingdom.

This brief allusion to the letter of Laodicea introduces the possibility that the messengers of the time of the end could succumb to the lure of the great assembly of the nations. The prophecy speaks directly to them. The advice is not without irony. They are to take heed not to parade their nakedness as though it were designer clothes. The believers of the last days face the powerful temptation to think that they have achieved ultimate knowledge and piety, that they "do not need a thing" (Rev. 3:17). The call of the Apocalypse seeks to awaken them out of their torpor. No more hopeless case can exist than that of those who worship the god of Babel while standing among the ranks of Jerusalem. Their feeling of self-righteousness and the comfortable conviction that they have the truth powerfully blinds them to their idolatry.

But the name of Armageddon evokes more than the concept of a battlefield. It also suggests the battle's outcome. Through the allusion to Hadad Rimmon that reminds us of the context of Zechariah's prophecy, Armageddon recalls to mind a gripping scene of mourning: "They will look on me, the one they have pierced, and they will mourn for him as one mourns for an only child, and grieve bitterly for him as one grieves for a firstborn son. On that day the weeping in Jerusalem will be great, like the weeping of Hadad Rimmon in the plain of Megiddo" (Zech. 12:10, 11).

In his oracle Zechariah announced to his people that they would experience a time of mourning comparable to that involving Hadad Rimmon. The prophet here alludes to an old Canaanite legend, one well-known to the Israelites and found in the Ras Shamra tablets.[19] It is the story of the god Hadad, god of the thunder, who weeps over the death of his only son, Aleyin, killed by the goddess Mout. As for Rimmon, he is an Aramaic god (2 Kings 5:18). He became associated with the Canaanite god Hadad because of the cultural ties between the two cultures. Rimmon, from the root *rmm*, was often identified with thunder in western Semitic literature (Isa. 33:3), and is therefore another name for Hadad.[20] The myth of the god Hadad (Rimmon) fits very well with the ancient Palestinian cult of Baal, the fertility god, whose death Canaanite worshipers mourned every year.[21]

But beyond the reference to the pagan myth, the text of Zechariah points to another event, one that belongs to the Israelite tradition itself. The valley of Meggido witnessed one of the most dramatic incidents of mourning of Israel's history. It was there that the Egyptian pharaoh Neco killed King Josiah in 609 B.C.E. The passage in Chronicles relating the event (2 Chron. 35:20-27) shares several common themes with the text in Zechariah. Both mention the participation of women in the act of mourning (2 Chron. 35:25; cf. Zech. 12:12-14); both identify the mourning of Megiddo with that of Jerusalem (2 Chron. 35:24; cf. Zech. 12:11). And both texts are the only ones in the Bible to use the expression "the plain of Megiddo" (2 Chron. 35:22; cf. Zech. 12:11). Such parallels suggest that both passages refer to the same event—the death of Josiah.

The king who reigned longest over Israel, Josiah was also per-haps the greatest reformer in the history of ancient Israel. He single-handedly united the northern and southern parts of the kingdom in a spiritual, moral, and political alignment. According to the book of Chronicles, he was the last king to do "what was right in the eyes of the Lord" (2 Kings 22:2). His tragic death marked the beginning of the end of the kingdom of Judah. Its people commemorated his death yearly "to this day" (2 Chron. 35:25), according to the testimony of the chronicler (a century later).[22]

If the expression "plain of Megiddo" does indeed refer to the death of Josiah, its association with Hadad Rimmon increases even more its dramatic character, since Hadad Rimmon was the "firstborn son" of the god. And now not only the king of Israel, but the whole people of Israel with its Messianic hope are being mourned.

The name Armageddon conveys then the destiny that awaits the idolaters of Babel: a day of mourning like no other. Later, in chapter 18, the Apocalypse confirms this warning as it describes how the fall of Babylon leads to extraordinary mourning. The key word "mourn" appears several times in the passage (Rev. 18:7, 8, 11, 15, 19). It mentions the traditional rituals of mourning—weeping, ashes, and lamentations (verses 9, 10, 15, 19).

Through the mention of Hadad Rimmon, evocative of the death of the firstborn, Armageddon also directs us back to the tenth plague of Egypt (Ex. 12:29-36). The coincidence is too strong to be unintentional. The death of the firstborn of Egypt has no precedent: "There will be loud wailing throughout Egypt—worse than there has ever been or ever will be again" (Ex. 11:6).

Here we encounter the other lesson of Armageddon (via Hadad Rimmon)—the fall of Babel will inflict a loss equal in nature and intensity to what the ancient Egyptians experienced. For them the death of the firstborn entailed much more than the simple loss of a loved one or the end of the family name. The death of the firstborn was the death of their religion. Significantly, the text of Exodus interprets the last plague as a "judgment on all the gods of Egypt" (Ex. 12:12). The Bible applies the notion of firstborn to the priest,[23] to Israel,[24] to the Messiah,[25] and, in the New Testament, to Yeshua Himself.[26] The great significance of the firstborn makes this loss all the more dramatic. It signifies the death of hope.

On the other hand, any allusion to the last plague of Egypt would not be a completely negative one. Scripture associates the last plague of Egypt with the Pessah (the passing over) of God's people. Israel, the firstborn of God, is spared and now stands, cloak tucked in, sandals on its feet, staff in hand, ready for action (verse 11). It is the day the Lord has chosen to bring "the Israelites out of Egypt by their divisions" (verse 51). The tenth plague liberates the people of God from their wretchedness and brings them victory over their enemy.

Actually, the battle of Armageddon breaks out only at the seventh cup. For the first time God Himself initiates the punishment, and its effect is final. The voice we hear is God's: "It is done!" (Rev. 16:17). The expression is idiomatic. We hear it again in Revelation 21:6. There the passage associates it with the God of the beginning and of the end, the "Alpha and the Omega." The stubbornness of God's enemies has reached its "final" stage. For the first time, the camp of Babel declares open war on God. Blasphemy against God has never been so overt. In the fourth plague the people blasphemed against the "name of God" (Rev. 16:9), and in the fifth, against the "God of heaven" (verse 11). Now with the seventh plague they curse Him directly. We note that the progression of the references to God goes from the most specific to the most universal and abstract. The "name of God" has become the "God of heaven," and finally just "God."

For the first time, the plague affects the totality of the universe and not just the human race. Nature turns to chaos. The islands and mountains disappear (verse 20). Incidentally, one notes yet another allusion to the plagues of Egypt: hail. Huge hailstones bombard the earth (verse 21; cf. Ex. 9:22ff.). The Exodus account twice mentions the ravages of this plague that befalls "men and animals and . . . everything growing in the fields of Egypt" (Ex. 9:22, 25).

The wrath of God that had so far only been announced (Rev. 14:8, 10) has now reached its full impact: "God remembered Babylon the Great and gave her the cup filled with the wine of the fury of his wrath" (Rev. 16:19).

As with the ancient story of Babel, God's descent scatters the builders. The unity they had sought now lies completely destroyed: "The great city split into three parts" (verse 19). The alliance between the three powers—the dragon (occult powers), the beast (official Christianity), and the false prophet (the United States)—now dissolves.

The shattering of the three world powers brings about the fall of the nations (verse 19). The event echoes the sixth shofar, in which the three powers also dominated the world scene (Rev. 9:13, 14).

This confusion is the very sign of the fall of Babel.

Interlude: The Beauty and the Beast

In the midst of chaos, the prophetic word marks a pause: "One of the seven angels who had the seven bowls came and said to me, 'Come, I will show you the punishment of the great prostitute, who sits on many waters. With her the kings of the earth committed adultery and the inhabitants of the earth were intoxicated with the wine of her adulteries'" (Rev. 17:1, 2). It is no coincidence that the angel speaking is associated with the seven bowls, or cups (verse 1). What he reveals will justify the punishment of the seven cups that he helps dispense.

God does not behave as some great dictator who knows what He is doing and has His reasons. Instead, He loves and respects His people and wants them to understand and support His actions.

This is the last structural interlude. Up to now they have concerned the redeemed, who were living on hope and were not yet saved (Rev. 7; 15:1-5), while Babel continued its treacherous acts through history. But the third and last part of the Apocalypse (Rev. 15–22), presents the vision of the redeemed as a historical event. The book now has Babel existing as a mere interlude. The very structure of the Apocalypse thus indicates hope and judgment.

The Beauty

The Apocalypse here depicts the Babel of the interlude as a woman resembling her rival, the woman of chapter 12 who symbolized God's people and their role in human history. Both have a cosmic dimension—they occupy a central place in the universe—and both are associated with the desert (Rev. 17:3; cf.12:6, 14) and the dragon (Rev. 17:3, 7; cf. 12:4, 13ff.).

But the contrast between the two women is more striking. The first woman was suspended in the skies, surrounded by planets (Rev. 12:1), while the second is seated on the waters, surrounded by degenerate kings (Rev. 17:1, 2). The dragon attacks the first (Rev. 12:4, 13-17), and the second is dragonlike in nature (Rev. 17:3) and oppresses God's people (verse 6). The first flees into exile (Rev.

12:6); the second reclines as a queen (Rev. 17:3, 4). The first suffers alone in the desert (Rev. 12:6, 14); the second is ready for a party in the city (Rev. 17:4). The first has the hand of God feed her (Rev. 12:6, 14); the second is drunk with the blood of the saints (Rev. 17:2). The first is the mother of the Messiah and of the remnant of Israel (Rev. 12:5, 6); the second is the madam of prostitutes (Rev. 17:5). Clearly the woman of chapter 17 is the antithesis of the woman of chapter 12.

The marriage metaphor helps us to understand these contrasts. The Old Testament, as we have already mentioned, often portrayed Israel as God's bride and compares its infidelity to adultery or prostitution.[27] The Apocalypse employs the same language. The identity of the prostitute is certain. She is neither a pagan nor a political power. In the line of biblical tradition, the prostitute of the Apocalypse embodies the infidelity of God's people, and in the perspective of the New Testament, she represents the church who has flirted with and succumbed to worldly lovers. The Apocalypse identifies the prostitute with the power of Babel. Called "Babylon the Great" (Rev. 17:5), she incarnates both religiosity and Satan's desire to usurp God's role.

Such a revelation is indeed shocking. Since the prophet lives in the time of the early church, the concept leaves him "greatly astonished" (verse 6).

The Beast

To solve the riddle of the woman that puzzles the prophet, the angel refers to the mystery of the beast associated with the woman. He gives the formula of the creature's nature in a sequence of four phases:

A. 1. The beast, which you saw, once was,
  2. now is not,
  3. and will come up out of the Abyss
  4. and go to his destruction (Rev. 17:8).

It mirrors that of God who "was, and is, and is to come" (Rev. 4:8; cf. 1:4, 8), confirming the beast's ambition to replace God. This is the same beast as the sea beast of chapter 13 that, we remember, sought to receive worship like God (Rev. 13:4). Both beasts are likewise "blasphemous" (Rev. 17:3; cf. 13:6). At the same time the "scarlet beast" (Rev. 17:3) reminds us of the "enormous red dragon" (Rev. 12:3). Furthermore, like the beast that emerges out of the land, this creature has the character of a political power whose function is to back up the other religious and occult powers—the woman and the dragon (Rev. 17:2, 12; cf. 13:11, 12). Indeed, the 10-horned dragon of chapter 12 has echoes in both the sea beast, also 10-horned (Rev. 13), and in the land beast, who spoke like a dragon. In other words, the scarlet beast of chapter 17 regroups all three powers—all of God's enemies—into a real coalition.

The enigma of Revelation 17:8 further develops in two successive and parallel waves (verses 10 and 11). The first unfolds the same history in a pattern of four, this time in regard to seven kings:

> B. 1. Five have fallen,
>   2. one is,
>   3. the other has not yet come;
>   4. but when he does come, he must remain for a little while (verse 10).

The second wave also unfolds the same history in a sequence of four, but this time it combines the general theme of the beast (verse 8) with the particular theme of the kings (verse 10).

> C. 1. The beast who once was,
>   2. and now is not,
>   3. is an eighth king. . . .
>   4. and [he] is going to his destruction (verse 11).

A chart combing the three prophetic formulas (ABC) will help us decipher the riddle.

First Phase
> A1. The beast . . . once was
>> B1. Five [kings] have fallen
>>> C1. The beast that was

Second Phase
> A2. Now is not
>> B2. One [king] is

C2. And is not

Third Phase
A3. will come up out of the Abyss
B3. [a king] has not yet come
C3. an eighth king

Fourth Phase
A4. Go to his destruction
B4. Must remain only a little while
C4. Is going to his destruction

To decode the history represented by this beast, one must go back to its description in chapter 13. The 10-horned beast covers the historical period announced in the vision of Daniel 7. Not only is it similar to the fourth beast (cf. its 10 horns, Dan. 7:7) and to the little horn (cf. its arrogant and usurping behavior, verse 8), but it possesses all the characteristics of the animals that precede it—the leopard, the bear, and the lion.

The 10-horned beast of Revelation 13 covers the five historical periods predicted by Daniel 7: Babylon, the Medes and Persians, Greece, Rome, and the little horn.[28] This is the first phase, the five kings mentioned in Revelation 17:10.

The second phase predicts a period of absence that corresponds to the fatal wound of the beast (verse 11)—the time of the sixth king. The prophet observes the paradoxical state of this king, who "exists" even though he looks as if he is dead (Rev. 17:8, 10, 11; cf. 13:3).

The third phase announces that the wound has healed and the beast goes up from the Abyss (Rev. 17:8; cf. 11:7). Because the seventh king lasts until the end, the Apocalypse also describes him as the eighth king (Rev. 17:11), for his reign lasts beyond the seven kings. The seventh king represents the church that has been reinstituted until the end.

The fourth phase projects the vision to the time of the end, when the eighth (seventh) king, who represents the church at the end of time, shall go to "his destruction" (verse 11). The reign of the eighth (seventh) king coincides with that of the 10 kings, the two periods of time being both situated in the "not yet" (verse 12; cf. verse 10). Both periods are characterized by their brevity: a "little while" for the eighth (seventh) king (verse 10) and "one hour" for the 10 kings (verse 12). The symbolic language signifies a very short time. Revelation 18 renders the brevity of the judgment that causes the fall of Babylon in the same way—"in one hour" (Rev. 18:10, 17, 19).[29] Earlier, in the same chapter, the expression "in one day" captures the same idea (verse 8). The 10 kings represent the last political world powers. Having already encountered them in Revelation 16 in the context of Armageddon (Rev. 16:12), we shall meet them again in chapter 18 in which they fight the last battle of Armageddon (Rev. 18:9).

Armageddon—Part I

This last phase has the prophet's undivided attention. After a brief huddle, during which the kings of the earth agree to govern together under the authority of the beast (Rev. 17:13), they declare the war of Armageddon (verse 14). God, however, vanquishes the world's armies (verse 14). Bitterly defeated, the kings turn against their leader, the woman they had crowned queen (verses 17, 18). The prophecy predicts that the 10 horns (the kings of the world) "will hate the prostitute. They will bring her to ruin and leave her naked; they will eat her flesh and burn her with fire" (verse 16).

Curiously, we know nothing of what happens next with them. For now the prophecy focuses on God's judgment and adds simply, "Fallen! Fallen is Babylon the Great!" (Rev. 18:2). The proclamation of the angel echoes word for word that of the second angel (Rev. 14:8), suggesting that the prophecy has been fulfilled. It could not have been otherwise, for God Himself had "put it into their hearts to accomplish his purpose by agreeing to give the beast their power to rule" (verse 17).

As in the case of the hardening of Pharaoh's heart, God assumes the whole responsibility, defying thereby the usurping nature of Babel. Babel's iniquities have reached the point of no return. The very tone of the passage—calculating and precise—supports this.

In contrast to this cold and hard determinism, we find the prophetic words intertwined with paradox and irony. The beautiful woman, dressed in queenly garb and precious stones, daintily drinks from a cup "filled with abominable things and the filth of her adulteries" (Rev. 17:4). She sits elegantly on a hideous beast scarred by "blasphemous names" (verse 3). The woman and the beast are as one (verses 17, 18), yet that very beast will later turn against her in raging bitterness (verse 16). "Babylon the Great" is about to collapse in ashes (Rev. 18:2).

This paradoxical and disturbing language testifies to a philosophy of history that perceives the hand of God even in political chaos and evil intentions. God ultimately sorts out history's tangles. History has a direction—its present absurdity will eventually resolve into God's plan, testifying to His justice and to the hope of new meaning.

Come Out of Her

The prophecy now takes on a tone of urgency. The call resonates throughout the earth: "Come out of her, my people" (verse 4), an expression borrowed from the prophet Jeremiah. He intended it for the exiled Israelites, warning them to flee Babylon (Jer. 51:45). Not only did the summons seek to help them escape the wrath of God about to befall the city and to prepare them to return to their homeland, it reminded them of the even more urgent need to avoid the corrupt influence of Babylonian idolatry (verses 47, 52).

The same call has sounded all through Israel's history. Abraham received it in Ur of Chaldea (Gen. 12:1), Lot in Sodom (Gen. 19:12), and the Israelites in Egypt (Ex. 12:31). In the New Testament Christians receive this same summons to separate from the world (2 Cor. 6:14; Eph. 5:11). It is always the same disturbing message that leads both to the uprooting of lives and to unexpected adventure. But it is not a request to emigrate to another country. Ever since Babylon's historical collapse, the call to come out of Babylon does not necessarily entail moving vans and plane tickets.

In fact, Babylon is everywhere. Of course, Babylon represents the religious institution of Christianity. But it is not enough to step out of any particular church to escape Babylon. Babylon is also a mentality. To come out of it is to reject a whole way of thinking that the church has clung to through the centuries. It means to stop considering the church as the door to God (Babel) and to stop replacing Him with the church and faith with politics. To come out of Babylon is to rejects its imperialism and arrogance. It is to take a stand against anti-Semitism, to remember the church's Jewish roots. To come out of Babylon is to adopt a critical stance toward it while remaining open to revelation from God. And it is the risk taken by those for whom comfort and tradition are not enough.

Thus to come out of Babylon is to experience total conversion. It is the only way to escape the end-time massacre, the only way to survive, and the only way to recover one's true identity.

To come out of Babylon is a shout of hope ringing in the very streets of Babylon, a call for each and every one of us while the opportunity continues.

The Mourning of Babylon

And as though to back the argument, the voice from heaven destroys the last illusions of a future for Babylon. The whole earth is in mourning (Rev. 18:9-20). The post-Babylonian era is an unhappy one. The kings of the earth (verse 9), the merchants (verse 11), and the sailors (verse 17)—all who have benefited from its wealth and influence—weep over what they have lost. None of them have anyone to blame for the tragedy but themselves. They are its cause, the ones who threw it into the fire (Rev. 17:16). Like capricious children who whine about the toy they have just broken, the lovers of Babel weep in vain.

Earth's inhabitants have destroyed their only god. But they continue to adore it. Even their mourning has a worshipful attitude to it. The exclamation "Was there ever a city like this great city?" (Rev. 18:18) mirrors the ancient formula of adoration to the Beast: "Who is like the beast?" (Rev. 13:4); thereby also paralleling the ancient Israelite stance of worship: "Who is like God?"[30]

It is a day of mourning unlike all others, as indicated by the expression of Armageddon. And it is the mourning of a god, like that of Hadad Rimmon. But the god of our passage will not resurrect in

166

springtime as did its Canaanite counterpart.

Unlike traditional mourning rituals, this one contains no comfort. Our story has a tragic and hopeless ending. Its closing act features an angel who throws "a boulder the size of a large millstone" into the sea, symbolizing the great city's downfall: "With such violence the great city of Babylon will be thrown down, never to be found again" (Rev. 18:21).

The prophet Jeremiah made the same gesture to symbolize the fall of the historical Babylon. On God's order, he had thrown a large stone into the Euphrates, saying, "So will Babylon sink to rise no more because of the disaster I will bring upon her" (Jer. 51:64). The ritualistic acts and intentions in the two passages are the same. Only the object differs. This time a millstone is thrown into the sea, an important detail, since the image of a millstone symbolizes life (Rev. 18:22). The angel discards the millstone in the sea because no one remains to use it—Babylon's inhabitants have all gone. The millstone was such an important aid to survival that the law of Moses forbade anyone to seize it as security for a debt, "because that would be taking a man's livelihood as security" (Deut. 24:6). Now it is of no use to anyone.

Moreover, the "large" millstone is much heavier than the stone, therefore sinking much deeper into the sea. The angel hurls the millstone "with . . . violence" into the sea and not just into a local river (Rev. 18:21).

These contrasts all point to the finality of Babylon's collapse. The death of Babylon is irrevocable.

And there lies the consolation for God's people. They have nothing left to fear ever again. The prophecy reassures the "prophets and . . . the saints, and . . . all who have been killed on the earth" by this mighty city (verse 24). The Apocalypse receives the news with great rejoicing. The joys of justice combine with the eagerness of hope.

---

[1] Ps. 136:6; Isa. 40:12.

[2] See the Talmud of Jerusalem, *Berakot* 4. 5.

[3] Cf. Isa. 51:17; Zech. 12:2.

[4] Jacques Ellul, *Apocalypse: The Book of Revelation*, trans. George W. Schreiner (New York: 1977), pp. 183, 184.

[5] Doukhan, *Secrets of Daniel,* pp. 171-176.

[6] See Malachi Martin, *The Keys of This Blood: The Struggle for World Dominion Between Pope John Paul II, Mikhail Gorbachev, and the Capitalist West* (New York: Simon and Schuster, 1990).

[7] Ps. 36:8, 9; Jer. 17:8, etc.

[8] Doukhan, *Secrets of Daniel,* pp. 171, 175, 176.

[9] Wisdom of Solomon 17.

[10] *The Histories* 1. 191. 2-4.

[11] Doukhan, *Secrets of Daniel,* p. 98.

[12] See C. Thompson, *Semitic Magic: Its Origins and Development* (Jerusalem: 1971), pp. 28-32, 90.

[13] Doukhan, *Secrets of Daniel,* pp. 171-177.

[14] Joshua 12:21; 17:11; Judges 1:27; 5:19; 1 Kings 4:12; 2 Kings 9:27, etc.

[15] See Andrzej Strus, *Nomen-omen: La stylistique sonore des noms propres dans le Pentateuque,* Analecta biblica (Rome: 1978), vol. 80, pp. 199, 200.

[16] See, for instance, Deut. 32:15 *(wayishman/yeshurun)*; 2 Kings 8:28, 29 *(yoram/Aram).*

[17] See, for instance, the use of the ancient name Shinar in Dan. 1:2; see Doukhan, *Secrets of Daniel,* p. 13.

[18] Jezreel is thus composed of *zara* (seed) and of *El* (God) to express the fact that God shall give the seed (Hosea 2:22, 23); see Moshe Garsiel, *Biblical Names: A Literary Study of Midrashic Derivations and Pun* (Ramat Gan, Israel: 1991), pp. 229ff.

[19] H. H. Rowley, *The Re-discovery of the Old Testament,* Library of Contemporary Theology (London: 1945), p. 49; see also D. Winton Thomas, ed., *Documents From Old Testament Times* (London: 1958), p. 133.

[20] Jerome identifies the name of Hadad Rimmon with a city then called Maximianopolis (in *Commentariorum in Zachariam Prophetam* 3. 12. 11, 12 [*Patrologicae Latina,* vol. 25, col. 1515]) and located two miles south of Meggido. It is now named Rummaneh.

[21] See J. Aistleitner, *Die mythologischen und kultischen Texte aus Ras Schamra,* Bibliotheca orientalis Hungarica (Budapest: 1959), vol. 8, pp. 17, 18.

[22] The books of Chronicles, written during the time of Ezra and of Artaxerxes, date from the fifth century B.C.E., while the book of Zechariah dates from the sixth century B.C.E.

[23] Num. 3:11-13, 40ff.; 8:14-18.

[24] Ex. 4:22; Jer. 31:9.

[25] Ps. 89:27.

[26] Matt. 1:25; Luke 2:7; Heb. 1:6; Col. 1:18; Rev. 1:5; 1 Cor. 15:20.

[27] Hosea 5:3; Isa. 1:21; Eze. 16:15; 23:1-4, etc.

[28] Doukhan, *Secrets of Daniel,* pp. 29-36, 101-111.

[29] Cf. 1 Thess. 2:17.

[30] Cf. Ex. 15:11; Micah 7:18.

CHAPTER 8

STAR WARS

(Revelation 19; 20)

Pre-Sukkot

Once again the vision pauses for a scene of adoration. This introduction echoes that of the seven seals (Rev. 19:1-10), using the same themes: the heavenly throne, the 24 elders, the four living creatures, and the Lamb. But the Apocalypse now explicitly identifies the person on the throne: "God, who was seated on the throne" (Rev. 19:4). It is the last liturgical scene of the Apocalypse.

For the first time the book does not mention the Temple and its objects. All of the atoning rites of the Temple have been accomplished, and the Temple has no more "raison d'être." The judgment continues now outside its walls. The Kippur ritual set a ram apart (for Azazel), not to be sacrificed, but to be chased into the desert, bearing the sins of Israel (Lev. 16:10, 20-26). After Kippur the people were delivered from their sins. From a prophetic perspective, the lesson is laden with hope. God is not content merely to forgive us of our sins. He also wants to deliver us from them. The devil, embodied by the ram in the ritual of Azazel, gets chased from the camp to its death.

From now on, all becomes praise. According to Jewish tradition, the days following Kippur are joyous ones. The festival after Kippur, Sukkot (the Feast of Tabernacles), is also called *zeman simhatenou,* "time of our joy." People must not fast on the days devoted to the building of the huts (Sukkot).

We find our passage permeated with the joy that celebrates the destruction of evil and anticipates a new life with God. Babylon has fallen, and the New Jerusalem awaits. The prostitute is dead, the bride is carried in triumph through the streets. The heavens burst into five resounding "Hallelujahs" (Rev. 19:1, 3, 4, 5, 6).[1]

The English word "hallelujah" is a rough transliteration of the Hebrew expression *halelu Yah,* meaning "praise Yah" (Yah being an abbreviation of the name of God, YHWH). The expression dates back to the psalms, which, in Hebrew, are called *tehilim* (psalms, using the same root as *halelu*). The significance of hallelujah is implied in the words associated with the verb *hillel,* from which *halelu* derives:

"Sing" (Ps. 146:2; 149:1)

"Declare" (Ps. 22:22)

"Give . . . thanks" (Ps. 35:18)

"Revere" (Ps. 22:23)

"Extol" (Ps. 109:30; 115:18; 145:2)

"Joy" (Jer. 31:7)

The word *hillel* implies all of this. Hallelujah is a spontaneous shout of joy, a reflective meditation of the mind. This word of praise now resonates from the past into the future. We praise not only God the Creator (Ps. 104) or God the Savior (Ps. 105; 106; 135), but also the God whose "love endures forever" (Ps. 106:1; 107:1; 118:1, 2, 3, 4, etc.).

It is interesting to note with the ancient rabbis that the expression *halelu Yah* doesn't appear until the closing verses of Psalm 104, in which it immediately follows the extermination of the wicked: "But may sinners vanish from the earth and the wicked be no more. Praise the Lord, O my soul. Praise the Lord" (Ps. 104:35).

It is no coincidence that the hallel (Psalms 113-118) is the principal text of the liturgy of Sukkot. Jews traditionally recite the psalms during the eight days of the festival.[2] The way people employ them varies from tradition to tradition. Some communities sing them antiphonally. Others, such as the Yemenites, have the congregation interject hallelujahs between each verse. It is how we are to hear the hallelujahs sung in the Apocalypse—like the singing of the responsory by the Temple choirs.[3] Hallelujah was thus the congregation's *responsa* to the soloist. The very syntax of the expression presupposes a liturgical genre. *Halelu* is a plural imperative that incites the multitudes to praise God.

A number of voices sing the hallelujahs of Revelation 19. First, we hear the sound of "a great multitude" (Rev. 19:1, 6), identified previously as the 144,000 (Rev. 7:4, 9). Second, we listen to the 24 elders and the four living creatures (Rev. 19:4), representing the whole of creation. Finally, an anonymous voice issues from the throne of God (verse 5).

The first two hallelujahs, pronounced by the crowd, have to do with events of the past. The first hallelujah celebrates the death of the prostitute (verse 2). The second hallelujah rejoices over the fact that the "smoke from her goes up for ever and ever" (verse 3), a sign of her final destruction.[4] This vision anticipates the final destruction of evil and death. The expression "for ever and ever" to indicate eternity in Revelation 20:10 later applies to Satan's death, represented by the ritual of Azazel (Lev. 16:10, 21, 26).

Heavenly beings (the 24 elders and the four living creatures) pronounce the next two hallelujahs and direct them to God Himself. The third hallelujah expresses adoration of the "God, who was seated on the throne" (Rev. 19:4), the God who reigns and judges. The fourth hallelujah communicates the fear of God (verse 5) that characterizes "his servants" (cf. Rev. 1:1).

The fifth and last hallelujah is the loudest. The prophet hears what seems like "the roar of rushing waters and like loud peals of thunder" (Rev. 19:6). This hallelujah looks to the future and anticipates God's total reign. "For our Lord God Almighty reigns. Let us rejoice and be glad and give him glory! For the wedding of the Lamb has come, and his bride has made herself ready" (verses 6, 7).

The celebration of the prostitute's death and of the bride's wedding reintroduces the marriage metaphor. The multitude now proclaims Israel the legitimate bride of the Lamb. Our passage mentions that God's "bride has made herself ready" (verse 7). Salvation is therefore not a mere passive experience. God awaits the human response at each step of the way. On the day of her wedding, it was customary for the bride to adorn herself for her husband. She bathes, perfumes, and decorates herself with precious jewels.[5] The whole process requires the help of her friends. After they veil her completely, only her husband may unveil her in the nuptial chambers.[6] They fasten a belt around her waist that only her lover may loosen.[7]

The attendants give her "fine linen, bright and clean" for her to wear (Rev. 19:8). Not only the type of garment, but the act of draping it over her nakedness Scripture presents as a grace—as a gift—from above. The "fine linen" symbolizes the "righteous acts of the saints" (verse 8). The Apocalypse here contrasts her garment of "fine linen, bright and clean" with the garish robes, also of fine linen, of the prostitute (Rev. 18:16). The simplicity and modesty of the spouse stands in contrast to the pride and impudence of the prostitute.

The various comparisons show to what degree the biblical author parallels the two women in his mind. Like the spouse, the prostitute participates in the conjugal metaphor. Even the shouts of joy on the wedding day of the spouse (Rev. 19:7, 9) echo the lamentations mourning the death of the prostitute (Rev. 18:10, 11, 16, 19, 22). This joy now invades the earthly scene of Yohanan: "Blessed are those who are invited to the wedding supper of the Lamb!" (Rev. 19:9).

Happiness is contagious. It must be shared. The beatitude invites us all to participate in it.

Having heard those words, Yohanan falls to the feet of the angel "to worship him" (verse 10). The prophet seems to have gotten carried away with the emotion of the moment. "Do not do it!" the angel rebukes him. "I am a fellow servant with you" adding somewhat mysteriously, "For the testimony of Jesus is the spirit of prophecy" (verse 10).

His last words are enigmatic. We find them again in the conclusion of the book and in a similar context (Rev. 22:8, 9). There also a beatitude appears to incite the prophet to fall down in worship. And there also the prophet receives a rebuke from his "fellow servant." The parallelism between the two passages helps clarify the strange expression:

Revelation 19:10	**Revelation 22:8, 9**
I fell at his feet to worship him.	I fell down to worship at the feet of the angel. . . .
But he said to me, "Do not do it!"	But he said to me, "Do not do it!"
I am a fellow servant with you and with your brothers	I am a fellow servant with you and with your brothers . . .
who hold the testimony of Jesus.	**who keep the words of this book.**
Worship God!	Worship God!

The phrase "[those] who hold the testimony of Jesus" corresponds to "[those] who keep the words of this book." In other words, the "testimony of Jesus" is the equivalent of "this book," namely, the Apocalypse. To testify to Yeshua means, then, to proclaim the message of the Apocalypse—it is to announce the prophecy concerning the final salvation of the universe. The "testimony of Jesus" proceeds from Yeshua Himself (in Greek, a subjective genitive; cf. Rev. 1:1, 2). The passage here also identifies the testimony as the "spirit of prophecy"—namely, the divine inspiration of the prophetic word.[8] Revelation 19:10 confirms that "the testimony of Jesus is the spirit of prophecy." The testimony of Yeshua is thus more than an ethic or a tradition—it implies inspiration from above.

In another passage the Apocalypse associates the testimony of Yeshua with obedience to the commandments (Rev. 12:17). To keep the commandments of God—to live according to the divine criteria—is to confirm the prophecy. The "testimony of Jesus" is then also the testimony *about* Yeshua. A moral life is a sign of the spirit of prophecy, namely, of divine inspiration. In other words, we cannot lay claim to the spirit of prophecy without actually embodying its divine principles in our life and existence. Scripture here denounces fanaticism and other religious excesses that sacrifice ethics for prophetic pretensions.

The expression "the testimony of Jesus" thus has two facets.[9] It is no coincidence that the Apocalypse associates the "testimony of Jesus" and the "spirit of prophecy" with the "rest of her offspring" (Rev. 12:17). The last witnesses for God's coming reveal not only their faithfulness and righteousness, but also their awareness of prophecy, which guides them through the last spasms of history.

Victories of Heaven

The next vision comes upon Yohanan while he bows down in adoration (Rev. 19:10). Looking beyond the angel, Yohanan sees the heavens "standing open" (verse 11). As of yet, the heavens have opened only for voices and angels. Earlier a door had stood open (Rev. 4:1), and the temple had been opened (Rev. 11:19; 15:5). This time the entire heavens swing open. The revelation is complete as the vision reveals the infinity of the heavenly kingdom.

Across the horizon emerges a white horse, galloping to his last military campaign. The victories of heaven follow the structure of the seven seals:

The Seals	The Victories
1. White horse, crown, victory (Rev. 6:2)	1. White horse, crowns, victory (Rev. 19:11-13)
2. Horse of blood, war, sword (Rev. 6:3, 4)	2. Armies, bloodbath, war, sword (Rev. 19:14-16, 19-21a)
3. Spiritual famine (Rev. 6:5, 6)	3. Man-eating orgy (Rev. 19:17, 18; cf. 21b)
4. Death, dwelling of the dead (Rev. 6:7, 8)	4. Abyss (Rev. 20:1-3)
5 Souls, slain because of their testimony, waiting in death (Rev. 6:9-11)	5. Souls, beheaded because of their testimony, come to life (Rev. 20:4-6)
6. Battle of Armageddon (Rev. 6:12-17)	6. Battle of Gog and Magog (Rev. 20:7-10)
7. Empty skies, silence, parousia (Rev. 8:1)	7. Great white throne, earth and heavens empty (Rev. 20:11-15)

The White Horse

The white horse takes us directly back to the historical development of the seals. In the seals, the white horse inaugurated the triumphant beginnings of the church (Rev. 6:2) and covered only the first moments of history. Now the white horse symbolizes the triumphant return of the heavenly host and represents the totality of history. The last white horse thus takes over and finishes what the first white horse began.

In the cycle of the seals a rider of peace without any weapons mounted the white horse. Now it carries a bloodthirsty warrior who uses his sword against the nations and spills blood (Rev. 19:13, 15). The first rider merely wore a crown of laurel (Rev. 6:2) while the last rider now has many crowns (Rev. 19:12). A laurel marked the brief victory of a sports competition, but the many crowns now express the permanence of royalty. The Apocalypse mentioned the first rider only in passing—he was just a shadow. Now we can discern His features. The book explicitly describes His head and eyes (verse 12), His mouth (verse 15), and His thighs and clothing (verse 16), clearly revealing His identity.

He receives four names, expressing the proximity of the incarnated God as well as His grandeur. The first name, "Faithful and True" (verse 11), affirms the certainty of God's presence—His coming is certain.[10] The second name, "that no one knows" (verse 12), expresses the distance of the invisible God and His otherness. His coming will be unexpected. The third name, "Word of God" (verse 13), affirms that God has manifested Himself in the flesh, that He is a God who revealed Himself in the words and actions of His people. He is the personal God of history and of existence. And the fourth name, "King of kings and Lord of lords" (verse 16), expresses the sovereignty of the Master of the universe. It is also the name of the Lamb, Yeshua the Messiah (Rev. 17:14).

Our passage interweaves both God's transcendence and immanence. God is both near and far. The prophet couples the incarnation and the proximity of God with His sovereignty, justice, and grandeur. This was what Yeshua meant in praying "our Father" (the proximate God) "in heaven" (the distant God) (Matt. 6:9).

Likewise, the kingdom of God is both present and future, existential and cosmic. Right after teaching the Pharisees that the kingdom of God was "within" them (Luke 17:21), Yeshua added: "For the Son of Man in his day will be like the lightning, which flashes and lights up the sky from one end to the other" (verse 24).

It is the awareness of this tension that characterizes our worship of God. Indeed, this revelation comes to Yohanan while he still bows in worship (Rev. 19:10), the very moment where it reaches its climax in the coming of God.

Armageddon—Part II

In a typical Hebrew manner, the prophet now backtracks from the vision of victory to the events leading up to it.[11] The fresh blood on the clothing of the rider (Rev. 19:13) shows that He has used His sword, bringing us back to the second seal. The blood of the oppressors is spilled for the blood of the martyrs (Rev. 6:3, 4). The white rider wars against those who waged war against the saints. The sword leads to the sword.

The gathering of the "kings of the earth" against the divine warrior (Rev. 19:19) points to a similar assembling of the "kings of the whole world" on the mountain of Megiddon against the God who comes like a thief (Rev. 16:14-16). Our passage shares a number of common themes with that of the sixth cup—it is the same battle of Armageddon.

The Apocalypse does not describe the details of the battle. The prophet is content to give us the ending: God is totally victorious over His enemies. The beast and the false prophet now join forces with all the others. Chapters 17 and 18 were but an incomplete account of the war of Armageddon. We witnessed the defeat of Babel and the ensuing doom of the kings of the earth, but Scripture said nothing about the final outcome of those kings. The angel now concludes the story. He reminds us of the defeat of Babel and its ally, the false prophet (Rev. 19:20; cf. 17:16; Dan. 7:11). The earlier account (Rev. 17 and 18) did not even mention the false prophet. We now witness the downfall of both powers.

As for the others—"the kings of the earth," the political powers—they perish from "the sword that came out of the mouth of the rider on the horse" (Rev. 19:21). Their punishment is different from that of the beasts. The sword attacks the "kings of the earth." God engages each power within its own sphere. The cosmic power of the God-judge annihilates the religious powers, and the military power of the God of armies vanquishes the political powers.

The fatal weapon is none other than the word of God. God created the world with His word (Gen. 1:3; John 1:1-3), and now He destroys the world with it. The word of God can both create and destroy. "Long ago by God's word the heavens existed and the earth was formed out of water and by water. . . . By the same word the present heavens and earth are reserved for fire" (2 Peter 3:5-7).

In Hebrew, "word" is more than a cluster of sounds. The *davar* (word) means also "history," "an event." The word is the expression of the soul, of the person. According to the Epistle to the Hebrews, "God . . . has spoken to us by his Son" (Heb.1:1, 2).

The Parousia is God's most *outspoken* moment. That is why humanity cannot endure it (Isa. 33:20; cf. 1 Tim. 6:16). They either change or die. The coming of God entails either transformation (1 Cor. 15:51, 52) or death.

People-eating Orgy

For the "kings of the earth" the Parousia leads to a violent death. And for the first time, God is the direct cause of the punishment. In fact, He is the only one left on the scene. As of yet, the judgments have followed the principle of reciprocity, operating according to factors inherent to the human condition. But God Himself administers the last judgment. "The rest of them were killed with the sword that came out of the mouth of the rider on the horse" (Rev. 19:21). Then "all the birds gorged themselves on their flesh" (verse 21).

Babylon had ended up the same way. The 10 horns and the beast had feasted on its flesh (Rev. 17:16). Now it's their turn. This event parallels a vision of Ezekiel but with some differences. The Hebrew prophet assembles the birds and all the beasts of the field, while Yohanan's vision mentions only the birds. Ezekiel limits the massacre to that of the princes, heroes, horses, and warriors (Eze. 39:17-

20). The Apocalyptic vision, however, has cosmic dimensions, adding to the list of casualties "the flesh of all people, free and slave, small and great" (Rev. 19:18). The destruction is total.

Ironically, this "people-eating" orgy that consumes the kings of the earth echoes the spiritual famine in the third seal (Rev. 6:5, 6). At the same time it also alludes to the wedding banquet of the Lamb by using the same Greek word (*deipnon,* translated as "supper") to describe the event (Rev. 19:17; cf. 19:9). The symmetry between the two banquets points to the dual character of salvation—it both saves and destroys. The wedding banquet of the Lamb replenishes its guests with joy and eternal life. The orgy of Armageddon devours its guests in a mood of bitter and absolute mourning. Nothing remains of their bones. They are not even properly buried, a fundamental concern of the ancient world. The vultures devour them completely. The "kings of the earth" disappear completely from the face of the earth.

The Devil and Nothingness

It is in this desert of death and nothingness that God arrests His supreme enemy. As in Revelation 12:9, Revelation 20:2 calls him "the dragon, that ancient serpent, who is the devil, or Satan." Of God's three enemies (Rev. 16:13), the dragon is the sole survivor. The two others—the sea beast and the land beast (the false prophet)—have both been destroyed, and with them the last kings of the earth.

The "key to . . . the Abyss," which had been lost to the fallen star, the prince of the earth (Rev. 9:1), is now returned to the angel of God (Rev. 20:1). The passage alludes to the pre-Creation state of the earth. The Greek of the Apocalypse implies the same Hebrew word *tehom* (Abyss) of Genesis 1:2. The devil is thrown there.

The earth has returned to its original state of nothingness and void. God is absent, as is life. Heaven has condemned the devil to the desert and to the void, just as the serpent had been reduced to the dust (Gen. 3:14). He has no one left to seduce. Unlike the situation in Genesis, there is no one left to tempt. Evil is thus neutralized.

It is a lesson of hope already hinted at in the ritual of Kippur. It also condemned the ram for Azazel, representing Satan, to the desert (Lev. 16:20-22) as part of the ritual of salvation. The expulsion of evil enacted in the Azazel ritual finalized the atonement of the people's sins and the cleansing of the sanctuary.

The Gospel of John pronounces the same prophecy. During the "judgment on this world," Satan "the prince of this world will be driven out" (John 12:31; cf. 16:11). Jewish tradition also develops the idea in the book of 1 Enoch, in which God orders Raphael to bind Azazel and cast him into the desert.[12] In his vision of the judgment of God for "the time of the end," Daniel, who associates the judgment with the ritual of Kippur (Dan. 8),[13] must have also implied this other side of salvation, namely, the expulsion of Azazel, the devil, to the *tehom* of the desert.

The Apocalypse speaks of this expulsion as a concrete event in time. It is to last a thousand years. In the context of Revelation such a rounded-off figure is symbolic. The "thousand[s]" that make up the 144,000 signify multitudes. In Hebrew tradition the number 1,000 often represents the notion of multitude.[14] Such symbolism can refer to time. "Better is one day in your courts than a thousand elsewhere" (Ps. 84:10), or "For a thousand years in your sight are like a day that has just gone by" (Ps. 90:4). Likewise in the book of Ecclesiastes: "Even if he lives a thousand years twice over but fails to enjoy his prosperity" (Eccl. 6:6) echoes the preceding verses, "A man may . . . live many years; yet no matter how long he lives, if he cannot enjoy his prosperity . . . , I say that a stillborn child is better off than he" (verse 3).

In light of such verses, we have strong reasons to understand the number "one thousand" in terms of "many years." Significantly, the end of the verse contrasts "the thousand years" with "a short time" (Rev. 20:3), confirming once again the idea that "one thousand" means "many."

The prophet Isaiah had a similar vision. In a passage called by commentators "the small Apocalypse" (Isa. 24; 25), the prophet identifies a desert of "earth," a key word in the passage (17 occurrences), with *tohu* (formless), a quality of the earth before Creation (Isa. 24:1, 10; cf. Gen. 1:2). Again, the prophet pronounces God's judgment against Satan and his subjects: "In that day the Lord will punish the powers in the heavens above and the kings on the earth below" (Isa. 24:21). As with the Apocalypse, we find an imprisonment during a long period of time—"many days" (verse 22)—that confirms our understanding of Revelation 20:3 in terms of a long period of time.

The Apocalypse does not clarify what will take place on earth during the millennium. What matters is that, for a period symbolically defined by the Apocalypse as a long time, evil will have no power over humanity. The symbolic connotation of the 1,000 years does not exclude the possibility that the period will be literally 1,000 years. But that is not what is important. At this stage in history, from the perspective of eternity, time is conceptualized differently.

Yet, a "thousand years" also approximates the age attained by the first generation before the Flood (Adam, 930 years; Jared, 962; Methuselah, 969; Noah, 950, etc.). The mention of "a thousand years" signifies then a return to the antediluvian era, the time of the Garden of Eden. The book of Isaiah uses the same language (Isa. 65:17) to present the hope of a "new heavens and a new earth." It describes that new world in terms of the golden age before the Flood. At that time, to die at 100 was to die young (verse 20), and human beings lived to be as old as the trees (verse 22).

Our passage might thus be announcing a return to that golden age in which life was good and long. The millennium would hence represent humanity's first steps into eternity.

The Living Dead

From the desolate abyss, the vision takes us to the heavens bursting with life. We first encounter those we least expected—the oppressed, the humiliated, those "beheaded because of their testimony for Jesus" (Rev. 20:4) and who had pleaded for justice under the fifth seal. But along with the martyrs and heroes we also find the simple and the humble, those who remained true to themselves (verse 4). Thus we meet the righteous in every form and manner.

The angel announces: "Blessed and holy are those who have part in the first resurrection" (verse 6). It is the fifth of the seven beatitudes in the Apocalypse, and like the others, the book again associates it with the return of the Messiah. The connection between resurrection and the coming of the Savior is not new. The book of Daniel had already established it: "Multitudes who sleep in the dust of the earth will awake" (Dan. 12:2), an extraordinary event attributed to the coming of Michael. Significantly, the last chapter of Daniel begins and closes on this particular theme. The warrior angel, Michael (verse 1),[15] who rises (in Hebrew *amad*), leads to the rising *(amad)* "at the end of the days" (verse 13). Likewise, the Apocalypse associates the resurrection of the righteous with the victory of the warrior on the white horse. The apostle Paul develops the same belief: "We who are still alive, who are left till the coming of the Lord, will certainly not precede those who have fallen asleep. For the Lord himself will come down from heaven, with a loud command, with the voice of the archangel and with the trumpet call of God, and the dead in Christ will rise first. After that, we who are still alive and are left will be caught up together with them in the clouds to meet the Lord in the air. And so we will be with the Lord forever" (1 Thess. 4:15-17).

The resurrection is the only explanation for the presence of these living dead in heaven. They are present body and soul. Their soul has not survived their destroyed bodies as those who believe in an immortal soul infer. Instead, they are wholly and fully present, both physically and mentally.

We should understand the word "souls" here (Rev. 20:4) in the Hebrew sense. The soul, in the Hebrew mind, designates the whole person. The Hebrew word *nephesh,* generally translated in the Septuagint by the Greek word *psuchē* and in English Bibles by "soul," implies the human being as a total unit. All the physical, mental, and spiritual components are present. The *nephesh* (soul) suffers from hunger (Ps. 107:9; Deut. 12:20) or thirst (Ps. 143:6), is satisfied (Jer. 31:14), and is full (Isa. 55:2). The *nephesh* also loves (Gen. 34:3; S. of Sol. 1:7), is moved emotionally (Ps. 31:10), cries out (Ps. 119:10), knows (Ps. 139:14), and adores and praises God (Ps. 103:1; 146:1). The Bible presents a wholistic conception of human beings. When the body dies, so do the mental functions (Eccl. 9:5). Death involves the complete person, just as does life.

181

Deeply rooted in the Hebrew scriptures, the Apocalypse speaks of resurrection as an event comprising both the physical and spiritual dimensions, both the body and the human consciousness. For the Bible, the body is not distinct from the soul. The body is the soul, and the soul is the body.

We now better understand the concept of resurrection as developed in our passage. In the Bible, life implies both the sensory body as well as emotions and thoughts. The angel does not hint at the exact nature and process of the resurrection. As always, the focus lies less on the process than on the result—a fact true of all biblical miracles, whether it is Creation, the dividing of the Red Sea, or the resurrection of Yeshua. The inspired author testifies to the event without resorting to scientific explanation.

What matters is that the resurrected are present—in the flesh. The very fact that they are in heaven at all proves that resurrection has occurred. Scripture posits God and the creation of the earth and of humanity as irrefutable realities. The human being and the historical event need not be validated by external proof. Their existence speaks for itself.

The prophetic vision therefore shifts to the resurrected humanity. "I saw thrones on which were seated those who had been given authority to judge" (Rev. 20:4). The victims have become judges. With the roles reversed, justice is done. God summons them to share the responsibility of sentencing the wicked. Yet the Lord has already given the sentence. The first resurrection shows that a judgment has taken place. The coming of the Messiah itself separated the just from the wicked. The prophet Daniel implies this, since he situates the event of God's judgment before the coming of the Son of Man (Dan. 7). Likewise, the Armageddon account, when it groups the wicked in opposition to the just, implies that the two camps are already defined.

In any case, the judgment belongs to God—to the Creator. He alone is capable of searching "hearts and minds" (Rev. 2:23). The Lord is the only one able to combine grace and justice and the only one capable of forgiveness. His purity is the only guarantee of true discernment between good and evil. Thus He is the only one who has the right to judge (John 8:7).

God wants, however, to justify Himself before His people. He brings forth the records and opens them (Rev. 20:12) to the redeemed, giving them equal power to judge as they reign with Him (verses 4, 6). The Lord wants them to be informed, to understand why He made the decisions He did.

His people will partake not only of His royalty and power, but also of His holiness. Scripture identifies them as priests—"priests of God and of Christ" (verse 6). The book of Leviticus often pairs the functions of the priests with the term qodesh (holiness).[16] Also, there the key phrase "be holy, because I am holy" and its variants express a repeated theme.[17] Significantly, the beatitude in the Apocalypse that introduces the promise about being priests links the adjective "blessed" to that of "holy" (verse 6). By qualifying the resurrected as "priests," the Apocalypse closely relates them to God. Holiness (qodesh) is the essential attribute of God.[18] God gives it to the resurrected so that—like Him—they will be able to distinguish between good and evil.

But the Lord does not merely endow them with the means to judge. He also gives them the time to do so—1,000 years. Not only do their fellow humans judge the wicked, but God submits Himself to their judgment.

Gog and Magog

The Lord respects their judgment to the point that He waits 1,000 years to implement the sentence. The final destruction could have occurred at the Parousia. God had then all the necessary data. Nevertheless, He needs humanity to give the final seal of approval and to understand His decision. A new start is possible only after all doubts have been dispelled. God thus holds back for the 1,000 years. And even then, the final destruction comes in response to the initiative of the wicked. After the millennium the remaining dead are resurrected. They are a multitude "like the sand on the seashore" (Rev. 20:8).

Satan makes a flamboyant entrance onto the world scene as the great seducer (verse 7). His intentions are clear: to gather the nations for battle (verse 8). The scenario is similar to that of Armageddon's. Both feature the gathering of nations for conflict and their tragic end in the lake of fire (Rev. 20:10, 13, 14; cf. 19:20). And both battles receive a Hebrew name. The name of the new battle, "Gog and Magog," derives from Israel's history (Eze. 38:2).

The two conflicts do have some differences, however. Whereas the battle of Armageddon pits Israel against a well-defined enemy—Babylon—the battle of Gog and Magog, as described by Ezekiel, features an indefinite enemy, whose only objective is to destroy a kingdom of peace: "On that day thoughts will come into your mind and you will devise an evil scheme. You will say, 'I will invade a land of unwalled villages; I will attack a peaceful and unsuspecting people—all of them living without walls and without gates and bars'" (verses 10, 11). In the battle of Armageddon, the armies of Babel fought against a Savior from the East (Rev. 16:14, 16), and the invaders had to use strategy to penetrate Babylon's walls. In the battle of Gog and Magog, the armies of the dragon are already within the walls of the "camp of God's people" (Rev. 20:9). The "kings of the earth" led Armageddon under the supervision of the beast, the false prophet, and the dragon. The war of Gog and Magog involves "the nations in the four corners of the earth," whose number resembles "the sand on the seashore" (verse 8). The "nations" as a great multitude is the dominant theme of Ezekiel's vision about Gog and Magog: "On that day I will give Gog a burial place in Israel. . . . Gog and all his hordes will be buried there. So it will be called the Valley of Hamon Gog" (Eze. 39:11; "Hamon Gog" means "hordes of Gog" or "multitudes of Gog").[19]

The transition from Armageddon to Gog does not lack irony. God's enemies wanted to conquer the mountain (har) of God—they end up in a valley. An irony also occurs within the battle of Gog itself. The multitude begins as a symbol of power, but becomes—in a landscape of death—one of horror. The mighty hordes of Gog turn into hordes of corpses (Eze. 39:11, 13, 15). The Hebrew words for "Valley of Hamon Gog" (Gey Hamon Gog) echo Gey Hinnom (Valley of Hinnom), where Judah sacrificed infants to Moloch (2 Chron. 33:6).[20] The latter valley eventually inspired the concept of "Gehenna" or "hell" (see, for example, Matt. 5:22).

The name of "Gog and Magog" itself evokes the multitude. Its numerical value—70—represents in Jewish tradition the number of nations outside of Israel.[21] This suggests a reason for the unique association of the two names in our passage. It is an interpretation in tune with apocalyptic literary style, in which numbers often have a symbolic value (for example, 666; Rev. 13:18).[22] Therefore, in the apocalyptic symbolism, "Gog and Magog" signify the multitude of nations, the *goyim,* who, according to traditional Jewish terminology, are those foreign to the covenant of the God of Israel.

The Death of Death

The vision of the "great white throne" (Rev. 20:11) that concludes the cycle echoes the "white horse" that introduced it. The victory of the warrior leads to the throne. "Earth and sky" flee from his presence, plunging us back into the silence of the seventh seal (Rev. 8:1). The traditional formula "the heavens and the earth" used in the Creation story the Apocalypse now reverses as "earth and sky." Our universe, our environment, our niche—they all disappear.

The survivors of Armageddon, after a thousand years of scrutinizing the books, come to the simple conclusion that "each person was judged according to what he had done" (Rev. 20:13). The death that now destroys God's enemies is final. Beyond this last death, "the second death" (verse 14), there is no more death. The last death includes the death of death itself. The prophet describes the event in metaphorical language: "Then death and Hades were thrown into the lake of fire" (verse 14). We remember the cries of the prophet Hosea that the apostle Paul would later repeat: "Where, O death, are your plagues? Where, O grave, is your destruction?" (Hosea 13:14; cf. 1 Cor. 15:55).

Ezekiel's vision of Gog and Magog had already alluded to the total destruction of the wicked. According to this vision, the troops of Gog and Magog, unlike those of Armageddon, would have no survivors from their camp to mourn them: "The house of Israel will be burying them" (Eze. 39:12).

In the end, only Israel survives. The Jews, the Christians, and all others that remained faithful to God are spared. Israel—in the context of the Apocalypse—is more than an ethnic entity. According to the definition given at the beginning of our chapter, Israel consists of those who "had not worshiped the beast or his image and had not received his mark on their foreheads or their hands" (Rev. 20:4). The angel had already described them as those bearing the seal of God on their foreheads (Rev. 7:2, 3), the "144,000 from all the tribes of Israel" (verse 4).

The Apocalypse understands Israel in a spiritual and symbolic sense as designating the survivors of human history. Now the prophet focuses all his attention on them. As with Ezekiel's vision, the tragic scene of Gog and Magog makes way for the New Jerusalem in all her splendor and beauty (Rev. 21:1–22:5; cf. Eze. 40–48).

---

[1] The Greek expression for "praise God" (Rev. 19:5) means essentially the same thing as hallelujah.

[2] The Babylonian Talmud dates this tradition as far back as Moses (*Pesahim* 117a); see also Matt. 26:30.

[3] See Ps. 135:19-21; cf. 1 Chron. 16:25, 36.

[4] It would be an error to deduce from this expression the existence of an eternal hell, as taught later by the church and imagined by the Italian poet Dante Alighieri. The Bible commonly uses the expression to indicate total annihilation. Scripture employed it with the city of Babylon (Rev. 14:11) and the cities of Sodom and Gomorrah (Jude 7; cf. 2 Peter 2:6).

[5] Isa. 61:10.

[6] Gen. 24:5; S. of Sol. 4:1, 3; 6:7.

[7] Jer. 2:32.

[8] We find this definition of the "spirit of prophecy" attested in the Aramaic Targum. See Strack and Billerbeck, *Kommentar zum Neuen Testament,* vol. 2, pp. 128, 129; cf. J. W. Etheridge, *The Targums of Onkelos and Jonathan Ben Uzziel on the Pentateuch* (London: 1862), vol. 1, pp. 131, 556; vol. 2, p. 442.

[9] See, for example, 1 Cor. 1:6; cf. W. de Boor, *Der erste Brief des Paulus an die Korinther,* Wuppertaler Studienbibel (Wuppertal: 1968), p. 28; cf. Gerhard Pfandl, "The Remnant Church and the Spirit of Prophecy," in *Symposium on Revelation—Book 2,* ed. Frank B. Holbrook, Daniel and Revelation Committee Series (Silver Spring, Md.: Biblical Research Institute, General Conference of Seventh-day Adventists, 1992), vol. 7, pp. 310, 316.

[10] Later, the two adjectives qualify the Word (Rev. 22:6) to express the veracity of the kingdom of God and of the New Jerusalem (verses 1-5).

[11] See Doukhan, *Secrets of Daniel,* p. 155.

[12] 1 Enoch 10:4, 5; cf. 88:1.

[13] Doukhan, *Secrets of Daniel,* pp. 125-133.

[14] Ps. 91:7; 119:72; 1 Chron. 16:15; Eccl. 7:28.

[15] See Doukhan, *Secrets of Daniel,* pp. 183.

[16] Lev. 8:10, 12, 30; 21:6, 7.

[17] Lev. 11:44, 45; 19:2; 20:7, 26.

[18] Isa. 6:3; 57:15; Ps. 99:5.

[19] Cf. Eze. 38:4-9, 13, 15, 16, 22, 23; 39:2, 11, 12, 15, 16.

[20] The valley of Hinnom, south of Jerusalem, served as the border between the tribes of

Benjamin and Judah (see Jer. 15:7; 18:15, 16). It became so infamous that Jeremiah did not even need to mention it by name when condemning the cults of "the valley" (Jer. 2:23).

[21] The concept derives from the fact that Genesis 10 mentions 70 nations. The number also matches that of the members in the family of Jacob (Gen. 46:27; Ex. 1:5; Deut. 10:22). Jewish tradition has interpreted this agreement as the application of the principle in Deuteronomy that the number of the nations are determined "according to the number of the sons of Israel" (Deut. 32:8). The motif "seventy nations" appears widely in rabbinical literature. Thus priests and Levites wrote the Decalogue in 70 languages so as to be understood by the 70 nations (Mishnah *Sotah* 7:5). For similar reasons, people heard the divine voice at Sinai in 70 languages (Babylonian Talmud, *Shabbath* 88b). The 70 sacrifices offered in the sanctuary are destined to atone for the 70 nations (Babylonian Talmud, *Sukkah* 55b).

[22] From the most ancient times Hebrew letters have had a numerical value (*alef,* 1; *bet,* 2, etc.). The rabbis often found significance in the numerical value of a word, a system of interpretation called *gematria* (a Hebrew word that is perhaps a corruption of the Greek word from which we derive "geometry"). A classical example of *gematria* concerns the 318 servants in Genesis 14:14. Interpreters saw a connection between them and Abraham's servant, Eliezer, whose name has the numerical value of 318 (see Babylonian Talmud, *Nedarim* 32a; Midrash Rabbah, *Genesis* 43. 2).

CHAPTER 9

GOLDEN JERUSALEM

(Revelation 21–22:5)

Sukkot

The descent of the New Jerusalem is the last prophetic event of the Apocalypse (see the "Prophetic Events" table, p. 189) and is the structural counterpart of the seven churches that introduced the Apocalypse. The two accounts share several common themes: The New Jerusalem (Rev. 21:10), the radiance of God (Rev. 21:23; cf. 1:16), the name of God inscribed on His people (Rev. 22:4; cf. 3:12), the tree of life (Rev. 22:2; cf. 2:7), and the book of life (Rev. 21:27; cf. 3:5). Both accounts pronounce a blessing over "he who overcomes" (Rev. 21:7; cf. 2:7, 11, 17, 26; 3:5, 12, 21), and call God "the Beginning and the End," the "Alpha and the Omega" (Rev. 21:6; cf. 1:17; 2:8). The two accounts are among the few in the Apocalypse in which we hear God's voice directly (Rev. 21:3; cf. 1:10).

Moreover, a reference to God's presence precedes both accounts. The account of the seven churches has the Son of Man walking among the candelabras of the earth (Rev. 1:13). Now the prophet sees a new heaven and a new earth and the Holy City coming down from God (Rev. 21:1, 2). And he hears a loud voice from the throne (verse 3). Here then, in the context of the New Jerusalem, we see God Himself dwelling among the people of the earth (Rev. 21:1-8).

Again, a liturgical setting introduces the vision. The festival of

Pessah, the first in the Jewish calendar, preceded the seven churches. Similarly, the New Jerusalem evokes Sukkot, the Feast of Tabernacles, the last in the Jewish calendar.

The Apocalypse employs language similar to that used in the context of Sukkot, the Feast of Tabernacles, thus associating the

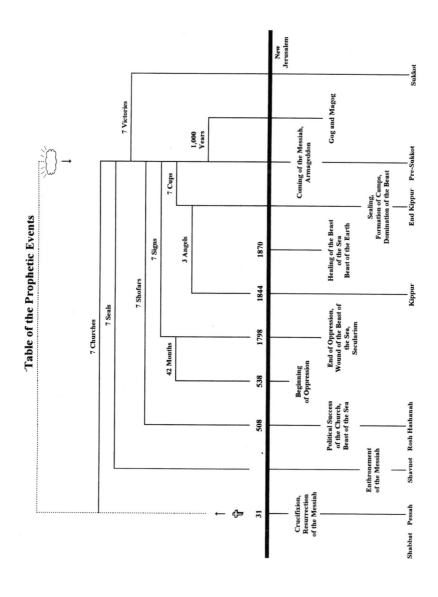

Table of the Prophetic Events

New Jerusalem with the festival. A key passage in this regard is: "And I heard a loud voice from the throne saying, 'Now the dwelling [or tabernacle] of God is with men, and he will live [or dwell] with them'" (Rev. 21:3).

The word "dwelling" or "tabernacle" translates the Greek word *skene*. The Greek word echoes the Hebrew word *shekinah,* the physical sign of God's presence among His people (Ex. 40:34-38). Also, the word *shekinah* derives from the same root as the Hebrew verb *shakan* (to dwell), rendered by the Greek *skenoun* (to dwell, to spread the tent).[1] Such background suggests that Revelation 21:3 is emphasizing that God will actually be with humanity.

The New Jerusalem will be God's actual presence and not simply a symbol of that presence, as was the case with the Temple. Later, the text is even more explicit: "I did not see a temple in the city, because the Lord God Almighty and the Lamb are its temple" (Rev. 21:22). Here is the principal difference between the New Jerusalem and the old. In the new city God's literal presence replaces the Temple, which had functioned as the symbol of His dwelling. The book of Ezekiel follows the same pattern, concluding likewise with God's presence in the city: "And the name of the city from that time on will be: the Lord is there" (Eze. 48:35).

God is finally here. True communion is at last possible between Him and His people. The Apocalypse expresses this in the language of the covenant: "They will be his people, and God himself will be with them and be their God" (Rev. 21:3). "I will be his God and he will be my son" (Rev. 21:7).[2] It is one of the favorite themes of the Song of Songs: "My lover is mine and I am his" (S. of Sol. 2:16; cf. 6:3; 7:10).

Both the conjugal metaphor and that of the father testify to the proximity of a God with whom it is at last possible to have a direct and reciprocal relationship without the problems of distance, sin, and error, and without the intervention of a priest or a ritual. What God had to refuse to Moses (Ex. 33:20-23) now becomes an everyday occurrence: "They will see his face" (Rev. 22:4).

God will be there—physically present—like the man or woman that we live with, with whom we converse, laugh, eat, and think. It is a new experience that we cannot express in either words or thought. But it infinitely magnifies that of the Feast of Tabernacles, which owes its name (*Sukkot,* tabernacles) to the makeshift dwellings from branches and vines that the people built for the celebration. The custom commemorated Israel's wandering in the desert and the construction of the sanctuary, the *sukkah* of God, a symbol of God's presence among His people: "Then have them make a sanctuary for me, and I will dwell *[shakan]* among them" (Ex. 25:8).

In Jewish tradition, the *sukkah,* like the sanctuary, symbolized the *shekinah*.[3] The psalms read in the *sukkah* testify to such symbolism—they all speak of His protective presence (Ps. 23; 27; 36; 57; 63; 91). Furthermore, the fragile nature of the *sukkah* recalls the precariousness of the world's cities while it strengthens the longing for the heavenly kingdom. The branches of the roof must always retain open space, so that we may see the heavens through the holes. Significantly, the liturgical readings of the Feast of Tabernacles cover the book of Ecclesiastes, in which everything—our lives, our deeds, our dwellings—is vanity (see especially Eccl. 2:4ff.). We find the same lesson of hope inscribed in the other name for the festival—the "Feast of Ingathering" (Ex. 23:16; 34:22)—for it also marked the end of the harvest.

In the Apocalypse, the allusion to the Feast of Tabernacles is particularly appropriate. After Kippur (Rev. 11:19), the harvest of grain and grapes (Rev. 14:14-20; 16:17, 18), the rite of Azazel (Rev. 20:2, 3), and the purification of the camp from evil (Rev. 20:7-15)—after these things follows the great gathering of God's people from the four corners of the earth. We see the universality of the assembly hinted at in the general expression "the dwelling of God is with men" (Rev. 21:3). The prophet Zechariah had already foreseen the Messianic overtones of the Feast of Tabernacles: "Then the survivors from all the nations that have attacked Jerusalem will go up year after year to worship the King, the Lord Almighty, and to celebrate the Feast of Tabernacles" (Zech. 14:16). The prophet of the Apocalypse uses similar language: "The nations will walk by its light, and the kings of the earth will bring their splendor into it" (Rev. 21:24).

Humanity's thirst for God is finally quenched: "To him who is thirsty I will give to drink without cost from the spring of the water of life" (Rev. 21:6; cf. 22:1). The image also appears in the context of the Feast of Tabernacles. On that occasion it was customary for the priest to draw water from the pool of Siloam with a golden jar during the morning and evening rituals of the daily sacrifices. The people greeted his return by singing: "With joy you will draw water from the wells of salvation" (Isa. 12:3).[4] It was the custom Yeshua alluded to during the Feast of Tabernacles when He said: "If anyone is thirsty, let him come to me and drink" (John 7:37).

A New Jerusalem

The Apocalypse gives the fulfillment of all hopes, the answer to all the longings of the world, the quenching of all thirsts (Rev. 21:6), the descent of the city of God, as a final point: "It is done" (verse 6). And indeed, the city's name—Jerusalem—is laden with meaning. First and foremost it is the city of peace, as connoted by its ancient name "Salem." It is the city of Melchizedek, the king of justice who supported Abraham in his military campaigns (Gen. 14:18; cf. Heb. 7:1). The city of Jerusalem was also built on Mount Moriah (2 Chron. 3:1), alluding thus to the sacrifice of Isaac (Gen. 22:1-18).[5] Jerusalem was also the place where God stopped the deadly sword about to decimate the people of Israel (1 Chron. 21:14-16). David conquered it and made it the first capital of Israel (1 Chron. 11:1-9), then kept the ark of the covenant within its walls (2 Sam. 6:12-23). But the collective memory of Israel primarily associates Jerusalem with the Temple. Jerusalem is a place of prayer and worship (Ps. 48:2; 122:1). The city is also the antithesis of Babylon and the symbol of the return from the exile and the end of oppression. It is the city that incites nostalgia—God's people cannot forget Jerusalem (Ps. 137).

Through these memories, the people of Israel came to identify Jerusalem with God's presence. The city stood for God's dwelling place in heaven, the place where the saints could shelter resplendent in God's inconceivable glory (Ps. 48:1-3).

The prophet Daniel also envisioned the heavenly Jerusalem. Beyond the earthly kingdoms that finally disappear without a trace (Dan. 2:35), the prophet sees "a kingdom that will never be destroyed" (verse 44), in the shape of a mountain (verses 35, 45), the traditional symbol of Zion, or Jerusalem.[6]

In the spirit of the biblical tradition, Jewish tradition affirms the reality of the "Jerusalem of above" *(Yerushalayim shel Maalah)* that existed even before the creation of the world,[7] and inspired the poets of love.[8] Jewish apocalyptic literature views the heavenly Jerusalem and its temple as coming down onto the cities of the world, "for no human work may compare to the dwelling place of the Most-High."[9] According to the Kabbalistic rabbi, Bahya b. Asher, the plural form of the Hebrew word for Jerusalem *(Yerushalayim)* alludes to there being two Jerusalems, one on the earth and the other in heaven.

The Jerusalem of the past, however, hardly compares with the New Jerusalem. Nothing is the same. The very first words of Revelation 21 describe the New Jerusalem in terms of creation: "Then I saw a new heaven and a new earth, for the first heaven and the first earth had passed away, and there was no longer any sea" (Rev. 21:1). The parallel text in Isaiah makes an explicit reference to creation: "Behold, I will create new heavens and a new earth. . . . But be glad and rejoice forever in what I will create, for I will create Jerusalem to be a delight" (Isa. 65:17, 18).

The new earth will be radically different. The "sea" is no more (Rev. 21:1), the first characteristic of this new universe. The "sea" in the Hebrew mind-set had a negative connotation, representing void and darkness (Gen. 1:2; Ps. 18:12; Job 26:10; Prov. 8:27), death and "nonbeing"[10] (Eze. 26:19-21; Jonah 2:6; Hab. 3:10), and evil (Isa. 27:1; 51:9, 10). Scripture also associates "sea" with Babylon (Rev. 16:12) and, in the Apocalypse, to the origins of the beast (Rev. 13:1).[11]

The Greek word *neos* that qualifies Jerusalem means radically and "totally other."[12] God gives the new Jerusalem a new configuration and lowers it down to earth from the heavens (Rev. 21:2; cf. Rev. 3:12). It is not the Jerusalem of the Six-Day War, neither that of the Mosque of Omar, of the Wall of Lamentations, nor that of the Holy Sepulcher. The New Jerusalem is more than a new coat of paint or some new roadwork. The change is radical and affects everything: "I am making everything new!" (Rev. 21:5).

On a personal level, the Jerusalem of above means first of all great consolation. It is the first truth that the Apocalypse infers: "He will wipe every tear from their eyes" (verse 4). The tears here do not concern the massacre of Gog and Magog and the memory of those who disappear forever. The context suggests instead that "every tear" accounts for the wounds of the past. Like death and suffering, tears also shall be no more.

Human suffering is certainly humanity's oldest and most serious grudge against God—the God who remains silent in the presence of suffering. Where was God during times of pain and oppression? The tears of the little girl tortured by the soldiers had gone unseen, but now God wipes them with His own hand. He offers no words, no explanations—only a gesture, accompanied by the promise that there are to be "no more tears." It is the ultimate consolation, the only possible answer to the problem of suffering.

Thus it all comes down to God. That is why the prophet postpones the description of the splendor of the New Jerusalem until later in our passage. For the first time in the Apocalypse, the vision of the prophet does not follow a chronological sequence, but focuses on one particular entity—golden Jerusalem. Here is humanity's final destination. Nevertheless, the description of the city progresses from the general to the particular. The prophet depicts the city as it approaches him from the heavens.[13] The vision divides into two panoramas, each introduced by the formula "[the angel] showed me" (Rev. 21:10; 22:1).

As it proceeds from the periphery to the center, it successively unveils seven marvels. The first panorama (Rev. 10:10-27) presents (1) the city as a whole shining like crystal with (2) its gates and walls of precious stones and (3) its main square of gold. The second panorama (Rev. 22:1-5) reveals the center of the square with (4) its river of the water of life, (5) the tree of life, (6) the throne of God, and finally (7) the Lord God Himself.

City of Light

The New Jerusalem is a new and perfect environment that inspires trust, admiration, and enjoyment. "A great, high wall" securely protects it (Rev. 21:12). Each side of the city (verse 16) measures 12,000 stadia (about 1,400 miles). Its wall (verse 17) stretches across 144 cubits (about 200 feet) and rests on 12 foundations (verse 14). The entire city is built on the basis of the number 12, the number of the tribes of Israel, whose names are written on the gates (Rev. 21:12; cf. 7:4-8, in which 12 x 12,000 saved = 144,000), as well as that of the apostles, whose names are engraved upon the foundations of the city (Rev. 21:14).

God has designed the city with its inhabitants in mind. It could not be more adequate. The architect is the Creator Himself, perfectly acquainted with His creatures' needs and desires. The 12 gates open to the four cardinal directions (verses 13, 25), testifying to a spirit of receptivity and trust between the inhabitants of the New Jerusalem.

The gates and each foundation consist of a different stone (verses 19-21). Each stone contributes to an aspect of the city, implying no competition or favoritism. Peace and trust now characterize all human relations. Significantly, all three lists of those evildoers excluded from the city culminate with the category of liars (Rev. 21:8, 27; 22:15).

But the architect does not limit the scope of His work just to practical needs. The city is also beautiful—"prepared as a bride" (Rev. 21:2). The Greek verb *kosmeo* (the source of our word "cosmetics") renders the aesthetic character of the city. We notice already its harmonious and symmetrical proportions—"as wide and high as it is long" (verse 16). The city forms the perfect cube, just as did the Holy of Holies of the ancient Temple (1 Kings 6:20). As with the candelabra, the Holy of Holies evokes the New Jerusalem awaited by humanity. The connection again testifies to the relationship between the human act of worship and the kingdom of God, for religion takes on meaning only in light of God's kingdom.

We note also the valuable materials used in the city's construction. The city consists of pure gold and precious stones (Rev. 21:18-21). Their diversity is emphasized only by what unites them—God's brilliant presence, "for the glory of God gives it light" (verse 23). The city stands like a golden temple with stained-glass walls, reflecting the light in a panoply of rich tones and colors.

City of Life

The New Jerusalem also brings with it a new life. It reminds us of the Garden of Eden (Gen. 2; 3) with its flourishing vegetation, its crystal waters, and particularly its "tree of life" (cf. Rev. 2:7). "Then the angel showed me the river of the water of life, as clear as crystal, flowing from the throne of God and of the Lamb down the middle of the great street of the city. On each side of the river stood the tree of life, bearing twelve crops of fruit, yielding its fruit every month. And the leaves of the tree are for the healing of the nations" (Rev. 22:1, 2).

The prophet Ezekiel had already foreseen such a marvelous garden with its rivers and miraculous trees: "Fruit trees of all kinds will grow on both banks of the river. Their leaves will not wither, nor will their fruit fail. Every month they will bear, because the water from the sanctuary flows to them. Their fruit will serve for food and their leaves for healing" (Eze. 47:12).

Tree symbolism permeates the Bible[14] and is present in different forms throughout the ancient Middle Eastern civilizations. In all cases the tree symbolized life, a concept that first appeared in the Garden of Eden. The man and the woman lived on its fruit. Death threatened them the moment they lost access to it (Gen. 3:22).

The tree in the New Jerusalem is wholly beneficial. Both its fruits and its leaves serve a purpose. Our passage does not have much to say about the nature of the fruit, except that it ripens all year long, sustaining the biological life of the city's inhabitants. On the other hand, the leaves provide for the "healing of the nations." The text is not referring to herbal remedies or other forms of medical treatment through plants. The disappearance of death implies the absence of any malignant germs or other diseases. Rather, the context suggests a different interpretation.

The preceding verses associate the "nations" with God's glory or radiance. "The city does not need the sun or the moon to shine on it, for the glory of God gives it light, and the Lamb is its lamp. The nations will walk by its light, and the kings of the earth will bring their splendor into it" (Rev. 21:23, 24; cf. 21:26). The "healing of the nations" thus involves the enlightenment of the nations by God Himself. It is one of the miracles of the New Jerusalem, marveled at by the prophets and inscribed in the heart of the Feast of Tabernacles: "Then the survivors from all the nations that have attacked Jerusalem will go up year after year to worship the King, the Lord Almighty, and to celebrate the Feast of Tabernacles" (Zech. 14:16).

The nations *(goyim),* traditionally excluded from the covenant and ignorant of God's laws and truth, now participate in His worship. Isaiah 60:1-19 presents a variation on the same theme: "Arise, shine, for your light has come. . . . The Lord rises upon you and his glory appears over you. *Nations will come to your light. . . .* The sun will no more be your light by day, nor will the brightness of the moon shine on you, for the Lord will be your everlasting light."

In the New Jerusalem God will "heal" the nations in the sense that He will enlighten and take care of them.[15] This nuance we find confirmed by the structure of our text in which the first part of our passage, ABC (Rev. 22:1-3a), is paralleled by the second part, A'B'C' (Rev. 22:3b-5). The "healing of the nations" in B corresponds to the "servants" who serve and are enlightened by God in B'.

A//A'   ◆"The throne of God and of the Lamb" from which the river of life flows to irrigate the trees of life (A, Rev. 22:1-2a), corresponds to

◆"the throne of God and of the Lamb" in the city (A', Rev. 22:3b).

B//B'   ◆The "fruit" yielded every month and the "leaves . . . for the healing of the nations" (B, Rev. 22:2b), correspond to

◆the "servants" that shall serve God and see the face of this one who "will give them light" (B', Rev. 22:3c-5b).

C//C'   ◆"No longer will there be any curse" (C, Rev. 22:3a), alluding to the curse of Gen. 3:14 that denies humanity the tree of life, corresponds to

◆"they will reign for ever and ever" (C', Rev. 22:5c).

The parallelism between B and B' then relates light to life, concepts associated together in biblical thought.[16] Thus the author of the Gospel of John speaks of Yeshua as the "life, and that life was the light of men" (John 1:4). Likewise, Yeshua promises His disciples that "whoever follows [Him] will never walk in darkness, but will have the light of life" (John 8:12).

The superposition of the two images—the tree of life with its leaves and the light of God that enlightens—elucidates the symbolism of the seven-branched candelabra, the famous menorah of the ancient Temple. Shaped like a tree with its branches of light, the candelabra was the sign of hope.[17] A symbolic reminder of the Garden of Eden with its tree of life and light, it kindled in the hearts of the people of Israel a longing for the lost Paradise.

The life given by the fruits and the leaves of the tree is full and complete. The tree of life nourishes both the body and the soul. Such a wholistic approach to life is typical of Hebrew thought. It considers spiritual and biological life as identical. Hebrew employs the same word, *ruah,* for the physiological breath of life (Gen. 6:17; 7:15) and for the psuchē, the soul, or the spiritual dimension (Num. 27:18; Isa. 63:10, 11). The *ruah* that enables humans to breathe and gives them life proceeds from God—it is the *ruah,* or Spirit of God. The psalmist closely identifies the two *ruahs:* "When you take away their breath *[ruah],* they die and return to the dust. When you send your Spirit *[ruah],* they are created" (Ps. 104:29, 30).

In other words, human beings exist only inasmuch as they are in a relationship with God. The religious dimension is not limited to the domain of spiritual needs—it is a biological necessity, a truth proclaimed from the very first pages of the Bible. God created the human being, breathing life into him. Thus every human being is biologically dependent on God. When humanity cuts itself off from God, it dies (Gen. 2:17; cf. 3:17, 19). Now the last pages of the Bible proclaim the same truth. Spiritual and physical life are intertwined.

The New Jerusalem is not the paradise of bodiless souls and of ethereal beings, and neither is it the Muslim paradise of sensual pleasure. Life is total. The senses are immersed in the experiences of touch, smell, taste, and beauty. The redeemed no longer experience fatigue, disgust, or suffering. The body has never been so strong. But the intellect is also revitalized. Thoughts go deeper, and life's mysteries become clearer to the perception. The saved more readily assimilate and understand God's Word. The spiritual and mental faculties have never been so acute. Memory, intelligence, and the passion for learning revive.

But for now, we linger in a world of struggle and suffering. Beauty must share reality with wretchedness, palace doors shelter beggars, lies pollute truth, and the odor of death permeates all life. It is a world screaming for change, screaming for the coming of God.

[1] Cf. comments on Rev. 7:15.

[2] Cf. Hosea 2:25; Zech. 13:9.

[3] Babylonian Talmud, *Sukkah* 116a-b.

[4] Mishnah, *Sukkah* 5. 1.

[5] The Midrash finds within the name of Jerusalem allusions to Melchizedek and the sacrifice of Isaac: Jeru, from the same root as Moriah, alludes to the sacrifice of Isaac; and Salem hints at Melchizedek (Midrash Rabbah, *Genesis* 56. 16).

[6] Ps. 24:3; Isa. 2:3; Zech. 8:3; Isa. 27:13; cf. Dan. 9:20; 11:45, etc.

[7] *Midrash on the Psalms,* Psalm 122, section 4; *Midrash Tanhuma,* ed. Salomon Buber (1885), Numbers, pp. 34, 35.

[8] Babylonian Talmud, *Taanith* 5a; *Tanhuma, Pekudei,* 1.

[9] 4 Ezra (2 Esdras) 10:54; 7:26; 1 Enoch 90:28, 29.

[10] The expression is borrowed from Johannes Pedersen, *Israel: Its Life and Culture* (London: 1926-1940), vols. 1-2, p. 464; cf. Reymond, *L'Eau sacrée,* p. 213: "The Old Testament often identifies the ocean with death . . . a place of no return . . . a place where there is no communion, neither with humans nor with God."

[11] See Doukhan, *The Genesis Creation Story,* p. 70ff.

[12] Kittel, ed., *Theological Dictionary of the New Testament,* vol. 3, pp. 447-450.

[13] See Roberto Badenas, "New Jerusalem—The Holy City," in *Symposium on Revelation—Book 2,* ed. Frank B. Holbrook, Daniel and Revelation Committee Series (Silver Spring, Md.: Biblical Research Institute, General Conference of Seventh-day Adventists, 1992), vol. 7, p. 246.

[14] Ps. 1:3; Isa. 65:22; cf. Lev. 26:4; Judges 9:8-13.

[15] The original Greek *therapeia* and the related verb *therapeuo* (cf. our word "therapy") also contain the same sense. Both words can involve the ideas of "taking care of [something or someone]" or of "serving [something or someone]" (see Acts 17:25; Luke 12:42, etc.). Consequently, in the Septuagint these words and their cognates render the Hebrew root *'bd,* which involves the ideas of service or a servant (see Gen. 45:16; Isa. 5:2, etc.).

[16] Job 3:20; 33:30; Ps. 49:19; 56:13, etc.

[17] See Carol L. Meyers, *The Tabernacle Menorah,* American Schools of Oriental Research Dissertation Series (Missoula, Mont.: 1976), no. 2, p. 118ff.

"I AM COMING"

(Revelation 22:6-21)

From the heavens, the vision now takes us back to the earth. The book's last prophetic words echo its first. This rhetorical method *(inclusio)* is very ancient. Hebrew poetry often used it[1] and even classical literature under the pen of Plato.[2] It also appears in the writings of Flavius Josephus[3] and third-century rabbis.[4] The author employs *inclusio* to indicate both in the introduction and in the conclusion the fundamental truth that has inspired and directed the whole writing.

The conclusion of the Apocalypse corresponds to the introduction in a number of common expressions and themes.[5] But the major echo between them is the coming of the Lord:

Introduction	Conclusion
"From him . . . who is to come" (Rev. 1:4)	"Behold, I am coming soon" (Rev. 22:7)
"Look, he is coming" (Rev. 1:7)	"Behold, I am coming soon" (Rev. 22:12)
"The Lord . . . 'who is to come'" (Rev. 1:8)	"The Spirit and the bride say, 'Come'" (Rev. 22:17)
"On the Lord's Day" (Rev. 1:10)	"Yes, I am coming soon" (Rev. 22:20)
	"Amen. Come, Lord Jesus" (Rev. 22:20)

Note, however, an interesting difference in the language. The introduction emphasizes Christ's return in the third person: "who is to come," "he is coming." The conclusion repeats the coming in the first person: "I am coming." The grammatical contrast suggests that the Second Advent has now become personal and direct. It is no longer a mere external testimony about the event. Now the one who comes—the subject of the event—speaks of His advent. And this affects the tone of the last message.

So far the apocalyptic discourse has been full of imagery, symbols, and fantastic visions that took us beyond immediate physical reality. Now, in the conclusion, it suddenly turns personal and insistent as it enters our present reality. "Come," the key word of the passage, appears seven times as a refrain. It concentrates the central message of the Apocalypse. The lesson we heard in the beginning of the book is the same one we hear at the end of the book and, therefore, the one we should retain as we go back to our daily routine, cares, and sorrows:

"Behold, I am coming soon!" (Rev. 22:7)

"Behold, I am coming soon!" (verse 12)

"Come!" (verse 17a)

"Come!" (verse 17b)

"Let him come" (verse 17c)

"Yes, I am coming soon" (verse 20a)

"Amen. Come, Lord Jesus" (verse 20b).

And if we follow closely the path traced by this key word, we discover a back-and-forth movement between the divine and the human spheres, suggesting a reciprocal relationship. To the shout of heaven that starts the series of "come" and sounds twice as a promise—"Behold, I am coming soon!" (verses 7, 12)—answers twice the call of the earth, "Come!" . . . "Come!" (verse 17). The heavens then reassure the earth—"Yes, I am coming soon" (verse 20a)—and the human prayer responds, "Amen. Come, Lord Jesus" (verse 20b).

The interwoven voices teach us an important lesson.

1. The divine promise always precedes human desire for God. Human beings do not initiate the desire to encounter God, nor do they inaugurate the prayer. God has spoken first, and that is why we

believe Him. Faith does not rest on human subjectivity, but on the divine word that existed before humanity.

2. On the other hand, God reassures those who call on Him. His saying "Yes, I am coming soon" strengthens the faith of those who await Him. One must already believe in God and live according to His will to actually long for His return.

3. Finally, those who pray for the return already believe in it. Prayer arises from a conviction, not from theological or historical data. Those who believe in the coming of God are those who pray for it.

The prayer that concludes the Apocalypse contains all the others that have gone before it—it is the prayer par excellence: "May your kingdom come" (cf. Matt. 6:10; Luke 11:2). It constitutes both a response and a plea. Christianity boils down to these words. Because we are accustomed to pray for happiness and success, prayer has often taken on the character of a magical formula for our desires and caprices. This last prayer, however, is neither a blessing for the daily bread nor one for our work in this life. Rather, it is a desperate plea for change. We cry "Come!" in response to the "I am coming soon," not because we want a better life, but because we desperately seek *another* life—the life promised by God.

This prayer is so important that the first Christians turned it into a greeting: *Marana tha!* "Come, O Lord!" (cf. 1 Cor. 16:22). The concluding words of the Apocalypse, *Amen Marana tha,* marked the end of each eucharistic service. We know this through the testimony of the Didache,[6] one of Christianity's most ancient documents, preceding even the Apocalypse in composition. Yohanan deliberately sought to place his book in the liturgical context[7] of the Lord's Supper that commemorated the "Lord's death until he comes" (1 Cor. 11:26).

But prayer and rituals are not the only answers to the promise from above. In the midst of the five last "comes"—interwoven with the "Come!" of the Spirit and of the church calling for the appearing of God (Rev. 22:17)—resonates a "come" of a different nature: "Whoever is thirsty, let him come; and whoever wishes, let him take the free gift of the water of life" (verse 17).

The coming of God and His people's desire for His return are not only future occurrences. The water that quenches the thirst is accessible to us in this present life and is more than the future fulfill-ment of the promise of salvation and eternal life (Rev. 21:6). The verb is in the present tense and situates the experience in our cur-rent situation.

The Hebrew Scriptures generally associate "the water of life" with YHWH and apply it to our present existence. "For with you is the fountain of life" (Ps. 36:9). Jeremiah 2:13 and 17:13 also con-nect the concepts.

In the New Testament Yeshua unites the same image with Himself when He offers the Samaritan woman "living water" (John 4:10-15) and summons the Temple crowd to drink from Him (John 7:37, 38). Yohanan explains that the water symbolizes "the Spirit, whom those who believed in him were later to receive" (verse 39).

Similarly, for the ancient rabbis and the Jews at Qumran, drink-ing the living water represents the religious life led according to the guiding principles of the Torah.[8] In all these cases such water can quench our thirst on this earth in our present experience.

In other words, God's people already sample the living water of the New Jerusalem here and now. The "Come!" of God implies the "Come and drink!" The religion of hope is not passive, cannot be diluted into some futuristic utopia. God offers us the "water of life" today (Rev. 22:17). This miracle has nothing to do with magical for-mulas or technological genius. To drink from the water of life sim-ply means to live with God. The God of life—the eternal God whom we shall meet face to face in the New Jerusalem—meets us in this existence.

Miracles already punctuate our journey on earth. We experience the invisible God in daily life through precise and direct answers to our prayers and in the joy we find in our hearts. Each one of us may feel His protection, guidance, and comfort even in the depths of de-spair and solitude as we have the deep conviction and intuition of His presence.

But God does not give this spiritual water arbitrarily. We must experience thirst, and we must "come"—we must desire the water. Life with God does not consist solely of grace, miracles, emotions, and comfort. An intense desire for change and a will for action are also part of the religious experience. The encounter with God requires our participation. And His presence can never be exhausted. We must desire it forever. Our thirst must remain unquenched. Paradoxically, the very presence that is supposed to satisfy our thirst will actually intensify it. Men and women have a role to play in their encounter with God. Many Christians have misunderstood this dimension and have reduced religion to a dogma or to a good feeling.

The religion of the Apocalypse comprises both the "coming" of God and the "coming" of humankind. The hope of the coming God permeates the longings of believers, their ethics, their choices, and their existence. Because of the gift of the "water of life," the return of God is real and historical—it flows already in the existence of those who drink of it.

It is not enough to merely read the Apocalypse—we must "drink" its words and treasure its message. This is what Yeshua meant when He said: "Blessed is he who keeps the words of the prophecy in this book" (verse 7). The angel repeats this lesson when he speaks of those "who keep the words of this book" (verse 9), and the author echoes it in the conclusion of the book in the form of a warning and a curse: "I warn everyone who hears the words of the prophecy of this book: If anyone adds anything to them, God will add to him the plagues described in this book. And if anyone takes words away from this book of prophecy, God will take away from him his share in the tree of life and in the holy city, which are described in this book" (verses 18, 19).

The Apocalypse does not have in mind the scribe whose function is to preserve the integrity of the text. Yohanan addresses "everyone who hears the words of the prophecy of this book" (verse 18)—everyone who reads the Apocalypse. The book of Deuteronomy uses the same language and has the same intention: "Do not add to what I command you and do not subtract from it, but keep the commands of the Lord your God that I give you" (Deut. 4:2; cf. 12:32).

The parallels between the two passages invite us to read the Apocalypse in much the same way that the Israelites read the book of Deuteronomy—as a covenant involving every aspect of existence. To "keep the words of this book" is to embody them in the flesh of existence.

We must first understand the prophetic word. It involves all the exegetes and commentators on the Apocalypse (including myself)—in fact, all the biblical book's readers. The work of the authentic exegete necessitates a critical mind, but also a humble heart. Goodwill and piety are not enough. To read the Apocalypse is not enough. We must read it in the right manner. The Apocalypse repeatedly warns against subjective, personal, and wild conjectures. The curse against those who add or subtract applies to all those interpretations that do not follow the direction of the text, but take off in the wrong direction.

To "keep" the words of this book implies that we have understood their significance in our lives. What is at stake in the Apocalypse is too important to be misunderstood. The life of the reader must respond to its vision. It is easy to become somewhat elated by the ecstasy of the "Amens" and "Hallelujahs" that resonate throughout the book. Or blinded by the celestial visions, it is easy to remain on a mystical level and to forget our responsibility as human beings to testify to the coming kingdom in our own lives.

The Apocalypse calls for a consistent and well-balanced religion. The vision of hope does not obliterate present reality. The book gives both perspectives together, and we should measure them against each other. The authenticity and truth of religion depends on such discipline. Without the prophecy that sustains hope, religion shrinks to relativism, humanism, and subjectivity. God is absent, opening the door to the oppression and abuse of a totalitarian society. Truth becomes the product of a majority as it seeks to assimilate or annihilate the minority. On the other hand, without the corrective of the human reality, religion degenerates into a fanatical—if not pathological—delirium, as we observed in the victims of a Messiah complex or in certain apocalyptic sects.

As this strange and threatening book comes to its conclusion, from the sky comes a last cry of warning. God meant the words of the Apocalypse to leap from their page into action. They should propel God to "Come!" and men and women to "Come!" to the God who comes. The book ends in a truly Hebrew perspective. It does not conclude with a word of wisdom to make us think, or with a beautiful song to make us dream, or even with a spiritual message to make us pray. Rather it finishes with an event to make us wait . . .

---

[1] See, for example, Gen. 1:1 and 2:4; Isa. 1:2 and 66:22; Job 1, 2 and 42:7-17; Eccl. 1:2 and 12:8ff., etc.

[2] Plato *Laws* 4. 7.

[3] Josephus *Antiquities* 8. 2. 2.

[4] Midrash Rabbah *Genesis* 31.

[5] Compare Rev. 22:6 and 1:1; 22:7, 18, 19 and 1:3; 22:16 and 1:4-6; 22:13 and 1:7, 8 and 1:9, 10, etc. See K. A. Strand, *Interpreting the Book of Revelation* (Ann Arbor, Mich.: 1976), p. 45.

[6] *Didache* 10. 6.

[7] See Pierre Prigent, *L'Apocalypse de saint Jean,* Commentaire du Nouveau Testament, Second Series (Paris: 1981), vol. 14, pp. 361, 362; cf. O. Cullmann, *La foi et le culte de l'église primitive,* Bibliothèque théologique (Neuchâtel-Paris: 1963), pp. 111-115.

[8] See Hugo Odeberg, *The Fourth Gospel: Interpreted in Its Relation to Contemporaneous Religious Currents in Palestine and the Hellenistic-Oriental World* (Amsterdam: reprint 1968), pp. 149-169; cf. *The Dead Sea Scrolls,* trans. Millar Burrows (London: 1956), pp. 353, 356.